ROUTLEDGE LIBRARY EDITIONS: LIBRARY AND INFORMATION SCIENCE

Volume 3

ACCESS SERVICES IN LIBRARIES

ACCESS SERVICES IN LIBRARIES
New Solutions for Collection Management

Edited by
GREGG SAPP

LONDON AND NEW YORK

First published in 1992 by The Haworth Press, Inc.

This edition first published in 2020
by Routledge
2 Park Square, Milton Park, Abingdon, Oxon OX14 4RN

and by Routledge
52 Vanderbilt Avenue, New York, NY 10017

Routledge is an imprint of the Taylor & Francis Group, an informa business

© 1992 The Haworth Press, Inc.

All rights reserved. No part of this book may be reprinted or reproduced or utilised in any form or by any electronic, mechanical, or other means, now known or hereafter invented, including photocopying and recording, or in any information storage or retrieval system, without permission in writing from the publishers.

Trademark notice: Product or corporate names may be trademarks or registered trademarks, and are used only for identification and explanation without intent to infringe.

British Library Cataloguing in Publication Data
A catalogue record for this book is available from the British Library

ISBN: 978-0-367-34616-4 (Set)
ISBN: 978-0-429-34352-0 (Set) (ebk)
ISBN: 978-0-367-36951-4 (Volume 3) (hbk)
ISBN: 978-0-367-36959-0 (Volume 3) (pbk)
ISBN: 978-0-429-35203-4 (Volume 3) (ebk)

Publisher's Note
The publisher has gone to great lengths to ensure the quality of this reprint but points out that some imperfections in the original copies may be apparent.

Disclaimer
The publisher has made every effort to trace copyright holders and would welcome correspondence from those they have been unable to trace.

Access Services in Libraries: New Solutions for Collection Management

Gregg Sapp
Editor

The Haworth Press, Inc.
New York • London • Norwood (Australia)

Access Services in Libraries: New Solutions for Collection Management has also been published as *Collection Management*, Volume 17, Numbers 1/2 1992.

© 1992 by The Haworth Press, Inc. All rights reserved. No part of this work may be reproduced or utilized in any form or by any means, electronic or mechanical, including photocopying, microfilm and recording, or by any information storage and retrieval system, without permission in writing from the publisher. Printed in the United States of America.

The Haworth Press, Inc., 10 Alice Street, Binghamton, NY 13904-1580, USA

Library of Congress Cataloging-in-Publication Data

Access services in libraries : new solutions for collection management / Gregg Sapp, editor.
    p. cm.
    Includes bibliographical references and index.
    ISBN 1-56024-417-8 (acid-free paper)
    1. Libraries-United States-Circulations, loans. 2. Libraries and readers. 3.Libraries-United States. I. Sapp, Gregg.
Z712.A26 1992
025.6'0973-dc20   92-34445
                                                                                                                                   CIP

Access Services in Libraries: New Solutions for Collection Management

CONTENTS

Preface *Peter G. Watson-Boone*	ix
Foreword	xiii
Access: The Key to Public Service *W. Bede Mitchell*	1
From Circulation to Access Services: The Shift in Academic Library Organization *Deborah Carver*	23

Management Challenges and Issues in Access Services Administration
    Karen S. Lange
    Linda D. Tietjen
	37

Quality Access Services: Maximizing and Managing *Amy Chang*	63
Information Delivery in the Evolving Electronic Library: Traditional Resources and Technological Access *John B. Harer*	77
Access to Library Materials in Remote Storage *Claire Q. Bellanti*	93
The Impact of Networked Information on Access Services *Greg R. Notess*	105

The Role of the Access Services Manager in Policy
  Formation   119
    Alberta S. Bailey
    Lora L. Lennertz

Changing Circulation Policies at an ARL Library:
  The Impact of Peer Institution Survey Data
  on the Process   133
    Merri A. Hartse
    Daniel R. Lee

Traditional Access to the Library via Telephone Service:
  A Case Study   149
    Tammy Nickelson Dearie
    Alice J. Perez

Planning for Success: Documenting Workflow
  in the Circulation Department   167
    Brenda Cameron-Miller

A Library Shelver's Performance Evaluation
  as It Relates to Reshelving Accuracy   177
    S. Celine Sharp

Measuring and Managing Circulation Activity
  Using Circulation Rates   193
    Matthew S. Moore

Triage Assessment and Management Measures
  for Access Services   217
    Barry Brown

Access Services: The Development of a Holistic
  Approach to Convenience Information Services:
  An Editorial Essay on the Future of Access Services   237
    Pat Weaver-Meyers
    Virginia Steel

Preface

The concept of *access to library resources* has for most of this century been growing in importance as a philosophical underpinning of librarianship. "Access" provides a useful perspective, for it allows us to examine everything connected with library service. Access is increasingly recognized as one of the noble purposes for which we practice our profession: from building design to collection management to cataloging, circulation, reference and instructional services. It can help each of us to bring our own focus both to broad professional issues such as intellectual freedom, scholarly communication, copyright, and preservation of materials, and to local practicalities like misshelved books, wrongly-transcribed call numbers, policies for purchasing microform, and library hours.

Influenced chiefly by one of the great prevailing facts of contemporary librarianship, namely the relentless, steep increases in the cost of periodical subscriptions, the concept of access has extended its hold on our imaginations in recent years. No longer just a pious general creed, it has become headline news, a matter of direct urgency and accountability–rather like the institutional shift some years ago from relying upon *implicit* ideas of fairness and decency, to setting in motion specific, results-oriented programs such as Affirmative Action or barrier-free *physical* access. For at least ten years either side of 1990, one of the biggest challenges for libraries of all types has been, and will continue to be, solving the new, more complex equation of "Access versus ownership."

Libraries can no longer adequately serve their users' needs for access by just "being there" with a conventional collection and a settled interlibrary loan service. To do a good job in the provision of access to information demands its own brand of Affirmative Action by all library managers. And one of the most dynamic ways in which this is happening is the creative regrouping of certain

© 1992 by The Haworth Press, Inc. All rights reserved.

components of a library's organization into an "Access Services Department," intended to be an operation subset of the larger array of access concerns outlined above. But the effort is still young, so there are definitions to be agreed upon, experiments to be conducted, a literature to be assembled and developed, practice to be shared, new training and skills to be sought.

What constitutes "access services" is itself a matter of local choice. At the heart of the idea is the concentration upon physical access, at the time of need, to existing materials in a collection; therefore the acquisitions, cataloging, and reference functions are not usually part of the structure. The circulation unit is normally central to the grouping, though anyone who thinks of all this as merely a trendy renaming of circulation is missing the point–there's a new mentality driving it. In academic libraries, other likely components are current periodicals, microforms, reserve, and media. Interlibrary loan services also contain dimensions of access services. Since its beginnings, ILL work was so closely dependent on manual verification activities using book and card catalogs that it was typically a sub-function of a reference unit. Now, with the maturity of massive online bibliographic utilities, that link is not as important. Circulation is the basic service of lending to one's own user something that is in the building; classical interlibrary borrowing is just the extended circulation service of lending to that user something which happens to be kept in a different building. Similarly, interlibrary lending is the provision of a reciprocal circulation service to a user at another library, with the umbilical connection to one's own circulation operation amply demonstrated by having the ILL office registered in the main circulation files as just another borrower.

Should the ILL unit now be subsumed under "access services"? By juxtaposing an access service and an ownership service, this example indicates how the concepts meet. Ownership is something libraries engage in precisely because it is a most efficient way to provide access, particularly for a user group large enough to be called "a public." (This is the very foundation of the public library idea.) In other words, access has been the reason for ownership all along. Access of some type is the goal–ownership, despite all the tremendous intellectual structures we have built to support it, is merely a mechanism, an instrument. And if, in a given situation, ownership cannot achieve the goal, then what we must provide surely falls within the definition of access service.

Considerable discussion among access services managers at professional meetings is still apt to be devoted to sharing information on what has been grouped together to form their units ("Do you have Microforms?" "No, but I do have ILL," and so on). For some time yet, we must realize that we may be talking about different brands with the same generic name when we try to generalize and compare access services experience.

Hence the special value of what a group of leading managers and practitioners is telling us in this compilation. I believe it is the first of its kind to give a clear, in-depth and as comprehensive as possible overview of the field as we now see it. Here is displayed the fresh thinking that is re-examining previous writings, presenting new experimental designs and results, creating contemporary organizational solutions, and adopting innovative techniques for increasing our users' access to library materials within constrained budgets. (Which library these days is free of a sense that it isn't spending enough on reshelving, on binding, on other forms of preservation, etc.?)

There will be many more full-length discussions of this highly interesting and challenging branch of modern library service. I expect to see books, manuals, proceedings and dissertations appear, as they have done for other recent large-scale professional advances such as online search services, online catalogs and bibliographic instruction. This volume is notable for charting a new current of thinking and practice that is moving swiftly into the mainstream. It substantially documents the state of the art, and should bring increased clarity and focus to the debates now proceeding in many libraries about how we are to honor our commitment to the "access" concept in the era when it will challenge the "ownership" concept as never before.

Peter G. Watson-Boone
Library Director
University of Wisconsin–Milwaukee

Foreword

Access is quite possibly the most powerful word in contemporary librarianship. Several well known factors from both within and external to the profession have collectively worked to create an information environment in which the traditional library goal of providing access to materials takes on entirely new dimensions of complexity and significance. Since these very factors will be addressed in a number of the essays and articles in this anthology, I will not belabor them here, except to state, in summary fashion, that libraries everywhere, from the smallest and most selective to the largest and most voracious, have been forced to reexamine the means by which they meet this goal. Providing access means shelving books so that patrons can find them and checking them in/out for patron use; but providing access in an electronic era also means exploiting online and networked alternatives that exist for making information available. The job of an access services manager straddles these poles, and in that sense represents the past, present, and future of the library profession.

The word "access" also unites and encompasses virtually everything that we do in libraries. Appropriately, even though there is a growing tendency toward institutionalizing access services in libraries, there is very little consensus on what units or departments belong under that administrative umbrella. As the contributors to this volume will show, access services might fall within the realm of public services, or of technical services, or indeed might legitimately constitute a third, distinct and independent component of library services. Some have expressed concern that the concept of access services lacks focus and definition because it does not have a consistent or universal reporting structure. I believe, however, that its versatility is the strength of the concept. While the components of public or technical services are, for the most part, the

© 1992 by The Haworth Press, Inc. All rights reserved.

same from library to library, regardless of the institution's size, resources, or mission, those of access services are flexible, established on the basis of what makes good sense in terms of local conditions or priorities. Thus, what comprises access services can be any library's decision, depending on the unique access issues it faces, and always considering the needs of the library user. As Alberta Bailey and Lora Lennertz state in their article from this collection, "The access services manager represents empowerment for the user when there is a true commitment to the access services concept."

The totality of this access services concept is perhaps beyond the scope of any single volume. Thus, there may be aspects of what have been called access services in various libraries that receive just passing mention here. There are many different visions of this concept, many different realities. With a concept that is evolving as rapidly as that of access services, no truly comprehensive handbook is possible. The largest goal of this anthology is not to define access services–such a effort would be futile and pointless. Rather, this volume seeks to serve two purposes. The first of these is to demonstrate, through discussions such as Deborah Carver's, that the foundations of what are now called access services are deeply ingrained in library practice and literature, and, second, to provide practical and intellectual models for the future development of the field.

The volume is arranged around two complimentary themes. The articles which appear earlier are those of a more philosophical or theoretical nature. It is vital that the practice of access services in libraries, however defined, has a cogent theoretical basis. This is important because, in the past many of the components of access services have been viewed as routine, purely clerical functions, and continuing to think in these terms diminishes the larger concept. In this category, W. Bede Mitchell's article sets the tone for the ensuing collection. Deborah Carver discusses the historical antecedents of access services. John Harer does a excellent job of describing a conceptual balance between tradition and innovation in how we in the library profession interpret the concept of access.

Theory should be linked with an overall philosophy of management. In their review article, Karen Lange and Linda Tietjen set a broad agenda of management issues for access services practitioners. Building from these themes, Amy Chang puts forth some of the ways in which the concept of "quality service"–a prominent theme in the recent literature of business and management–can be applied to library management in access services. Alberta Bailey and Lora Lennertz take these principles one step farther by showing how they figure into the processes of policy formation and revision. Barry Brown's concluding piece discusses some interesting techniques of operations management and evaluations. And Brenda Cameron-Miller brings the perspective of a circulation department head from a mid-sized public library to her article on planning and workflow analysis.

Finally, access services managers often find themselves thinking on a theoretical level, but acting on a purely practical one. The design, delivery, and evaluation of responsive library services is first priority and ongoing challenge of access services. Articles such as those by Claire Bellanti on access to materials in remote storage, Greg Notess's on networked information resources, Merri Hartse and Daniel Lee's on policy analysis and revision, Celine Sharp's on shelving accuracy, Tammy Nickelson Dearie and Alice Perez on telephone access, and Matthew Moore's on calculating circulation rates provide useful information on just a few of the current and emerging issues related to delivering access services.

Special thanks and acknowledgements are due the following: Virginia Steel and Pat Weaver-Myers, the consulting editors of this volume, for their numerous fine contributions; Bruce Morton, Assistant Dean for Public Services at Montana State University Libraries, for support and advice; Peter Gellatly of the Haworth Press for giving me the opportunity to compile the volume; Kathy Miller and Beverly Marsh for clerical and secretarial assistance, and the entire access services staff at MSU–Kathy Aden, Pat Engbretsen, Shari Grubb, Mary Anne Hansen, Camille Jackson, Dineen Kailey, David Martinez, Ellen Palmer, Todd Stewart, and Bob Tetro. Finally, my wife, Beatrice, and children, Kelsey and Keegan, deserve my deepest appreciation; I look forward to having more time on weekends now that this project is finished.

I hope that the articles in this volume further the development of the still-young concept of access services. To date, there has been a paucity of writings in library literature about access services; in that sense, the literature has lagged far behind actual practice. As more and more libraries reorganize around access services, however, practitioners and administrators will use and build upon this literature. Clearly, access services is an idea whose time has come.

Gregg Sapp
Head of Access Services
Montana State University Libraries
Bozeman, Montana

Access:
The Key to Public Service

W. Bede Mitchell

SUMMARY. S.R. Ranganathan's five laws of library science are examined for the implications they hold for determining access services policies. A number of theoretical and practical problems are discussed in light of the insights gained from Ranganathan's laws.

INTRODUCTION

It seems appropriate to begin by defining the term "access" as it is used in the library context. *Webster's New Collegiate Dictionary* says that access is having the opportunity or permission to enter, approach, speak with, or use. Thus "library access" could mean permission to use the collections and the opportunity to approach and speak with library staff in order to seek assistance. The opportunity to seek assistance is the aspect of access that leads me to regard it as the key to public service. Permission to use the collection may mean nothing more than opening the library. However, when a library is open but assistance is unavailable the public soon finds it has been granted limited access. Many library users need help to find what they need in the library, and they would not be

---

W. Bede Mitchell is Associate Librarian for Public Services, Appalachian State University, Boone, NC 28608. He earned his MLS at the University of Michigan and his EdD at Montana State University. This paper is adapted from an address delivered March 15, 1991 at the conference "Access Services: Circulation and Beyond" sponsored by the School of Library and Information Science, University of Iowa.

well served by having access that is limited to "permission to use."

In order to seek a more complete view of what is meant by access, I turn to S. R. Ranganathan's 1931 set of five laws of library science.[1] His laws remain one of the best guides to the role of librarianship, and they go a long way toward showing why access is the key to public service:

1. *Books Are For Use*. We should evaluate collections and services in terms of user needs. Preservation needs are important but should not be considered primary. Objective and empirical investigation should replace subjective, impressionistic approaches. The purpose of all our policies and procedures should be to ensure that users' needs are satisfied.
2. *Every Reader His/Her Book*. We are obliged to help find the resources that meet a user's information need.
3. *Every Book Its Reader*. We should be concerned with exposure as well as accessibility. Library materials should find their potential users.
4. *Save The Time Of The Reader*. Information services must satisfy needs as efficiently as possible.
5. *The Library Is A Growing Organism*. The library must be willing to adapt to new social conditions, technological developments, needs of clientele, etc.

I think these laws constitute a sound philosophy of public service because they clearly and concisely emphasize that the primary role of librarians should be to assist users in accessing information. Maurice Line made the same point about the importance of maximizing access by identifying five laws which he claimed are more likely to be observed by academic libraries:

1. Books Are For Collecting.
2. Some Readers Their Books.
3. Some Books Their Readers.
4. Waste The Time Of The Reader.
5. The Library Is A Growing Mausoleum.[2]

Line may have been speaking with tongue slightly in cheek, but his laws complement Ranganathan's. These two sets of laws imply that the effectiveness of our public services should be measured by the extent to which library materials are accessible to the public. Because Raganathan's laws constitute a philosophy of public service defined in terms of access, I will examine each law in turn, in search of implications for access services.

BOOKS ARE FOR USE

As already noted, this law stresses that preservation should not take precedence over use. We must define our services in terms of user needs. It seems to follow that we should try to avoid creating access barriers that are intended to protect materials from the public. For example, placing certain sexually-oriented materials in closed stack collections appears to violate this law. Not allowing preservation to take precedence over use also has implications for collection development. Access services librarians should be well acquainted with the 80/20 rule of collection use, which was articulated and documented in the studies of Richard Trueswell and others.[3] Without claiming that the figures would be the same in all libraries, Trueswell told us that if we studied the actual use of our collections we would find that something like 80% of all use would be of only about 20% of the total collection. Most of Trueswell's research focused on circulation data, but he also found that usage patterns of books and journals that are used in-house tend to conform to the 80/20 rule.[4] Thus it may appear that in order for us to obey Ranganathan's first law we should eliminate all barriers that are intended to protect library materials and concentrate our collection development efforts on supporting the needs of our patrons that are expressed through use patterns.

However, I think this "strict constructionist" interpretation of the first law fails to take into account the way in which Ranganathan's fifth law must be applied to Ranganathan's other four laws. That is, our understanding of what these laws are intended to do must be predicated on our understanding of how changing conditions are affecting access.

When Ranganathan told us that preservation should not be given primacy over access and use, perhaps he had in mind access barriers like closed stack collections. Certainly such collections make it more difficult for patrons to gain access to the materials in question. However, after I had to reorder Annie Leibovitz's collection of *Rolling Stone* photos for the third time because of mutilation, it was clear that I could not conform to Ranganathan's first, second and fourth laws by simply reordering the same book over and over again. If I kept the Leibovitz book in the open stacks in the face of my previous experience with that title, how would I be saving the time of the reader who finds the citation in the catalog, hunts the book down in the stacks, and finds it to be too mutilated to be of any value?

These failures to conform to Ranganathan's laws are the result of not interpreting his laws in light of current conditions. Similarly, perhaps when Ranganathan told us that preservation should not be given primacy over use he was criticizing the tendency of some libraries to collect arcane materials instead of purchasing more copies of high demand items. However, just as I objected to a slavish devotion to the belief that Ranganathan's laws forbid any kind of restricted access to certain materials, so do I reject the notion that Ranganathan wanted all libraries to collect only those titles that can expect frequent use. To adopt such a collection philosophy in these times would constitute a far greater violation of his laws. Specifically, in the words of Ann Okerson and Kendon Stubbs "the present system of scholarly publishing is in danger. Information overproduction, 'publish or perish' philosophy, the weakening U.S. dollar, skyrocketing prices and the increasing unaffordability of published research findings . . . all lead the Association of Research Libraries to believe that cancellation projects must be a way-station to longer-rage solutions."[5] The experience of the University of California at Berkeley illustrates the point: as Berkeley's subscriptions took an increasingly larger share of the materials budget, the number of monographs purchased went from 83,000 in 1981-82 to 42,000 in 1990-91.[6]

As these ominous trends continue, it has been suggested that future researchers will find yawning gaps in library resources when they attempt to study our era. We are buying fewer and fewer titles; books tend to go out of print relatively quickly due to changes in the inventory tax laws; and we are thus unable to retrospectively fill in collection gaps that are becoming larger every day. While Ranganathan said preservation should not be given primacy, surely that is not tantamount to ignoring completely our obligation to ensure access to information that is important but does not become part of the 20% that satisfies 80% of demand. Directors of ARL libraries, in attempting to find solutions to the crisis in scholarly publishing, are promoting

> a new paradigm for research libraries, with a shift from supply to access; sharing expensive international journals among several libraries statewide or in a multi-university region; exploring opportunities to facilitate transmission of information via developing networks and other technologies.[7]

Irene Hoadley and John Corbin struck a similar note in an article on library organizational structures. "Already libraries are experiencing a leveling off, if not a decrease, in the number of items added to the collection. At the same time there is an increasing number of access tools (such as CD-ROM databases) being added to libraries. There will probably never be as many dollars spent on access as are spent on acquisitions, but the prejudice in favor of acquisitions will disappear as the emphasis moves to fulfilling the needs of users rather than simply building larger collections."[8]

In a way, these quotes are basically restatements of Raganathan's laws, but they are based on a understanding of our present economic conditions and the current state of scholarly publishing. The question is how best to achieve the goal of meeting user needs in the face of our budgetary problems. The laws and issues relating to access must be understood in light of the kind of library under consideration. Any non-research library, whether it be a small public or college library, should interpret the "books are for use" law a bit differently than large research libraries. Even though no library can collect everything, major research libraries have an obligation to place greater emphasis on preservation than do other libraries. And this obligation is very much in keeping with Ranganathan's dictum that use be a higher priority than preservation, because one cannot use what is not available *anywhere*, and as all libraries try to cope with declining buying power we will all be more dependent on cooperative programs to ensure access for our users.

To summarize thus far, perhaps the most important lesson to be taken from the foregoing is that our users' needs must be the primary focus of our public services, but the way in which we go about meeting those needs will be affected by the kind of library we are administering, the resources that are available to us, the prevailing social and economic conditions, and user behaviors. Because Raganathan's first law stresses user needs over collection considerations, I will conclude this section with a comment about what constitutes a real need and why the concept of "real need" is important to access services librarians.

All of us have a real need for food because without food we would not survive. But if I say that I have a need for chocolate I am expressing a desire rather than a real need. To apply this distinction to access services, patrons try frequently to persuade librarians to change certain policies because those policies are interfering with patron needs. For example, some patrons may say the loan period should be lengthened because it is too short for them to use materials adequately. However, would changing the loan period really meet patrons' needs? Some studies, such as those by Buckland and Shaw, have concluded that the great majority of books loaned will be returned on, or very near, their due dates, and this pattern will remain even after the loan period is changed.[9] If this holds true, then lengthening the loan period would mean most loaned materials will stay out of the building for that much longer a period of time. The result would be a reduction in the overall level of book availability, i.e., a reduction in the level of patron access to the collection. I believe that access to the collection is the library equivalent of a true need, and in some cases lengthening the loan period can lead to the library's meeting that true need less effectively. By comparison, the convenience of the longer loan period for the patron is a desire, a desire that may lead to less library conformity to the rule that we should save the time of our patrons.

I am not claiming that there is no such thing as a loan period that is too short. My point is that we have an obligation to apply our professional expertise to solving library problems. We need to consider the possible negative effect of proposed policy changes on availability and then determine whether we can find better solutions. We are in a service *profession*, and we should exercise our professional expertise for the good of our users, even if in some cases the users do not recognize that our decisions are in their best interests.

Another way of making my point is to consider the difference between the attitude that says "the customer is always right," and the attitude of the professional, such as a physician, who attempts to influence the behavior of the patient by asserting greater medical expertise. An ethical physician should not prescribe an inappropriate treatment, even if the patient wants to take that treatment. Similarly, if a patron wants to use *Reader's Guide* because he or she is familiar with it but the librarian knows it is not the best source for the required information, the librarian has a professional obligation to explain to the patron why his or her particular need would be better filled by using, for example, *Psychological Abstracts*. Our access policies must be rooted in an understanding of our patrons' real library needs and the ways in which our policies, popular or not, will promote the satisfaction of those real needs.

Another reason why access services librarians must understand what constitutes a real need is that there is a tendency to equate use with need. More and more libraries are carrying out sophisticated use studies which indicate which subject areas and/or specific titles are most heavily used. I want to caution against the danger of assuming that use equals need. Suppose someone goes to the local library with a particular information need and, without consulting a librarian, concludes that the library has very little of value about that subject. That patron will likely leave the library without using anything, and therefore there has been a unmet need that will not show up in any use study. It may even be argued that use studies may skew our understanding of patron needs because some people will use what we do have, even if it is not what they needed.

Further discussion of determining our patrons' real needs leads us to an examination of Ranganathan's second law.

EVERY READER HIS/HER BOOK

I understand this to mean that the library must strive to help meet every patron's information need. Therefore we should ask ourselves, what percentage of the people who enter our library are able to access the information they need? We can try to measure the extent to which our materials are available or accessible, but as we have seen, we must also know what needs are not being met and are not being expressed to us. How do we go about gathering this information?

Our professional literature contains many books and articles that offer methods for conducting availability and failure rate studies, and I do not think this is the place to repeat them.[10] At this point I would like to discuss the problems inherent in trying to identify unmet and unspoken patron needs.

The first method of assessing patron needs involves the study of the subjects and formats of the materials we seek on behalf of our patrons' through our various resource sharing programs. For example, we can examine the subjects and formats of the materials which our patrons are ordering most frequently through interlibrary loan. Similarly, we can look for subject and format patterns in the referral letters we write to enable our patrons to arrow materials from other libraries, if we have such a service. The information about patron needs that can be gained through resource-sharing records is much too valuable to be discarded in the interest of reducing work.

The second method for determining our patrons' needs is designed to find out what unmet needs are not being communicated to us. This can be done by asking users to fill out a failure slip whenever they cannot find what they need. By indicating the nature of their failed search, patrons enable us to determine whether the patrons failed because:

1. our library does not own the items necessary to satisfy the need,
2. the items were owned but not available, or
3. the items were available but the user simply failed to search successfully.

Carrying out such an analysis of user failure is very labor intensive, especially if it is done all the time. However, Nancy Van House and her co-authors describe in two different books how such studies can be done in public and academic libraries using sampling techniques.[11]

Such studies can yield valuable information. In one such study reported by Schofield, Cooper and Waters, it was found that of all patron search failures, 13.5% were because the titles were not owned, 32.4% were due to inadequate patron searching, and 54% were because the titles, though owned, were not available.[12] These results raise many questions. Just to pose a few of them: Why were over half of the failures due to material unavailability? How much of the unavailability was due to misshelving, or to previous borrowing? Are there policies and procedures that the library can modify in such a way that material unavailability can be reduced?

Certainly there are other useful, if less comprehensive and systematic ways of identifying unmet user needs. We can take advantage of informal contacts with patrons outside of the library. We can invite representatives of groups with unique needs, such as disabled or minority patrons, to meet with librarians and discuss their perspectives on library services. But whatever combination of methods we use, the need to determine user needs can legitimately be considered to be one of the most important parts of our access services enterprise. If we want to help every reader gain access to his/her book, we must take the initiative to find out what needs are unmet and unspoken.

EVERY BOOK ITS READER

This law means we should be concerned with exposure as well as accessibility. Therefore libraries should be judged in part on the basis of how well they inform people about materials of potential use to them. Ideally we would familiarize ourselves with the interests of all of our users so that we can let them know when we identify sources of potential use to them. However, this is clearly an impossible goal for all but a few librarians, such as corporate librarians who support the research of relatively few people. Aside from such exceptions, the lesson of this law for the rest of us is that we must advertise our library resources and services in order to promote their use.

While I believe the other laws carry greater implications for access services, I would nevertheless like to draw attention to the way in which this law relates to a point made by Richard Dougherty: "There is a striking contradiction between our professional imperative of providing free and easy access to information and the rising tide of information that is rapidly engulfing us . . . We need to face the reality that more and more people haven't the time, the expertise, or the psychological make-up to find the information that best serves their needs."[13] A similar point was made by James Rice, who wrote: "End users . . . have little knowledge of how to narrow the search into a manageable and high quality result. We are a profession filled with people who could be helping end users make better decisions in their consumption of information."[14]

In this context, "Every book its reader" seems to imply that librarians have a responsibility to evaluate materials and recommend those with the most potential use to a patron. But this element of evaluation and selection takes place more appropriately during the process of identifying sources of information, rather than during the process of accessing or delivering those sources. The identification of information sources seems to involve a kind of professional judgment which is not among the professional judgments typically made during the process of delivering information sources. This fundamental difference explains in part why reference is rarely a part of access services. Another reason for that involves the law that states we must save the time of the reader. We will see why this follows by turning to a examination of that law.

SAVE THE TIME OF THE READER

In order to satisfy user needs as efficiently as possible, we need to identify the barriers to access. If we understand the nature of the barriers to efficient access, we can then design services which will mitigate the effects of the barriers. Access services as an organizational model is the result of such a design.

In his book *Library Services in Theory and Context*, Michael Buckland identifies six barriers to access:

1. Identification–A suitable information source must be identified.
2. Availability–The source must be physically available.
3. Price–The price of access, in terms of money, time, effort, and discomfort, must be acceptable to the inquirer.
4. Cost–The cost to the library of providing the access, in terms of effort, money, or inconvenience, must be acceptable to the library's view of its role, mission, and values.
5. Cognitive level–The source must not be too advanced or elementary for the inquirer.
6. Acceptability–The source may not be acceptable to the inquirer because the inquirer does not deem the source to be credible, or because the source gives the inquirer unwelcome information.[15]

Not all of these barriers are the responsibility of access services. As I have already said, the first barrier, "Identification," is *not* typically one of the access barriers with which access services is expected to deal. By virtue of their training, reference librarians continue to be responsible for helping patrons identify suitable sources of information. The justification for separating identification from the other aspects of access is articulated by Irene Hoadley and John Corbin.[16] In proposing a new library organizational structure they distinguish between access services (such as circulation, document delivery, interlibrary lending, reserve, and stack maintenance), and those units such as reference and instructional services, which are concerned with interpretation of materials:

> This proposed structure . . . moves almost solely to a functional structure, which brings about more centralization of activities. For example, since the circulation of all materials is in one unit, it is more likely that there will be uniformity

in circulation policies. Bringing together all interpretive or reference services in one location will benefit users by reducing the number of places they must go to find information, thereby decreasing the amount of time it takes.[17]

In short, the adoption of the access services model, with a separate interpretive services unit, is justified because this organization appears best suited to making patron access as efficient and effective as possible.

For reasons very similar to those just cited, I think it is clear why the fifth and sixth barriers to access–"Cognitive Level" and "Acceptability"–are also not normally the responsibility of access services. If an information source is unacceptable to a patron for whatever reason, then we must go back to the reference drawing board to identify a more suitable or acceptable source.

Within Buckland's paradigm, access services have come to concentrate on maximizing "Availability" and minimizing the "Price" of access to the user and the "Cost" of access to the library. We would approach the task of maximizing the availability of library materials most efficiently by diagnosing the extent to which we are failing to meet our patrons' needs for identified titles. Let us briefly consider how a properly designed and implemented user study can help us make such a diagnosis, and how we can respond to those results.

One of the most useful, detailed, and labor-intensive of the various availability studies is the one designed by Paul Kantor.[18] His study determines five separate sub-measures of availability. By analyzing user requests we discover the probability that the library has acquired a needed item, the probability that the user will locate the item in the catalog and get the correct call number, the probability that the needed item is not checked out, the probability that uncharged items are in their proper places on the shelves, and the probability that patrons will find items which are in their proper places. Although failures to find items due to any of these causes are undoubtedly access failures, only some can be directly affected by access services policies and procedures.

Access services librarians will be particularly interested in the probabilities of access failure due to items being checked out, uncharged items not being in their proper shelf locations, and patrons being unable to find materials that are in their proper locations. The latter problem is the simplest to address. The best methods for dealing with patron failure to find materials that are where they belong are to improve signage and other methods of leading the patrons to the location, and to work with bibliographic instruction staff members in order to educate users in understanding how call numbers work, how the range guides work, where are the library's more obscure locations, and so on. Unfortunately these steps will not solve the problem, but if carried out well they will reduce such patron errors dramatically.

The problem of uncharged items not being in their proper places on the shelves is due largely to stack maintenance failures. In my experience stack maintenance is the most important aspect of improving availability, not only because of the real improvements that superior stack maintenance brings but also because of the perceived improvements. By that I mean users know when books are not being regularly picked up off of tables, when sorting shelves remain full week after week, when sections of shelves remain in terrible disorder, and when their favorite areas have scores of books that are not in call number order. When users observe these conditions they not only infer correctly that their ability to find materials is being seriously hampered, but their overall confidence in the library's services is seriously undermined.

I urge access services managers to give greater attention to stack maintenance, even at the expense of public service desks if necessary. If the stacks are in terrible shape but we are truly so strapped what cannot add more staff to the shelving crew, then we should close some of the public service desks a few hours before the building closes (or not staff them until an hour or more after morning opening) and reassign the support staff to shelving during those periods. Remember that stacks which are in poor shape will harm considerably the morale of patrons, shelvers, and desk staff.

The probability that needed items are already checked out, what is sometimes called "circulation interference," can be addressed in a number of ways. In his book entitled *Book Availability and the Library User*, required reading for any access services librarian, Michael Buckland analyzes a wealth of data which lead him to conclude that the two most powerful tools for combatting circulation interference are the loan period and duplication of high demand titles.[19] Buckland regards the loan period as the more effective and precise method for increasing availability, with duplication serving as an important alternative method. The danger inherent in relying heavily on duplication is that it can quickly use up our materials budget, but for those public and academic libraries who do not serve as research libraries, duplication is an obvious and undeniably effective way to increase availability.

The importance that Buckland attaches to loan period is based upon his drawing a number of conclusions from this data, the most relevant being the following:

1. The longer the loan period, the lower the immediate availability. The shorter the loan period, the higher the immediate availability.
2. There is a marked tendency for materials to be returned or renewed when they are due back, and this holds true regardless of the length of the official loan period, the status of the borrower, or the subject matter of the books.

In other words, we can adjust our loan periods to maximize availability. However, if we adopt this approach we must do so with care. If we reduce loan periods too much we might find users responding with behavior changes that counteract the intended result of this policy. We must judiciously weigh the advantages and disadvantages of adjusting loan periods. If we choose to adjust the loan period for each title based upon the level of demand on the title, we must craft such a policy with special care or it will be unworkable because of the detail involved in managing it. Imagine the patron confusion that would result if every title in the library had a loan period that was periodically adjusted in light of current demand. It would seem wiser to use only two or three loan periods to accommodate demand, for even then there is a danger that adjustable loan periods will confuse and frustrate patrons to a degree not justified by the benefits. Nevertheless, in spite of findings such as Reginald Coady's, whose research indicated that due dates may be less likely to be observed in the cases of certain kinds of patrons and certain subjects of books,[20] Buckland has demonstrated that we have the potential to abide more closely to Ranganathan's fourth law by influencing materials availability through circulation policies.

There are many kinds of sanctions that libraries might use to improve availability rates. Take for example the patrons who fail to return books even though they have been told that other patrons have requested those books. I strongly endorse policies which revoke the borrowing privileges of such patrons. I also suggest that academic librarians look into the possibility of including a statement in the university's honor code, if there is one, that such behavior constitutes a violation of the honor code and is punishable by one or more of the honor code's typical sanctions. Certainly the most common sanction in use is the overdue fine. Even so, nobody really knows much about the effects of fines and we will probably never know much about their effects. Part of the problem is that it is very difficult to control all the variables that need to be controlled before it can be confidently concluded that changes in overdue rates were caused by the changes made in the fines policies. An exhaustive review of the literature yields a few articles which conclude that if you adopt a no-fines policy, one where the most serious sanction may be a processing fee for very long over-due books, you may have a higher probability of eventually getting your books back, but if you charge fines for each day or week that a book is overdue you may have a greater percentage of books returned on or near the due date.[21] There are no good rules of thumb for determining how big a fine is too big; the access services librarian must consider the profile of the library's patrons and make an informed judgment about what will be an effective deterrent without being cruel and unusual punishment.

I will conclude this discussion of sanctions by calling to your attention a system I devised that is predicated on the use of positive reinforcement to minimize overdues.[22] The system is as yet untried and therefore unproven, but I recommend it to any of you who are concerned with the problem of overdues if for no other reason than it may stimulate you to some creative thinking of your own.

Another barrier is the "Price" of access. Buckland tells us that price refers to the amount of time, effort, discomfort, and money that the patron must expend in accessing materials. For the purposes of our discussion I think we can treat time, effort, and discomfort together, although it is evident there are important distinctions between those factors.

Saving the time, effort, and discomfort of the user can be accomplished in so many ways that a entire book could (and should) be dedicated to the possible methods. However, there is one thing we can do to reduce the user's price of access that I think is far more important than any other method. I refer to ensuring that our public service desks are staffed by well trained, user-oriented personnel. It is amazing how much patrons will forgive if they know they can get help from friendly and capable staff who are motivated to satisfy the patron.

With this in mind it is important to note that the typical access services unit is made up predominantly of classified staff and student assistants, with an access services librarian and perhaps an assistant access services librarian running the show. Most of the real direct contact with the public is done by the non-librarians. This is why I think the training of these staff members is the most important means of controlling the price of access. Patrons are heavily dependent on these staff members for efficient and effective access, that key to public service, and yet these staff members are not librarians. These people usually do not come to their first day of work with a thorough understanding of the library principles, service philosophy, and overarching mission of libraries that we librarians are supposed to gain from our library school educations. Staff need to understand what are their library's stated mission and service goals, and they need to understand how their jobs relate to the accomplishment of those goals. They need to understand the fundamental concept of access and how the library's policies and procedures are intended to facilitate access.

Staff who lack this kind of background will be far less likely to realize that in some cases a rigid application of a certain library policy will actually run counter to the library's efforts to facilitate access. Sometimes it is appropriate to waive an overdue fine if there seem to have been certain extenuating circumstances beyond the patron's control. It may be that this patron will be more likely to comply with circulation policies in the future if we are willing to cut some slack in this particular case. In any event, I advocate designing staff training programs with more in mind than a concern that we cover all the how-tos and don't-do's. A library staff that understands the whys and wherefores is our single greatest weapon in cutting the price of access.

There is also the access issue of price to the user, which includes the debate over when user fees should be charged and when they should not. At the risk of oversimplification, I think the most compelling justifications for charging user fees for certain services have been the perceived need to control the level of use of a costly service, and the need to generate revenue to pay for the service when we lack any other means to pay for it. But in too many situations I fear that fees add to the split between the access-rich patrons and access-poor patrons and so are not justified by the alleged benefits. This reservation should receive greater weight in the future if we do in fact stress greater access at the expense of building collections. The greater emphasis on access implies that more than ever there should be a presumption against assessing user fees. The burden of proof should lie on the side of the debate that supports a proposed user fee.

To conclude this discussion of Buckland's barriers to access, let us consider "Cost." As I said previously, librarianship should have a professional service philosophy as opposed to a business, or "customer is always right" philosophy. If we determine that the resources necessary to offer service X are so great that we would be incapable of maintaining another service that is more in keeping with the library's mission and values, then we should not offer service X. Here I am using the term "service" to stand for any number of possible responses to user demands. A good example of what I mean might be a request that several expensive, highly technical journals be added to the library at which I work, the Belk Library at Appalachia State University. Our institution offers many masters programs and will soon have its first doctoral program, so we are what the Carnegie Foundation calls a comprehensive university–we are not a research university. This role is supposed to be reflected in the performance expectations of our faculty. Teaching is supposedly more important than research. If that is truly the case, then we in the library need to carefully consider the possibility that adding those expensive and obscure journals is not compatible with the mission of our university and our library. In this case, the cost of access to the institution may be too high for us to respond favorably to the request.

THE LIBRARY IS A GROWING ORGANISM

The library does not exist in a vacuum and must be ready to adapt to future needs, technologies, and political and economic realities. I am no futurist, but I will take a few moments to paint with a rather broad brush a picture of what I think will be the greatest future concerns to access services. As we have already seen, many librarians expect that providing means of access will become more important as our ability to build comprehensive collections continues to decline. Therefore access services departments will be under increasing pressure to use various technologies, cooperative resource sharing programs, and document delivery services to reduce the delays that are inevitable when a needed resource is not immediately available within the library. The growing dependence of libraries on vehicles of access will require that more budgetary and human resources will need to be allocated to access services. As access services personnel attempt to apply technology to meet the access challenges of the future, they will need to remain flexible and adaptable because technological changes can be as rapid as they are unexpected.

Changing technology will not only affect the way access services personnel do their jobs, but as Susan Martin pointed out, technology will continue to lead to new products, services, and methods of accessing information that bypass the library, enabling people to find information on their own, without ever coming to a library.[23] But these access opportunities will come at a cost that only some people, and perhaps only some libraries, will be able to afford. The gulf between the haves and have-nots, the access-rich and the access-poor, will widen. Libraries will find it even more difficult to provide their users with levels of access that are commensurate with the levels enjoyed by the access-rich.

We can further expect that technology will continue to make our retrieval tools more powerful and easier to use. Access services personnel will find that this leads to increasing demand and use in general, but in addition we may find that use increases as much in "depth" as it does in "width." Patrons will find more frequently information sources that are now difficult to retrieve due to limitations in printed indexes, card catalogs, and first generation electronic databases. The result could be *wider*, more dispersed collection use, perhaps making the 80/20 law of collection use obsolete. Still, I think access services personnel will continue to struggle with maximizing access to high demand materials because the more powerful retrieval systems are just as likely to lead to increased demand for the materials already in high demand. This is what I am calling *deeper* demand and use. After all, high demand materials are in high demand because they are, to use Buckland's terms, cognitively accessible and credible to a large portion of our users.

On the other had, we might look much further down the road and find that as more information becomes available in full text electronic databases, there will probably be a decline in demand for hard copy items. Patrons will come to expect the capability of downloading electronic text to their own disks, or the option of offprinting the text. Copyright considerations will eventually be worked out so that we will be able to offer these capabilities. As a result, access services personnel will gradually concentrate less on managing vehicles for making hard copy available, and will concentrate more on managing the means for patrons to access electronic text.

The shift from warehousing to access will cause more libraries to adopt the access services organizational structure, and it will create greater pressure on access services personnel when dealing with the public. Let me address this latter point first. In spite of our best efforts to keep our public informed about our budgetary problems, not all of our users are going to understand, or even be aware of, the sufficient reasons that libraries have for shifting to an access mode from a collection mode. And this shift will lead to some misunderstandings and frustrations, no matter how effective our access services. One example of this is described by Hoadley and Corbin: "At present, when a serial title is acquired it is considered a permanent, continuing commitment. Because of constant price increases and the proliferation of journal titles, libraries will be forced to change their attitude of permanency toward serials. Serials will be acquired as they are needed, not because they were needed at some point in the past. Selection of serial titles will be ongoing, not one-time decisions. This change in attitude will serve the users of the libraries better because there will be more flexibility in responding to current needs; it may even make the publishing world more responsive.''[24]

What Hoadley and Corbin are advocating will lead to many incomplete serial runs, a situation that is difficult to explain to a patron who needs a journal issue that we lack because of when we started or stopped our subscription. In the future, if we do shift paradigms, access services personnel are going to find that they spend a lot more time explaining why we must go elsewhere to obtain an information source. This will be a particular problem at larger libraries where regular users are accustomed to the libraries owning what the users need.

Finally, a word about my expectation that more libraries will adopt the access services organizational model. For the reasons given by Hoadley and Corbin, I think the access services model is logical and leads to better public service. For Hoadley and Corbin, the ideal access services model brings together circulation, document delivery, interlibrary lending, reserve, shelving, and stack maintenance, while at the same time bringing together in a separate but related unit all special formats, such as microforms, audiovisuals, software, maps, current journals, and documents. By centralizing responsibility for, and when possible the physical location of, our lending activities and special formats, we can free reference librarians to concentrate on their identification and interpretation functions. Further, we can realize the staffing advantages of cross-training personnel between access service units, we can increase understanding and communication between access service units, and we can benefit from the uniformity of policies and procedures that the access services librarian can impose on the different access units.

CONCLUSION

There are many other aspects of maximizing patron access to information beyond those that I have discussed in the foregoing pages. Some were not addressed due to space limitations, but others were neglected because they are not usually the responsibility of access services units, or indeed of other public service departments. As an example I refer again to the availability study designed by Kantor. We saw that by analyzing user requests we can gain a greater understanding of the reasons why patrons are often failing to find what they need. Many of those failures to access information are most likely to be overcome by the actions and decisions of librarians who do not work in the traditional public service areas. Therefore, if the name of the game is satisfying information needs quickly and efficiently, then I agree with Michael Buckland that the notion of access can provide a unifying concept for our whole field of librarianship.[25]

REFERENCE NOTES

1. S. R. Ranganathan, Five Laws of Library Science (Bombay: Asia Publishing House, 1931).
2. Maurice B. Line, "Review of Use of Library Materials: The University of Pittsburgh Study," College & Research Libraries 40 (November 1979): 557-558.
3. Richard W. Trueswell, "A Quantitative Measure of User Circulation Requirements and Its Possible Effect on Stack Thinning and Multiple Copy Determination," American Documentation 16 (January 1965): 20-25; idem, "Determining the Optimal Number of Volumes for a Library's Core Collection," Libri 16 no.1 (1966): 49-60; idem, "Some Behavioral Patterns of Library Users, the 80/20 Rule," Wilson Library Bulletin 43 (January 1969): 458-461.
4. Richard W. Trueswell, "Article Use and Its Relationship to Individual User Satisfaction," College & Research Libraries 31 (July 1970): 239-245.
5. Ann Okerson and Kendon Stubbs, "The Library "Doomsday" Machine," Publishers Weekly 238 (February 8, 1991): 37.
6. Ibid.
7. Ibid.
8. Irene B. Hoadley and John Corbin, "Up the Beanstalk: An Evolutionary Organizational Structure for Libraries," American Libraries 21 (July-August 1990): 676.
9. Michael K. Buckland, Book Availability and the Library User (New York: Pergamon, 1975); W. M. Shaw, Jr., "Loan Period Distribution in Academic Libraries," Information Processing & Management 12 no.3 (1976): 157-159.
10. Paul B. Kantor, Objective Performance Measures for Academic and Research Libraries (Washington: Association for Research Libraries, 1984); F. W. Lancaster, If You Want to Evaluate Your Library. . . . (Champaign: University

of Illinois Graduate School of Library and Information Science, 1988); Nancy A. Van House, Mary Jo Lynch, Charles R. McClure, Douglas L. Zweizig, and Eleanor Jo Rodger, Output Measures for Public Libraries: A Manual of Standardized Procedures, 2nd ed. (Chicago: American Library Association, 1987); Nancy A. Van House, Beth T. Weil, and Charles R. McClure, Measuring Academic Library Performance: A Practical Approach (Chicago: American Library Association, 1990).

11. Van House, Weil, and McClure, Measuring Academic Library Performance: A Practical Approach, pp. 60-76.

12. J. L. Schofield, A. Cooper, and D. H. Waters, "Evaluation of an Academic Library's Stock Effectiveness," Journal of Librarianship 7 (July 1975): 207-227.

13. Richard M. Dougherty, "Balancing Access and Overload," Journal of Academic Librarianship 16 (January 1991): 339.

14. James Rice, "The Hidden Role of Librarians," Library Journal 114 (January 1989): 59.

15. Michael K. Buckland, Library Services in Theory and Context, 2nd ed. (New York: Pergamon, 1988).

16. Hoadley and Corbin, "Up the Beanstalk."

17. Ibid. p. 678.

18. Kantor, Objective Performance Measures.

19. Buckland, Book Availability.

20. Reginald P. Coady, "Comparing Return Rates of Home Loans of Social Science Book Material," Library & Information Science Research 8 (January 1986): 41-52; idem, "A Comparison of Single Book Renewals by Subject and Patron Status for Similar Rates of Renewal and Return," Journal of the American Society for Information Science 37 (March 1986): 78-85.

21. Robert Burgin and Patsy Hansel, "More Hard Facts on Overdue," Library & Archival Security 36 (Summer/Fall 1984): 5-18.

22. W. Bede Mitchell, "On the Use of Positive Reinforcement to Minimize the Problem of Overdue Library Materials," Journal of Library Administration 9 no.3 (1988): 87-101.

23. Susan K. Martin, "Information Technology and Libraries: Toward the Year 2000," College & Research Libraries 50 (July 1989): 397-405.

24. Hoadley and Corbin, "Up the Beanstalk," p. 676.

25. Buckland, Library Services in Theory and Context.

From Circulation to Access Services: The Shift in Academic Library Organization

Deborah Carver

SUMMARY. This article traces the organizational shifts that have occurred in academic libraries with respect to the function of circulation. Up until WWII, the circulation department played a highly visible, central role in the mission of the academic library. The responsibilities assigned to the department were broad and included a variety of reader advisory services. Following WWII, the role of the department narrowed, and the work became mechanical and routine. The major forces affecting this change were the influence of scientific management, increasing specialization of labor, and the growing emphasis on unit efficiency. Since 1980, however, the function of the circulation department has begun to broaden once again. In many cases, new responsibilities have been added including interlibrary loan and document delivery. With the growth in the availability and cost of information and the decline in purchasing power, libraries have focused more intensely on broader goals and organizational effectiveness. Access services represents a renewed commitment to patron satisfaction and a willingness to experiment with different organizational structures to meet that primary goal.

INTRODUCTION

In the past ten years, a noteworthy variation has emerged in library organization. This change has been more apt to occur in large academic libraries, and while its appearance is not yet prevalent, it has become an increasingly common organizational structure. At the nucleus of this new structure is the circulation depart-

---

Deborah Carver is Assistant University Librarian for Public Services at the Knight Library, University of Oregon, Eugene, OR 97403.

© 1992 by The Haworth Press, Inc. All rights reserved.

ment; the other components vary, but the most common elements are stack maintenance, reserve collections, interlibrary loans, current periodicals and document delivery. The term often used to describe this new structure is "access services," and in most cases, it represents an enlargement of circulation's responsibilities. From the perspective of private enterprise, this variation in organization may seem like another incremental change that determines the meager progress of public bureaucracies. But compared to the relative stagnation that has gripped library organizations during the past fifty years, this change may be one of the more significant attempts to refocus library services through internal restructuring.

A review of the literature on circulation and access services quickly reveals the lack of printed information on either topic. Most of the articles and books that deal with this aspect of library service are concerned with specific automated systems, statistics for collection development purposes, loan rules governing non-traditional formats, etc. Very little has been written on this unit's broader purpose and contribution to overall library goals. Fortunately, it is still possible to trace the evolution of the circulation unit by reviewing a few basic texts and thoughtful articles published since the 1930s.

Perhaps the most intriguing discovery gleaned from the literature is that the structure and scope of the circulation department in academic libraries has come nearly full circle in the past sixty years. From the turn of the century until WWII, the circulation department was at the core of library services. Its responsibilities were broad and its professional status was unquestioned. For the next thirty-five years, however, the unit's scope narrowed and its functions became highly routinized. Beginning in the 1980s, another shift occurred. Some circulation departments were renamed "access services" and reorganized around a larger purpose. This essay describes these organizational shifts that have occurred and explores some possible reasons behind the formation of access service departments.

CIRCULATION: THE CORE OF LIBRARY SERVICES

During most of the nineteenth century, academic libraries were primarily concerned with preservation. Undergraduate borrowing was very restricted, and in many universities students were allowed to visit the library only once a week. The books were considered precious artifacts for a handful of privileged researchers; they were not necessary for a general education. Beginning in the late-1800s, some institutions began to loosen these restrictions, and the collections were viewed from a more practical and utilitarian perspective. Emphasis was placed not just on undergraduate teaching, but on undergraduate scholarship, which necessitated wider access to library materials.

This shift in higher educational theory and practice created an organizational change within academic libraries. The circulation or loan department took on greater responsibility and became the core of public services. The heyday of the circulation librarian is described in quaint detail by Brown and Bousfield in their classic 1933 text, *Circulation Work in College and University Libraries*.[1] Brown and Bousfield saw the loan department as the most important unit of the library. "Whatever the position of the library in the institution may be, the loan department should be the center of the activities of the library."[2]

The circulation or loan librarian was in the best position to know the students' needs and to recommend specific titles for their general edification. Circulating books and maintaining records was only an incidental part of the librarian's responsibility. Brown and Bousfield describe the department as much more than a passive agency. "Not only should it apply books wanted, it should stimulate, expand, and increase the intellectual needs of its readers.[3]

The loan librarian played an active role in library orientation. Reference staff worked primarily with graduate students, but in many colleges and universities, the loan librarian was responsible for instructing undergraduates. In most academic libraries, there was very little differentiation between the reference and the loan librarian. Another major function of the department was to track patrons' unsuccessful searches and analyze their causes. This responsibility put the loan librarian in a position to recommend specific remedies including the purchase of new titles, investigations into binding delays, and faster cataloging procedures.

Brown and Bousfield predicted that the role of the circulation department would expand further as a result of continued experiments in certain prestigious institutions such as the University of

Chicago, Harvard, and Johns Hopkins. Following the spirit of Bertrand Russell, who saw a regrettable tendency in newer universities to embrace the lecture method and insist on class attendance, these institutions were emphasizing the acquisition of knowledge through the wide use of books and research.[4] Brown and Bousfield expected these changes in teaching to have a profound impact on the library. The loan librarian would need to provide greater personalized service, more guidance, and intellectual discussion of the best books.

CIRCULATION: SCIENTIFIC MANAGEMENT AND ROUTINE LABOR

Soon after Brown and Bousfield published their text, however, the function of the circulation department began to change. Frederick Taylor (1856-1915), whose ideas on scientific management had revolutionized private industry, was beginning to influence the service sector and public bureaucracies.[5] Brown and Bousfield recognized a certain division of labor between public services and cataloging, but they did not envision the dramatic growth in departmentalization based on the principles of scientific management that took place following WWII.

Prior to Taylor, few rational theories of management existed. The tremendous growth in manufacturing following the industrial revolution necessitated some form of managerial control to maximize output. The cornerstone of scientific management was the quest for efficiency. The techniques involved the separation of planning from the execution of tasks, close examination of discrete functions, and the application of minor andjustments to improve productivity. Advocates of this theory argued that both micro and macro management were necessary components, but it was not uncommon for only the micro aspects to receive attention. Although Taylor may not have advocated a hyper-subdivision of labor, his theories contributed to this development in many larger libraries.

In academic libraries, the interest in greater efficiency and at least some of the tenets of scientific management was fueled by two major developments: the growth in collections and the shortage of trained professional staff. Although many libraries hired more employees following WWII, it was still difficult to handle the physical and intellectual problems associated with the tremendous increase in published material. As libraries continued to grow in size, they continued to departmentalize. In public services, reference and information services were separated from circulation, and in technical services, the acquisition process was split from cataloging. In larger organizations, divisions were also made according to format (microforms, serials) and subject.

The professional who performed an array of services from charging books to providing reader services was seen as an inefficient use of skilled and higher paid labor. Specialization and the division of work resulted in breaking down some library tasks into several basic parts, each of which could be rapidly handled by easily-trained, relatively inexpensive clerical assistants. In an effort toward greater efficiency, the circulation department was eventually relieved of all functions save those associated with the charging of books. By the end of WWII, a stripped-down, mechanized, clerically-staffed circulation department hand replaced the broader concept so fondly documented by Brown and Bousfield. The atmosphere became businesslike and impersonal. Patron questions were discouraged because the clerical staff were not equipped to answer even general inquiries. Critics argued that effective service had been sacrificed, and fragmentation was destroying the unity behind a common service philosophy.[6] Despite these concerns, many academic libraries continued their march toward efficiency through specialization and division of labor under the banner of scientific management.

The interest in efficient use of trained staff sparked a lively debate concerning the role of the professional librarian in circulation. Alarmed by the threat to the professional status of loan librarians, Bousfield wrote an impassioned essay in 1944 calling for a halt in the current trend of relying primarily on clerical staff.[7] Bousfield used the same arguments favoring the division of labor and specialization to make his point. Of course, there should be some distinction between clerical and professional tasks, but the need for a professional loan librarian still existed and would likely increase in the future. Loan librarians should not be overly concerned with the routine procedures, but should concentrate on planning, supervising, and advising readers. Bousfield predicated that the post-war boom in college enrollments would intensify the need for professional assistance at the circulation desk and argued that the scope of the department needed to be broadened to meet the demands of more students. In an attempt to re-professionalize the department, Bousfield recommended that the circulation librarian advise on all reading assignments and recreational reading and keep in close contact with the collection and service needs of graduate students and faculty. The reference department, on the other hand, would maintain its usual passive function of "aiding persons who apply for information, but would not project itself into the teaching departments or student activities."[8] Bousfield advocated a new title to reflect these broader responsibilities. He suggested replacing "circulation department" with either "public service" or "public relations department."

Bousfield was unable to reverse the trend toward a narrower and more technical role in circulation. As the universe of published material continued to grow, library administrators became increasingly concerned with acquiring new titles, cataloging, and maintaining high production schedules. Budgets were relatively healthy, compared to present times, so the focus remained on collection building and efficient processing. Emphasis shifted from providing reader services to relying on the resourcefulness of patrons.[9] With some basic instruction, most students were expected to fend for themselves, and since a significant portion of retrievable information was locally-available, the task was less complex than it is today.

Several larger academic libraries retained at least one professional in circulation, but even this limited presence was increasingly criticized. Brown and Bousfield's earlier recommendation that all contacts with patrons in college and university libraries be handled by professionally trained librarians hand been largely dismissed. E. W. McDiarmid, speaking at a University of Chicago Library Institute in 1948, considered this recommendation excessive and wasteful. McDiarmid believed that most public contact at the circulation desk consisted of simple clerical or directional questions. "In the interest of efficiency, we should give up the idea of providing experts for every public contact," he told his audience.[10] In the same year, the ALA Descriptive List of Professional Duties in Libraries concluded that "registration and circulation is non-professional in nature, requiring first of all, familiarity with good clerical procedures."[11]

By the 1950s, most library administrators and educators recognized that a significant portion of circulation work was routine, yet some directors continued to see a need for a professional in the department. Advising and instructing patrons hand become the exclusive role of the reference department, but a professional in circulation might still be necessary to supervise larger staffs, establish policies, and improve relations with the public.[12] Despite some attempts to maintain and enrich the role of the professional circulation librarian, the job became categorized as "the most uninspired, unprogressive, and unrewarding" position in public services.[13]

The goal of efficiency and the attraction to scientific management prevailed into the 1960s and 1970s. It is likely that the steady increase in library loans during the period perpetuated this trend and preserved the clerical role of the department. Circulation staff had difficulty keeping up with the labor-intensive procedures of filing cards, typing notices, and reshelving books.[14] It did not seem practical or necessary to assign the department additional duties and more professional responsibilities.

During the 1970s, many academic libraries introduced some form of automation to their circulation procedures. The literature began to describe the application of systems analysis to circulation routines, but little attention was given to changes in staffing or functions as a result of automation. In a 1973 article, Laurence Miller attempted to answer some new concerns regarding the purpose, function, and staffing patterns of circulation departments by conducting a survey of 126 major university libraries.[15] Miller discovered that the limited purpose (checking out books, stack maintenance) of circulation remained firmly entrenched. Most administraors, including those who employed professional circulation librarians, clearly favored a restricted and largely technical/clerical role for the department. Despite the lack of functions requiring the specific assignment of professionals, Miller's Survey indicated that over half the libraries responding still employed such personnel in their circulation departments. Most of these libraries reported that policy making and supervision justified a professional presence. Miller took exception with this position. He argued that policy making should take place at a higher level within the organization, and supervision did not require a professional degree.

Although Miller's survey confirmed the status quo, it also indicated a slightly different trend among those libraries that had more experience with automation. Of the 41 libraries that had undergone some form of computerization and systems analysis, Miller reported that 13 had broadened the range of functions allocated to the circulation. Only two indicated that the scope had been narrowed.[16] Miller found this result "surprising." At that time, many librarians expected automation to lead to a further diminution of circulation's responsibilities.

ACCESS SERVICES: BACK TO THE FUTURE

Miller's survey foreshadowed a new shift in the function and role of circulation departments in academic libraries. Since the mid-1970s, libraries have experienced several changes, both internal and external, which have had an impact on their mission, structure, and procedures. While the goal of unit efficiency seemed to dominate previous decades, in recent years libraries have been forced to examine their overall effectiveness. Library managers are still concerned with performing each task quickly without wasting resources, but they are becoming increasingly sensitive to broader priorities. Which tasks produce the most public benefit, and which tasks must we abandon to meet more important needs? The most significant developments shaping this shift include: the explosion of information in all formats, increasing costs of materials and labor, declining budgets, rising expectations on the part of the user community, and changes in library automation and the emergence of electronic and network technologies. In response to these changes, many academic libraries have reorganized and reassigned responsibilities. In the search for greater effectiveness, the goals and duties of the circulation department have broadened, and in some institutions, the term "access services" has been selected to reflect this new focus.

One of the first changes to occur which affected the function of the department was a reaction to the principles of scientific management. Several widely-read management theorists, including Taylor admirers such as Drucker, began to criticize some of the principles of Taylorism because they resulted in a fragmentation of jobs without regard for quality.[17] In libraries, those who were influenced by Drucker's persuasive reasoning began to wonder if the circulation department had been subjected to a level of micromanagement which resulted in increased efficiency without significant improvements in service. A few critics within the library profession argued that it did not matter how many items could be checked out in an hour or how many books were purchased if a significant portion of the users were unable to find the information they needed. In the mid-1970s, a few researchers including Buckland, Urquhart and Schofield began to look at failure rates, sometimes referred to as "frustration surveys."[18] Collections had become so large and complex, Buckland and others encouraged libraries to turn their attention to quality service and user satisfaction. How many times did students and faculty leave the library without the information in hand, and what prevented their success? Why did some students elect not to use the library? This type of analysis revived interest in user satisfaction and the larger service role of the circulation department.

In 1976, Betty Young wrote an article which questioned the limited clerical function of the circulation department.[19] The few studies that evaluated user satisfaction indicated a growing criticism of the level of assistance provided by the largely clerical and student staff at the circulation desk. Young made a connection between the reduction of circulation services to mechanical operations and a decline in user satisfaction:

> After reading user criticisms of service, it would seem that another look should be taken at the role of this library service point, where users have their heaviest contact and where judgements tend to be made about the entire library. Much of the dissatisfaction expressed with librarians is based on the com-

mon misuderstandings as to who are the librarians, a confusion easily explained when it is remembered that the primary contact users have with the library is with the circulation staff. Should not, then, professional librarians be returned to circulation, the nerve center of the library?[20]

This renewed interest in the quality of service has accelerated in the last decade in response to changing economic conditions. In the past, the organization of libraries reflected a production orientation allowing for consistency, control, and considerable job specialization. With the decline in purchasing power and the proliferation of information being produced, access has become as important as ownership, and service programs have become as important as production schedules.[21] The documentation on price increases has been prolific and shocking. Data reported by the *Serials Librarian* show an average price of $34.55 for a U.S. journal in 1975; by 1988, the average cost was $117.75. The falling dollar helped to bring absurd increases–as much as 200 percent since 1985–in the cost of foreign subscriptions. Since 1986, the number of monographs purchased by research libraries has decreased 19 percent while the cost per title has increased 38 percent.[22] Libraries have been spending more and getting less. It became clear to many leaders that organizational survival depended upon the ability to redefine the library's mission and enhance the delivery of service. Thus, the concept of access acquired new meaning and higher priority.

Growth tends to produce departmentalization and fragmentation; stagnation or economic retrenchment usually results in consolidation. The recent philosophy of combining the concepts of access and ownership has had significant impact on the organization of circulation departments. Circulation services have been combined with other functions, often interlibrary loan and document delivery. The role of access services departments has become larger than simply checking out books. These enlarged units have assumed responsibility for the final step in the provision of information, regardless of its format or location. The term "access services" also gives an important signal to the users: the patron can get assistance even if he has failed to find an identified title. The regrouping of certain functions represents an active commitment to improved service compared to the more passive and mechanical role of circulation departments during the middle part of this century.

Automation has been another important factor leading to broader responsibilities for many circulation departments. Manual files required considerable time and effort to maintain and could provide only minimal information. As a result, they had a limiting effect on the function of the department. Automation has helped to eliminate the labor intensity associated with manual files and opened the door to the possibilities of reorganization. Circulation departments were able to shed much of the routine labor and assume responsibility for more complex procedures which related to the work of other departments, particularly cataloging. The sophistication of integrated library systems required the circulation staff to have broader training and understanding of the techniques and principles of bibliographic control. Circulation's role in helping to create and maintain the bibliographic database has broadened the department's purpose and perspective. In some libraries, circulation units were transferred into technical service divisions; in other cases, the term "access services" was adopted to reflect the integration of technology and its impact on the traditional division of labor.

Automation has also provided complete inventory control systems that can generate a wealth of statistical detail, and has given circulation staff a more comprehensive understanding of the user's needs. Although this information is less personal, it is similar in some respects to the knowledge that loan librarians had of their patrons a century ago. The circulation librarian is again in a position to play a more active role in database maintenance, collection development, and the design of new services based on the availability of more useful information.

The creation of access services may be closely linked not only to the automation of circulation functions, but the growing complexity of tasks throughout the library and the existing distribution of professional staff. Prior to automation, the need for professionals in circulation was a debatable issue, but many academic libraries chose to retain these positions. Regardless of their necessity at the time, it is quite likely that professional circulation librarians have been in a position to accept greater responsibility such as stack maintenance, document delivery, and interlibrary loan. As their colleagues in reference and technical services become increasingly involved in more complex systems and services, the professional whose sole task it is to manage in-house loans may seem anachronistic. In those cases where the professional position exists, library administrators may see it as a perfect opportunity for job enlargement and a more equitable distribution of responsibility. For example, creating an access services department may justify removing interlibrary lending from an overburdened reference department and combining this service with in-house circulation.

Widespread implementation of computer systems throughout the library has highlighted the need to re-examine written policies and procedures. It is possible that the increased involvement of circulation librarians in policy analysis has increased their professional visibility within the organization and has made them likely candidates to assume greater responsibility. The creation of access services may also reflect the need to take advantage of experienced managers within the library. The head of circulation must be, first and foremost, an excellent manager. The largest task is to train and supervise a front-line staff ranging from the most inexperienced student assistant to the senior-level clerical employee. The head of circulation often has managerial expertise that is unmatched. These skills can be transferred to other situations, particularly those that require more managerial oversight rather than a significant commitment of professional time, such as stack maintenance, photocopy services, document delivery, and other responsibilities often grouped under the access services umbrella.

The creation of access services may also reflect a growing organizational philosophy that is based on the point of view of the user. It is unlikely that the user cares very much about who owns the information or how it is stored; the biggest concern is usually availability. How quickly can the information be obtained? During the era of departmentalization, libraries organized around function, format, clientele, and subject. During the current wave of consolidation, some library leaders are advocating a simpler approach that makes sense to the patron.[23] Moving to an organization based entirely on function might increase effectiveness by eliminating some of the confusion for the user. Access services can be a solution to some of the existing fragmentation by centralizing responsibility for the use of all library materials regardless of their format, location, or intended readership.

The anticipation of dramatic and sweeping organizational change as a result of automation may be fading. Although a few large university libraries experimented with some bold changes, most libraries have introduced only modest alterations to the existing structure. One possible explanation for this conservative response is the prevailing commitment to provide continuous access to collections and services. Libraries are more likely to introduce structural and job design changes in increments which include redundant and overlapping functions that reduce the risk of service interruptions and staff-resistance.[24] The creation of access service departments represents an incremental but rational change in library organizations based on a number of plausible reasons and benefits.

It is too early to predict how long this new organizational trend will continue or when it might become universal. Because there are several variations and no set prescription for its structure, access services will offer many libraries the opportunity to increase their effectiveness, focus more directly on the patron's information needs, and take advantage of professional staff with managerial skills and experience. Perhaps most importantly, access services represents a break from tradition and a end to a stagnant organizational structure that has dominated the past.

REFERENCE NOTES

1. Charles Harvey Brown and H.G. Bousfield. *Circulation Work in College and University Libraries*. (Chicago: American Library Association, 1933).

2. Ibid. p. 11

3. Ibid. p. 34

4. Bertrand Russell. *Education and the Good Life*. (London: Boni and Liveright, 1926): 308-309.

5. Frederick W. Taylor. *Principles of Scientific Management*. (NY: Norton, 1947).

6. Stanley E. Gwynn, "Departmentalization and Circulation Work: Problems and Relationships." *Library Trends* 6 (July, 1957): 92.

7. H.G. Bousfield. "Circulation Department: Organization and Personnel." *College and Research Libraries* 6 (December, 1944): 46-50.

8. Ibid. p. 49

9. Wayne S. Yenawine. "Introduction–Current Trends in Library Services." *Library Trends* 6 (July, 1957): 4.
10. Ralph E. McCoy, "Personnel in Circulation Service." *Library Trends* 6 (July, 1957): 43.
11. American Library Association. Board of Personnel Administration. Subcommittee on Analysis of Library Duties. (Chicago: American Library Association, 1948): 52.
12. Philip J. McNiff, "Administration of Circulation Services." *Library Trends* 6 (July, 1957): 15.
13. Margery Closey Guigley. "Reporter at Large." *Library Trends* 6 (July, 1957): 7.
14. Shiela Inter. *Circulation Policy in Academic, Public and School Libraries* (NY: Greenwood Press, 1987): 3-10.
15. Laurence Miller. "The Role of Circulation Services in the Major University Library." *College and Research Libraries* 34 (November, 1973): 463-471.
16. Ibid. p. 469.
17. Peter F. Drucker. *The Practice of Management.* (NY: Harper & Row, Pub., Inc. 1954): 282-286.
18. Michael K. Buckland. *Book Availability and the Library User* (NY: Pergamon Press Inc. 1975; John A. Urquhart and J.L. Schofield. "Measuring Readers' Failure at the Shelf in Three University Libraries" *Journal of Documentation* 28 (September, 1972): 233-241.
19. Betty Young. "Circulation Services–Is It Meeting the Users' Needs?" *Journal of Academic Librarianship* 2 (July, 1976): 121-125.
20. Ibid. p. 124
21. David Lewis. "An Organizational Paradigm for Effective Academic Libraries." *College and Research Libraries* 47 (July, 1976): 337.
22. Jeffrey Gardner. "The Challenge of Maintaining Research Collections in the 1990's." *Journal of Library Administration* 14 n.3 (1991): 18.
23. Irene B. Hoadley and John Cobin. "Up the Beanstalk: an Evolutionary Organizational Structure for Libraries." *American Libraries* 27 (July/August, 1990): 676-678.
24. Ann DeKlerk and Joanne R. Euster. "Technology and Organizational Metamorphoses." *Library Trends* 37 (Spring, 1989): 467.

Management Challenges and Issues in Access Services Administration

Karen S. Lange
Linda D. Tietjen

SUMMARY. This article identifies and discusses the primary issues associated with managing an access services department. Some of the issues presented include: (1) identification of functions reporting to access services, (2) organizational considerations, (3) role of access services manager including level of expertise and leadership/management characteristics and (4) managerial issues and recommended proficiencies. The article describes a general operational and informational framework for access services managers and recommends a research agenda for both short and long-term studies.

INTRODUCTION

The purpose of this article is to explore the challenges and issues characteristic of managing an access services department in a academic or public library setting. Since the body of literature devoted entirely to access services is very limited, the literature of library services and general management will be explored.

Only recently has much interest been shown in developing a body of literature concerning one of the most widely-misunderstood and perhaps undervalued functions in today's libraries. For exam-

---

Karen S. Lange (MA, University of Denver) is Assistant Director for Outreach Services, and formerly Head of Access Services at University of Wyoming in Laramie, WY, 82071.

Linda D. Tietjen (MA, University of Denver) is Coordinator of Access Services at Auraria Library, Lawrence at 11th Street, Denver, CO 80204.

© 1992 by The Haworth Press, Inc. All rights reserved.

ple, a SPEC Kit will be issued in 1992 examining the organization of access and circulation services departments in ARL Libraries. In preparing this SPEC Kit, Virginia Steel surveyed over 60 ARL libraries.[1] Another example is the CIRCPLUS bulletin board and discussion group which became fully functional in April, 1991 and has provided a lively "question and answer" forum regarding access services' issues. The need for more information, both operational, as well as more conceptual or philosophical, has become very apparent to current practitioners in access services.

The body of this paper consists of three sections. The first section, "Organizational Considerations for Access Services" lists and discusses various functional units which may report to access services, followed by an analysis of the importance of organizational placement for an access services department. This section concludes by introducing a managerial framework. The second section presents an overview of "The Role of the Access Services Manager." Finally, the third section discusses managerial issues pertinent to an access services department.

ORGANIZATIONAL CONSIDERATIONS FOR ACCESS SERVICES

Access Services Functions: As noted in the introduction, there is a growing need to define access services. To do so requires that access services be given an identity within the organization. While there is very little information available on the concept of access services, a review of two ARL SPEC Kit organization charts reveals that it is becoming a more commonly recognized service entity in academic libraries.[2,3] Of the 71 ARL libraries submitting their organization charts in 1986, only 12 (17%) indicated having an access services unit, department, or division. In 1991, 10 out of 29 (33%) ARL libraries indicated they had an access services unit, department, or division. It is even more interesting to note the diverse functions which have been placed under the administrative umbrella of access services.

In an overview of access/circulation services in ARL libraries, Virginia Steel received 76 responses from access service departments and discovered that there is indeed a wide range of functions reporting to this administrative unit.[4] Functions ranking the highest were circulation, stacks maintenance, reserves, billing and library security. Second tier rankings were library storage, current periodicals, interlibrary loan, photocopy services and document delivery. The functions noted least often were microforms, information desk, transporting materials, and bindery/labelling.

Similarly, in October, 1991 Richard Osen from Western Washington University queried managers on CIRCPLUS regarding the functions/units reporting to access services departments.[5] By November, 16 academic libraries had responded. Results revealed the following units reporting to access services:

Circulation	16
Reserve	15
Stack Maintenance	11
Interlibrary Loan	10
Microforms	7
Current Periodicals	7
Security	5
Storage	5
Document Delivery	5
Audiovisual	5

The other functions mentioned were branch supervisor responsibilities, microcomputer lab, information desk, photocopy center, and processing. Note that responses to Osen ranked interlibrary loan and microforms at a much higher level than the ARL libraries in Steel's study. In addition, audiovisual functions were identified in the CIRCPLUS query; they were not mentioned in the ARL survey.

Placement of Access Services: The placement of access services within an organization is important for a number of reasons. As mentioned by Godden, a organization's structure facilitates internal coordination and communication.[6]

For the organization to accomplish its goals and objectives, Godden contends, there is a two-stage process it must follow. The first stage involves analysis of: (1) workflow, (2) decisions, (3) communications and (4) personal interactions. As a result of this analysis, major functional divisions can be listed. The second stage of the process is to arrange the major functions into appropriate units and departments. The organizational structure should be designed to facilitate development of the organization's mission, goals, objectives, policies, and procedures.

Once divisions have been defined and placed within the overall structure, the organization can function as a system or set of subsystems. The placement of access services within the organization will influence its ability to (1) communicate and coordinate services, (2) maneuver with authority, and (3) actively participate in the decision making process. All are especially important because of access services' relationship with all other functional divisions in a library. These matters take on even more significance when the library has developed an integrated automation system.[7,8,9]

Within the public services division, access services must particularly interact and cooperate with reference services in many ways. As one example, the University of Wyoming recently initiated a university studies program which had two library assignments. The access services and reference departments cooperatively worked out the logistics of collecting assignments and assisting with students using with reserve materials. New programs and services such as this may ultimately impact the staffing patterns and quality of services provided in an access services department. Again, because of UW's university studies program library assignments, the activity at the circulation and reserve desks and stacks maintenance units has increased so dramatically that additional personnel are warranted. Finally, it is especially important in coordinated services such as this that when patrons experience problems in one service area, appropriate remedial steps be taken for both so that all parties can work toward the same goal of providing quality service to the patron.

Access services' relationship with collection development is another area requiring meaningful communication and coordination. Material use studies and other data collection and recordkeeping activities may be administered by access services, but ultimately the data is most useful to the collection development office, as is information-either quantified or anecdotal-about such matters as stack maintenance, building traffic, missing or lost books, and many others that relate to access services.

Depending on where access service falls within the organizational structure and the library's degree of decentralization, there may be an increased need for coordination between branch libraries. Some ARL libraries indicated the existence of an access services committee which provided the mechanism for branch libraries to coordinate operations and make decisions about service policies and procedures.[10]

Unquestionably, access services must have a high management orientation. It should therefore be positioned within the organization so as to support a clearly-defined level of authority. Three key reasons why access services managers need sufficient authority to maneuver within the organization are:

1. Constant interaction with the public requires knowledge and authority to enforce policy. Authority should be granted to make exceptions, deviate from established norms when warranted, and handle incidents on a case-by-case basis.
2. Policies and procedures are the very foundation of operations in access services. A manager's ability to obtain endorsement of access services' policy initiatives is extremely important.
3. Access services usually employs the largest number of student workers and/or part time help. This situation can give rise to high turnover rates, discipline problems, and other problems associated with managing a diverse staff. Vested authority is important for enforcing hiring, training, placement, and termination policies.

Authority and decision-making go hand in hand. Access services should be an active participant in the decision-making process both vertically and horizontally within the organization. Access services managers need to participate in decision-making at the administrative level to (1) initiate and influence changes, such as decisions related to automation, (2) influence the establishment of organizational goals and priorities (funding, staffing and personnel decisions), and (3) participate in policy formulation.

In 1986, Hoadley reported that access services departments appeared in 12 of the 71 ARL libraries.[11] Five of those departments reported to an associate or assistant director of public services and three indicated access service units/departments either at the branch or main library, but not both. Three libraries reported access services at the assistant or associate director level, reporting directly to the library director/dean. One institution had the title head of access services placed at the same level as the assistant director.

In 1991, ten ARL institutions (total 29 reporting) had designated access service components.[12] Six departments reported to the assistant or associate director of public services, two were at the assistant director level, one reported to the associate director for automated and administrative services, and one was designated the associate director of access services. This title also included technical services.

Steel's survey of ARL library access/circulation services departments also revealed that the majority (33 respondents) reported to the associate director for public services.[13] Eight reported directly to the library director, while four reported to the associate director for technical services. Interestingly, two noted they report to collection development directors, and one to the head of a branch library. Seven respondents indicated they report to "other" administrative units.

For the most part, access service departments report to the public services assistant or associate director. As libraries become more automated, a body of literature is appearing which advocates the placement of circulation in the technical services environment.[14,15,16] To date, however, it does not appear that there is a large-scale trend toward moving circulation units or access service departments to technical services.

Still, there are may sound and logical reasons for libraries to consider such a move. Intner (1989) asks if circulation is the "third" technical service.[17] She points out similarities in the areas of storage/retrieval of bibliographic data and asserts that circulation is, in fact, a bibliographic function. She notes that the very definition of an integrated automated system includes the cataloging, acquisition, and circulation modules (and, in some libraries, serials modules). The integration of these modules makes it possible to answer questions most often asked by the public, i.e., do you have this book in the library and/or is it checked out? The ultimate question of whether access services belongs in public services or technical services should continue to be debated.

Managerial Framework for Access Services: As the literature indicates, there continues to be confusion and lack of agreement on an acceptable definition of access services. The functions which fall, organizationally, within this realm are perhaps even less known and understood. Consequently, it becomes very difficult to present a "typical" management model for access services. However, there are some standard managerial and organizational elements that should be considered in the early stages of establishing an access services department. While these elements have been noted by Manning in the context of technical services, they may also be applicable to access services.[18] They include:

1. Scalar principal-Authority is delegated downward from an ultimate authority, e.g., head of access services, to subordinate positions through a hierarchial structure of supervisors and subordinates such as head of circulation to evening supervisor and on down to student assistants. Manning further notes that every employee must understand where they are in the line of authority, to whom they are responsible, and their relationship to the other employees.
2. Unity of command-This ensures that an employee has only one supervisor who assigns duties and evaluates his or her performance.
3. Span of control-This refers to the maximum number of employees a manager can effectively supervise. Span of control also depends on the amount of time required to communicate with each individual (pp. 23-24).

As current access service departments mature, a study of their organization and management structures would be especially useful to institutions considering the establishment of an access services department. It would be appropriate to study current management theory and practice in relation to access services. Circulation studies similar to Laurence Miller's, but in the context of access services, would also be helpful in analyzing the role of access services.[19]

ROLE OF THE ACCESS SERVICES MANAGER

Level of Expertise: A very high level of managerial expertise is needed for the operation of an effective access services department. This is in contrast to the recommendation of Laurence Miller, who, in 1973 (prior to any large scale adoption of the access services model) concluded that circulation services units can be adequately managed by paraprofessionals.[20]

A new access services manager will discover that there is very little information about access services in the professional library literature. The first and, to date, only book-length publication specifically addressing this topic is Paietta's *Access Services Handbook*.[21] Unlike many library specialties, there is no journal devoted to access or circulation services. In contrast, interlibrary loan has several journals as well as a electronic bulletin board.

CIRCPLUS was also created very recently. This electronic bulletin board addresses a variety of access services policy and procedural issues, as well as serves as a medium on which to submit queries for help/information regarding circulation, reserves, shelving, access services organization charts, student workers, library security, etc. According to Dan Lester, moderator of CIRCPLUS, between April 28, 1991 and December 5, 1991, 1,027 messages were posted to the list.[22] This averages five messages per day.

Access services managers, typically more than other library managers, must be able to deal with a large and diversified staff. In academic libraries often up to half (and sometimes more) of access services staff members are student workers. One FTE (full-time equivalent), applied to student workers, may equal three to four part-time people. Furthermore, tenure of student workers is generally shorter than that of full-time staff.

Continuous turnover of access services student workers calls for strong supervisory and management skills in screening, hiring, training, retaining, and evaluating staff. A clear, articulate statement of policy and handbook of procedures are highly recommended, as are "quick reference" materials (handouts, signs, cards, or information sheets) at each circulation and/or interlibrary loan terminal. At the Auraria Library, interlibrary loan circulation supervisors have created "orientation packets" which are given to each newly-hired student employee. Also at Auraria, a shelving supervisor has experimented with a student contract which each student must read and sign prior to employment. The contract explains the importance of the shelving job as well as guidelines for working effectively in that department.

The successful access services manager will utilize library resources (human, fiscal, space, equipment/supplies) very wisely. The access services manager may also wear many hats: coach, trainer, supervisor, policy-maker, policy-writer, policy administrator, customer service specialist, cheerleader, visionary, police officer, mediator, automation and systems specialist and sometimes even departmental counselor. The access services manager should strive to be as "hands-on" as possible, both to help maintain and improve departmental operations as well as to keep in contact with front-line staff and daily routines. In addition, it is imperative that the manager serve as spokesperson for all access services units and strive to maintain cordial relations with all other departments in the library. This may involve attending several meetings per week, or working through various other formal or informal channels of communication.

Leadership vs. Management: Stueart and Moran point out that leadership is just one possible component of a manager's skills.[23] Management, which has often been characterized as a science, is frequently described with a series of present participles: planning, organizing, budgeting, staffing, and controlling. Meanwhile, writers such as Tom Peters and Max DePree characterize leadership as an art. DePree, in his book, *Leadership is an Art*, suggests leaders "abandon themselves to the strengths of others."[24] Peters likewise suggests that the leader,

> via soul-searching listening, assessment of the external situation, and solicitation of all points of view, develop a succinct vision that is clear and exciting, and at the same time leaves wide latitude for the pursuit of new opportunities.[25]

These examples are in contrast to the often prescriptive language used in management treatises, wherein managers are advised to dictate organizational effectiveness in human, fiscal, computer and other areas. The great dilemma facing managers is how to become a good leader ("artist") as well as a good manager ("scientist")? Further, do the two concepts compliment--or contradict--each other?

Stueart and Moran articulate a common concern of library managers and would-be managers:

> Many managers would like to be told how to lead; the situational theories say there is no one right way. Instead, effective leaders will adapt their style of leadership behavior to the needs of the followers and the situation. Since these factors are not constant, discerning the appropriate style is a challenge to the manager who wants to be an effective leader.[26]

Thus, there are any number of management and leadership models available, but no single model can apply for every situation faced by access services managers. Many access services managers experiment with different management/leadership styles to determine "likeness of fit" for their own organizations or rely on methods learned in library school or on the job and find none of these altogether satisfactory. Historically, MacGregor's Theory X (which states that workers do not intrinsically wish to work, and must be coerced and manipulated into doing the jobs) and Theory Y (which posits that workers find intrinsic value in work) distinction has been useful. More recently William Ouchi's book *Theory Z* goes "beyond" MacGregor by focusing on group dynamics and quality issues.[27] Any management textbook can outline dozens more current and historical management theories and trends. Some of the management/leadership models currently available include: TQM (Total Quality Management), MBWA (Management by Wandering Around), MBO (Management by Objectives), Management by Empowerment, and Participatory Management.

The culmination of this quest for developing the manager/leader is perhaps to be found in Peter Senge's 1990 best seller *The Fifth Discipline*. Senge contends that all employees in an organization must take a "learning" approach to their jobs if they are to succeed in an ever more complex and global world. Senge defines a learning organization as "a place where people are continually discovering how they create their reality and how they can change it."[28] He discusses the limited effectiveness of short-range solutions to complex problems. According to Senge, "the easy way out usually leads back in."[29] He further asserts that "today's problems come from yesterday's 'solutions.'"[30] Senge suggests "systems thinking" (the ability to learn and to create realistic, long-range solutions based upon environmental feedback) as the best approach to effective problem-solving.

MANAGERIAL ISSUES/RECOMMENDED PROFICIENCIES

The remainder of this article provides brief discussions on the following managerial issues and recommended proficiencies pertinent to an access services manager:

- Planning
- Organizing
- Controlling
- Human Resource Management (Staffing)
- Budgeting
- The Physical Environment
- Automation Issues
- Coordination and Integration

Planning: A strategic approach to managing access services is recommended. Mission statements for each unit reporting to access services in the organizational structure would be helpful, as would written statements of a customer service philosophy for each unit. Unit mission statements should be related to and integrated with the overall library mission. At the Auraria Library, a group of upper-level administrators held several all-day retreats during the summer of 1991 to determine a set of specific strategies and a "Three-Year Plan" for implementing them. The next step is setting goals and objectives at the unit (e.g., circulation) and service area or departmental (e.g., access services) levels. In addition, staff members' annual goals and objectives should tie in with the library-wide strategies.

Other approaches to planning strategies include accepted project management techniques such as Critical Path Method (CPM) or Just-in-Time (JIT). Each of these methodologies stresses the importance of setting priorities, timing/scheduling activities, and allocating staff, equipment and monetary resources. Project management software is an appropriate tool for guiding a manager through this complex process.

Traditional managerial wisdom says that each hour spent in planning can save three to four hours in implementation. Project management techniques can enable the manager to identify all resource constraints and results in a road map for operations. This road map can be developed as a GANTT or PERT chart. Generating such a chart makes it easier for a manager to identify such typical project elements as wages, available staff hours, equipment capacities, target completion dates, and how all these interact. This additive process indicates the critical path and is the best route to the efficient and timely use of resources.

Organizing: The second issue in the management of access services departments is "Organizing." Again, the general management literature can provide some guidance. For example, automated systems theory offers such techniques as "systems analysis." This is a method of assessing current workflow procedures and recommending more timely, effective, and less expensive means of accomplishing tasks. Systems analysis techniques are often discussed in computer science textbooks. There are also entire books devoted to the topic, e.g., *Analysis and Design of Information Systems* by James A. Senn (1989) and *Operations Research for Libraries and Information Agencies* by Kraft and Boyce.[31,32]

The access services manager must seek ways for constant systems improvement. In addition, managers, staff and students should be kept updated and continually trained, due to the rapid development of automated systems. Changes are occurring at an unprecedented rate, and much effort has to be expended merely to "keep up" with the changes. To keep ahead of them and anticipate organizational and systems changes, constant attention must be paid to professional journals, electronic bulletin boards, and to fostering networks with colleagues. Or, to heed Tom Peters, organizations need to "Train Everyone–Lavishly."[33] He particularly emphasizes the need for training of supervisors, contending that:

There is no more difficult transition in a career then the one from nonboss to boss; the second-toughest is to boss of bosses. These passages should be marked by programs commensurate with their significance.[34]

An additional requirement is that the access services manager have excellent time management skills to juggle numerous, sometimes competing, responsibilities. On the one hand, access services managers may wish to have open doors, while on the other hand, there is always a very long "To Do List" of tasks which require privacy and an ability to concentrate.

Controlling: Controlling the "outputs" of access services involves technical and, ideally, statistical and other quantitative skills. Statistics generated by automated (and manual) systems need to be evaluated in terms of usefulness for improving or monitoring the operations they represent. For example, statistics can be used to analyze staffing patterns, for decision-making, and to justify budget requests. Still these data must be examined carefully. The sheer volume of reports and statistics automated systems generate can create "information overload" if irrelevant data is not identified and eliminated.

Ideally, the control function starts with a good planning tool (a written plan, a checklist of reports and statistics needed by each department, etc.). This is the opposite of what many access services managers have inherited: the old "cart before the horse" in which a set of reports appears each week or month, without having been appropriately evaluated. A more rational approach involves deciding at the outset what information is needed, in what format, and how often, then working with systems coordinators to tailor reports to meet these needs.

Another area of control is management of the overdue and fine payment process. Thus, a peripheral accounting function is often entrusted to access services staff at circulation and interlibrary loan. For that reason, a periodic systems analysis of the accounting tasks, in terms of staffing, equipment/supply needs, and volume of the operation should be conducted, and, if necessary, system improvements made.

Managing Human Resources (Staffing): Perhaps the most difficult managerial skills to acquire have to do with the domain known as (HRM) Human Resources Management. These skills are not easily learned, cannot be mastered by merely reading books or articles, and are often situational, i.e., what works with one person may not work with another person.

Despite the inherent difficulties of mastering HRM, there are some approaches to management and supervision of library personnel in the library literature. Examples of books and articles addressing this topic include Herbert S. White's book, *Library Personnel Management*, as well as at least two books (and numerous articles) on managing library student employees, including *Managing Student Workers in College Libraries*, which includes sections on job descriptions, applications and interviews, orientation and training, quizzes and tests, and evaluations, and *Training Student Library Assistants*, which goes into more detail about planning and setting up a student training program.[35,36,37]

Another challenging aspect of human resources management is coping with the problems associated with morale. How do managers keep front-line employees productive, effective, and reasonably happy? A perspective which is gaining recent attention is espoused by William Bridges in his books *Transitions*, and *Surviving Corporate Transitions*.[38,39]

In his books, Bridges recommends that managers take a very patient and sympathetic approach when introducing change to staff. He contends that any major changes to organizational structures, policies and procedures will be perceived by staff as "the end of their world." He suggests that managers introduce changes slowly, then provide a reasonable time for employees to assimilate the changes into their own jobs. He states that people going through changes often exhibit symptoms of bad morale, but suggests that this may, instead, be a natural grieving process which must be experienced before integration and a healthy "moving on" (acceptance of the changes) can take place.

Added to anxieties associated with major changes is the daily stress related to working directly with the public, and sometimes having to be the bearer of bad news (e.g., the patron owes $25.00 in fines). As a worst-case scenario, the demands of working with the public on a daily basis can lead to either a chronic low-grade stress and a concomitant lack of enthusiasm or to "burnout" (an inability to function up to capacity). In addition, there is the pressure for service desk employees to project a friendly, "service with a smile" attitude at all times.

Then, too, there is a propensity for access services staff to think themselves under-valued. They work very hard, under difficult and demanding conditions, but as Virginia Steel stated at the ALA 1991 Annual Conference, they often perceive themselves as "the Rodney Dangerfields of the library" (i.e., getting no respect).[40] It is a daily challenge to maintain good spirits for the difficult, frequently unrewarding, job of providing efficient service to an ever-increasing number of patrons.

Budgeting: In a recent survey of ARL access/circulation services departments, respondents were asked to note their budgetary responsibilities.[41] The majority, 50 respondents, mentioned they managed the student wages budget, 24 managed the supplies budget, 19 included the equipment budget and 18 managed the staff personnel budget. In addition to budgetary responsibilities, it is very likely that access service units will have other monetary responsibilities such as collecting fines, service fees (photocopy charges, interlibrary loan fees, equipment rentals, etc.), and lost or damaged material charges. Further, this department may be linked to the institution's accounting or bursar's offices. It is important that the head of access services has a clear understanding of the budgeting process and basic knowledge of managerial accounting methods.

Ramsey explains that the budget is a translation of the future plan of the library into financial terms.[42] With this in mind, access service managers need to be aware of the budget planning process and, furthermore, be prepared to participate in budgeting decisions. Front-line supervisors should be involved in the budget planning process, since they have the experience and knowledge necessary for determining peak usage periods and estimating the allocation necessary for optimum staffing. Circulation data can be a powerful tool when additional funds are needed for stack maintenance, the reserve area, or other units.

Manning identifies eight steps in the budget process which could also be applied to access services.[43] They are: (1) planning the request, (2) formulating the request, (3) reviewing, (4) defending, (5) approving, (6) monitoring, (7) modifying and (8) closing out the budget. Departmental managers also need to be cognizant of budgeting methods used within the libraries as well as the larger institution. Briefly, the most common budget systems used in libraries are:

1. line item or object of expenditure budgeting which is the grouping of funds into categories (equipment, supplies, travel, etc.),
2. lump sum budgeting employs the allocation of one flat sum of monies,
3. program budgeting is based on specific program areas within the library such as reference services, circulation, audiovisual, and so on,
4. program planning budget systems (PPBS), a refinement of the program budget method, relates the libraries goals and objectives to specific program areas,
5. zero base budgeting requires continuous and ongoing justification of each budget request for every activity and program.

In his *Managerial Accounting for Libraries and Other Non-Profit Organizations*, Smith explains managerial accounting principles and describes how accounting information and formats can best be used for planning and decision making purposes.

Awareness of management accounting systems is especially important in costing services and establishing fee structures. It is necessary to have a clear understanding of the process and a rationale for why certain fees are established, what current accounting mechanisms are in place, and who has the authority to encumber funds. With the development of integrated automated systems, there are increased capabilities for interfacing with campus computer systems to monitor the flow of funds to and from the library. This involvement expands the role and range of responsibilities of the access services manager and requires an understanding and a willingness to practice two-way communication with departments outside of the library.

Finally, as budget planning activities move to higher administrative levels, the access services manager ultimately becomes the spokesperson for a department comprised of several functional units that will likely have varying and perhaps competing budgetary requests. In this capacity, the access services manager may be called upon to make difficult budgetary decisions, then to explain and defend them, both to library administrators and to staff. To do so clearly requires superior analytical and communication skills.

Managing the Physical Environment: More and more access services departments are being charged with the responsibility of managing at least some portion of the library's physical plant. This task may include planning space and facilities, basic library-wide safety and security, ergonomics in the access services work areas, and handling other building responsibilities such as lost and found, opening and closing the library, making public announcements, etc.

Managing the physical environment can encompass a number of specific responsibilities. The journal *Library Archives and Security Systems* is a source of articles relevant to this task. This literature can also be extremely diverse. For example, according to Cohen and Cohen, in *Automation, Space Management and Productivity: A Guide for Libraries*, "more than 350 work analysis, work improvement, or time study titles are added to the Library of Congress each year."[45] In addition, a national professional organization, the International Facilities Management Association (IFMA) addresses such issues.

Thus, an area of responsibility so large it can be a career in itself in some organizations is entrusted to access services staff and regarded as a "peripheral" responsibility assigned on the basis of proximity to the front door. In many libraries these responsibilities can only be learned "on the job." Basic security and enforcement training may be provided by the organization's police and security unit. It is imperative that this aspect of access services management not be neglected since situations may arise that are, literally, life-threatening.

Automation: The days of the "Circ Desk" with files of checkout cards and a manual charge/discharge system are gone for most libraries. In its place are integrated computer systems, which may further be part of vast bibliographic networks and/or consortia. Many circulation tasks might also be done on personal computers, e.g., accounting, writing form letters to patrons, keeping professor lists for reserves, and preparing budgetary information student/staff schedules. It is now common for library personnel at all levels to have acquired skills on various databases, spreadsheets, word processing packages, and operating systems. Increasingly, all employees need to be computer literate–and the responsibility for providing such training and retraining may fall on the access services librarian.

In order to be able to provide computer training for staff and students, the access services manager must be as knowledgeable as possible about automated systems in general, and, more specifically, about the circulation, reserves, interlibrary loan and other subsystem "modules." Additionally, the manager must see to it that all access services personnel have a general understanding of necessary components of the automated system. For example, a circulation employee will need to understand the bibliographic record if s/he is going to perform a "temporary conversion" of an unconverted item which a patron wishes to check out. Searching the database to link appropriate records with item numbers calls for understanding of the underlying bibliographic principles used to catalog such an item. Interlibrary loan staff must be expert at searching the on-line catalog so they can locate and properly identify materials owned by their own and other libraries.

Coordination and Integration: The final issue or challenge is the integration and coordination that takes place within access services. As noted previously, access services relates with every department and operation of the library. Access services is also likely to be involved with other campus departments such as the accounting office, registrar, campus ID office, etc. Relationships may extend further to other libraries, networks, and consortia for the purpose of honoring reciprocal borrowing agreements for sharing databases.

The issue of coordination is important, and it has been discussed throughout this paper. Coordination occurs at the procedural level on up to the policy, objective, and goal identification level. The necessity to interact with other departments places a great responsibility on access services managers and their ability to assure that activities and future plans are indeed coordinated and clearly understood between departments and upper administration. In addition, the access services manager's work will likely involve the coordination of the budget for several functional units or perhaps functions that extend to branch libraries.

As libraries automate, the access services and circulation activities are further integrated into the library system and the campus computer system. In discussing the changes from an offline, manual circulation system to an integrated system, Griffin described the extent to which coordination is needed not only internally but externally with other campus systems.[46] For example, Griffin discusses the necessity for developing an interface which would channel library bills directly to the university's accounting office. The ability to tape load user data from the registrar's office and faculty and staff files and thus avoid manually creating patron information in the circulation system is also desirable.

As more and more universities and colleges change to one-card identification systems, access services should consider involvement with that system as it relates to photocopier services, patron status, and fine payments. Certain restrictions on the use of ID cards may also impact the policies of the library.

Finally, the interaction that occurs between libraries, networks, and consortia can be invaluable to access service personnel. Woodsworth, Allen, Hoadley et al., predict that the

> administration of the library will become more complex as a result of (1) the centralization of university-wide information technology decisions and related policies, and (2) the increased significance of interinstitutional systems and relationships in the provision of access to information.[47]

These predictions will also impact access services.

The manager of access services should have a broad knowledge of the major operations within the library. Access services is not a place for entry level librarians. In order to function effectively in the role of coordinator, the access services manager must have some knowledge of the related operations of reference, cataloging, collection development, and others. Thierer presented a paper on what she perceived as the functions, responsibilities, and role of access service departments. In describing that role, she noted:

First the administration will need to decide which areas of concern apply to the library and state which areas will be included in access services. Then ideally, locate someone who has had experience in all of these areas. If not, they should have experience in one or more areas plus be willing to learn about the others. But most importantly is their willingness to look at the library as an inter-related system, yet through the eyes of the very naive patron.[48]

Again, this emphasizes the important issue of coordination. There is clearly a great need for access service managers to build bridges which will ultimately enhance services at a system-wide level.

CONCLUSION AND FUTURE DIRECTIONS FOR ACCESS SERVICES

Access services faces many challenges. It is at a stage where extraordinary demands are being placed on libraries in general, and access services in particular. There is increased emphasis on cooperation and coordination with other departments, particularly technical services, collection development, and reference.

Automation has introduced new dimensions to circulation and other related services. With automation, there has been an increase in the number of patron requests and the demand for more information in a shorter period of time. Further, automation requires the establishment of norms, profiles or parameters which calls for a reexamination and perhaps complete overhaul of existing policies and procedures.

In his review of the circulation literature for 1988 Ryoko Toyama identified six areas of future study addressing long term problems that confront circulation and access services. His recommendations for future research include studying:

1. Impact of automated circulation systems on library users, especially with regard to personal satisfaction, access habits, and new expectations of the library

2. Impact on the circulation unit's working relationship with bibliographic control and collection development
3. Impact on human resource training, required talents, and operational standards
4. Impact of an increase of publications in nontraditional formats on access means and speed of delivery
5. Development and impact of fee-based services on the library and users
6. Copyright issues in relation to reserves and nontraditional publications.[49]

Similarly, at the 1991 ALA annual conference, several issues were discussed and additional research recommended. Some of these included (1) study the effectiveness of circulation policies and impact of policy changes, (2) consider developing standards for collecting data, and (3) review management ideas and methods applicable to access services.[50]

Some past studies which have dealt specifically with circulation include: Laurence Miller's research on the role of circulation services in large academic libraries; Betty Young's survey of circulation services and user needs; and James Martin's study of automation and the service attitudes of circulation managers.[51,52,53] Perhaps it would be worthwhile to revisit those studies and consider expanding their methodologies and purposes to address the broader needs of access services. For example, the purpose of Miller's study was to gather data from over one hundred academic libraries to (1) determine the role (functions) of circulation, (2) review staffing patterns, (3) determine causes for change, and (4) gather information on management attitudes toward the role of circulation. Could these same factors be applied to analyzing access services? Such analyses might be used to determine purpose, needs, goals, and objectives. They could also be used to construct an organizational model for access services.

Young's study discussed whether the services offered at the circulation desk were meeting user needs. She concluded that patrons were not satisfied with the services. Perhaps Young's study would provide the basis for determining user needs and evaluating the quality of services in access services. Similarly, Martin's study would be useful in conducting a review of service attitudes in general for all access service functions.

Taking these issues into consideration, it is possible to outline a research agenda appropriate for access services. A review of the literature reveals very few recent studies on the management and administration of circulation, and none on access services. In this regard, Toyama's remarks that "while practical reports are available and most of them are useful for short-term, there is need for serious studies with a long-range view" are significant.[54]

The following is an outline of broad categories in which research and longitudinal studies are needed. The five categories provide some guidelines for an access services research agenda. They are:

1. Studies at the policy, operational, and procedural level
    - Fines, overdues, loan periods, recalls
    - Stack maintenance
    - Interlibrary loan routines and protocols
    - Transaction analyses and models
    - Document delivery
2. Studies investigating the role of access services
    - Organization
    - Functions
3. Studies addressing management methods and practices of access services. Management models appropriate to access services (Includes reporting structure: should it report to public or technical services?)
    - Role of manager–planning, organizing, and implementation
    - Management of human resources–staffing, training, morale, etc.
    - Data management–coordination with other departments and development of standards
    - Budgeting and other monetary concerns such as fee-based services
    - Communication and coordination–internal, external, campus community, vendors, etc.
4. Use studies

- Effectiveness of access services
- Impact of specific changes, e.g., automation
- Service needs and expectations

5. Other recommendations/suggestions
   - Establish forum for access service librarians to discuss specific issues and concerns
   - Expand recent study conducted by Steel (forthcoming) to include non-ARL libraries and to obtain detailed information on the management of access services.

Access services managers can explore the challenges posed in this research agenda as a means of coming to grips with the rapid changes taking place in today's libraries. Information gathered from such inquiries is desperately needed and will be valuable for everyone involved in this exciting new service concept called access services.

REFERENCE NOTES

1. Steel, Virginia. (Forthcoming). "Survey of ARL Access/Circulation Services, SPEC Kit." Office of Management Studies (Washington, D.C.: Association of Research Libraries, 1992).

2. Hoadley, Irene B., comp. *Organization Charts in ARL Libraries. SPEC Kit 129* (Washington, D.C.: Association of Research Libraries, Office of Management Studies, 1986).

3. Poole, Jay M., comp. *Organization Charts in ARL Libraries. SPEC Kit 170* (Washington, D.C.: Association of Research Libraries, Office of Management Studies, 1991).

4. Steel, forthcoming.

5. Osen, Richard. "Access Services in Organizational Charts." Information requested on CIRCPLUS, October 1, 1991.

6. Godden, Irene P., ed. *Library Technical Services: Operations and Management* (Orlando: Academic Press, 1984).

7. Manning, Leslie A. "Circulation Functions." in *Library Technical Services: Operations and Management*, edited by Irene P. Godden. (Orlando: Academic Press, 1984).

8. Miko, Chris. "Libraries in Transition: Institutional issues." A paper presented at the annual meeting of the Michigan Academy of Science, Arts, and Letters. Eighty-ninth annual meeting, March 22-23, 1985 at East Lansing, Michigan. Also available as ERIC document ED313037 (microfiche).

9. Toyama, Ryoko. "The Years Work in Circulation Control, 1988." *Library Resources and Technical Services*. Vol. 33, no. 4 (February, 1989) p. 331-334.

10. Poole, p. 11-70.

11. Hoadley, p. 11-14.

12. Poole; p. 11-70.

13. Steel, forthcoming.

14. Manning, 1984, p. 249-250.

15. Intner, Sheila S. "Circulation: the Third Service." *Technicalities*. Vol. 9, no. 3 (March, 1989) p. 9-11.

16. Toyoma, 1989, p. 332-333.

17. Intner, p. 11.

18. Manning, Leslie A. "Technical Services Administration." in *Library Technical Services: Operations and Management*. 2d ed. Edited by Irene P. Godden (San Diego: Academic Press, 1991).

19. Miller, Laurence. "The Role of Circulation Services in the Major University Library." *College & Research Libraries*. Vol. 34 (November, 1973) p. 463-471.

20. Miller, p. 470-471.

21. Paietta, Ann Catherine. *Access Services: a Handbook* (Jefferson, N.C.: McFarland & Co., 1991).

22. Lester, Daniel. E-mail correspondence with authors, December, 1991. Note: to subscribe to CIRCPLUS, send request to CIRCPLUS%IDBSU.

23. Stueart, Robert D. and Barbara B. Moran. *Library Management*. 3d ed. (Littleton, Colorado: Libraries Unlimited, 1987).

24. DePree, Max, *Leadership is an Art* (New York: Bantam Doubleday Dell Publishing Group, 1989).

25. Peters, Tom. *Thriving on Chaos: Handbook for a Management Revolution* (New York: Knopf, 1987).

26. Stueart and Moran, p. 180.

27. Ouchi, William. *Theory Z: How American Business Can Meet the Japanese Challenge* (Reading, Mass.: Addison-Wesley, 1981).

28. Senge, Peter M. *The Fifth Discipline: The Art and Practice of the Learning Organization* (New York: Doubleday, 1990).

29. Senge, p. 60.

30. Senge, p. 57.

31. Senn, James A. *Analysis and design of Information Systems*. 2d ed. (New York: McGraw-Hill Inc., 1989).

32. Kraft, Donald H. and Bert R. Boyce. *Operations Research for Libraries and Information Agencies: Techniques for the Evaluation of Management Decision Alternatives* (San Diego: Academic Press, 1991).

33. Peters, p. 389.

34. Peters, p. 394.

35. White, Herbert S. *Library Personnel Management* (White Plains, NY: Knowledge Industry Publication, 1985).

36. Kathman, Michael D. and Jane McGurn Kathman. *Managing Student Workers in College Libraries. CLIP Note #7* (Chicago: College Library Information Packet Committee, Association of College and Research Libraries, 1986).

37. Boone, Morell D., Sandra G. Yee, and Rita Bullard. *Training Student Library Assistants* (Chicago: American Library Association, 1991).

38. Bridges, William. *Transitions: Making Sense of Life's Changes* (Reading, Mass.: Addison-Wesley, 1980).

39. Bridges, William. *Surviving Corporate Transitions: Rational Management in a World of Mergers, Layoffs, Start-ups, Takeovers, Divestitures, Deregulation, and New Technologies* (New York: Doubleday, 1988).

40. Steel, Virginia. Notes taken from a presentation at the annual conference of the American Library Association, Atlanta, Georgia, June 1991.

41. Steel, forthcoming.

42. Ramsey, Inez, L. and Jackson E. Ramsey. *Library Planning and Budgeting* (New York: Franklin Watts, 1986).

43. Manning, 1991, p. 18.

44. Smith, G. Stevenson. *Managerial Accounting for Libraries and other Not-for-profit Organizations* (Chicago: American Library Association, 1991).

45. Cohen, Elaine and Aaron Cohen. *Automation, Space management, and Productivity: A Guide for Libraries* (New York: R. R. Bowker, 1981).

46. Griffin, Mary Ann and Kathleen O'Connor. "Offline Circulation to Integrated Systems: Expectation and Reality." in *Conference on Integrated Online Library Systems*. 3rd ed. (St. Louis: Geneway, 1987).

47. Woodsworth, Anne, Nancy Allen, Irene Hoadley et al. "The Model Research Library: Planning for the Future." *Journal of Academic Librarianship*. Vol. 15, no. 3 (July, 1989): 132-138.

48. Thierer, Joyce. "Ever Hear of Access Services?" Paper presented at the Spring meeting, Nebraska Library Association, College and University Section, Peru, April 14-15, 1983. Also available as ERIC document ED234817 (microfiche).

49. Toyama, p. 332.

50. Mitchell, Bede W. "Circulation Norms-Brief Summary." ALA annual conference, Atlanta. Information available on CIRCPLUS electronic bulletin board, July 8, 1991.

51. Miller, p. 463-471.

52. Young, Betty. "Circulation Service-is it Meeting the User's Needs?" *Journal of Academic Librarianship*. Vol. 2, no. 3 (July, 1976): 120-125.

53. Martin, James R. "Automation and the Service Attitudes of ARL Circulation Managers." *Journal of Library Automation*. Vol. 14, no. 3 (September, 1981): 190-194.

54. Toyama, Ryoko. "The Years Work in Circulation Control, 1987." *Library Resources and Technical Services*. Vol. 32, no. 4 (February, 1988): 387-390.

Quality Access Services: Maximizing and Managing

Amy Chang

SUMMARY. The concept of "quality services" has proven useful in business and has applications in the development and delivery of library access services. This article describes some of the basic principles of quality services, with particular reference to how they have been implemented in the access services department at Texas Tech University Libraries.

INTRODUCTION

Today, various electronic databases and communication networks have become powerful vehicles connecting people to world information. Technology has created the demand for information at high speed and yielded new dimensions for information services. The library of today is far less of a warehouse for materials than an information access center. The vision of how libraries provide information services has been broadened by the debate of access versus ownership. One common response to these changes has been the organization of access services departments in libraries.

The components of what has come to be called access services are not entirely new. The organization of the department may vary from library to library. It usually consists of the merger of the circulation, interlibrary loan, reserve, stacks, current periodicals, document delivery, and/or copy service units, depending on the size, needs, and structure of the individual library. These areas are

---

Amy Chang is Head of Access Services at the Texas Tech University Libraries. The university's address is Mail Stop 2041, Lubbock, TX 79409-0002.

© 1992 by The Haworth Press, Inc. All rights reserved.

responsible for maximizing and managing access to research and teaching materials for library users by charging/discharging, borrowing/lending, organizing, locating, and delivering these materials.

Recently, libraries have experienced high inflation in the costs of materials and of maintaining current information technologies. These problems are compounded by overall budget reductions. Responding to this situation, library professionals have been forced to rethink many traditional library services, and this has led many access services departments to focus on providing "total quality service." When implemented, this concept can lead to the design of innovative services and make effective use of information technologies. A commitment to total quality services can also provide a philosophical foundation for access services. Further, once the concept has been articulated and endorsed by management, it can become a central philosophy for initiating positive change.

This article describes the general concept of quality services and, more specifically, how it has been integrated into certain operations in the access services department at Texas Tech University (TTU) Libraries and served to facilitate positive changes. The libraries at TTU have over 1,000,000 volumes and serve approximately 23,000 students, 900 faculty and a couple thousand staff. The access services department of TTU, which is centralized in the main library and reports to the associate director of libraries, includes circulation, interlibrary loan, reserve, and stacks units. The department has eleven full-time positions, plus a full compliment of student workers. Because of various recent developments in the department, the quality service concept has proven useful in designing services, managing staff and handling change. This article further suggests that a commitment to quality services can provide a positive service affirmation in libraries of all types and a tool for dealing with budgetary restraints.

MAXIMIZING QUALITY SERVICE

Needs for quality service: For many years, academic libraries had the central role of applying and making available physical collections. Enormous amounts of time and money were spent to build these collections and perform the services through which they could be made available for faculty and students. It can be argued that, at one time, especially during the era of closed stacks, perhaps the chief purpose of libraries was to serve as warehouses for information. The objective of providing physical access to needed materials from local collections was paramount, and thus there was a strong emphasis on acquisition and preservation. If the needed material was not available in the library, interlibrary loan provided the chief recourse. Still, it might take days or weeks for interlibrary loan to verify the title and process the request before receiving the item. Often, patrons have had to bear the costs of ILL. While these situations still exist to some degree in most libraries, new library services are increasingly providing alternative means of access to materials.

With the emphasis on access, a new vision of quality service for the library has emerged, thereby creating a dramatic shift in perspective and the development of new services. This is due in a large part to information vendors, who now offer various alternatives for acquiring full-text information via electronic databases and telecommunication networks that are sometimes linked with "just-in-time" document delivery service. The recognition is emerging that no library can be self-sufficient in supplying and storing all needed materials and that greater interlibrary networking and resource sharing must be relied upon to provide broader access to materials. "Access" has become central to library services.

Facing the uncertainties and future challenges of access services, library leaders and managers are being asked to build new service concepts, to develop new ideas and methods to increase the availability of materials, and to implement speedy delivery systems in order to meet users' demands. Basic to this new awareness, the dimension of total quality access service must be defined and evaluated systematically, and an implementation strategy must be planned and developed.

The new dimension of quality service: The concept of quality service in a profitable business means service which meets customer's needs, and thus the standard of quality varies from person to person and from situation to situation.[1] As the quality concept applies to access services, the goal is to achieve patron-centeredness. This involves providing effective and efficient services to information users that satisfy their requests in the most cost-effective and timely manner. Quality access services requires that a strong service ethic be both emphasized and enhanced. Emphasizing services means understanding the needs of the user community, while enhancing services means designing the most efficient and effective services to meet those needs and increasing service visibility in the community. The following three considerations are extremely important.

First, in emphasizing and enhancing service, it is important to analyze complaints, understand their causes, and take steps to minimize them. The service desk is the front line where patrons communicate with library staff and contact facilities and technology; it is also the place where complaints are encountered. Complaints are the negative response to service considered to be unsatisfactory. Staff should be trained to listen to complaints, consider their merits, and respond to them appropriately. Even when complaints are voiced against a legitimate library policy, staff should treat them as an opportunity to better understand patron situations and thus improve services. Evaluation and analysis of complaints can also lead to policy revisions for service enhancements.

Second, patterns of service demand should be monitored and analyzed in terms of how best to allocate staff and resources to service demand. For example, the department of access services at TTU Libraries has developed an ILL database management system to monitor borrowing activities of interlibrary loan based on the following: (1) the users' status–faculty, graduate student, undergraduate student, and staff, (2) academic schools and departments, (3) type of materials borrowed–book, periodical, or dissertation (4) classifications of materials–science, fine arts, humanity, social science, engineering, etc., and (5) delivery time, including dates of initial request and delivery.[2] Statistical information on the data is generated from the ILL automated system and given to librarians for consideration in collection development decisions. Further, demand patterns are viewed by administrators when considering service enhancements, such as implementing an ILL material delivery and subsiding ILL costs. Unfilled ILL requests likewise are analyzed by several categories in order to examine the causes of unfilled requests and delivery delays.

Third, when initiating a new service, marketing must be carefully planned. Many new service ideas are not implemented successfully simply because they have not been effectively introduced to users. The idea behind marketing a service is to attract the attention of information users, to reach out to the public, and to increase the visibility of a service within the community. Well designed brochures, bookmarks, newsletters, and press releases (with pictures and graphs describing service enhancement and details as to how users can make use of services) are just some ways that have been used by TTU Libraries to publicize services. Also, electronic bulletins posted via computer networks can transport timely messages to users in the local community and beyond. After the initial marketing effort, regular or continuous efforts may follow.

Cost analysis for maximizing service: The full dimensions of quality service might not be considered when the library faces financial constraints. Managers may fear that maximizing service will increase demand and therefore increase costs, or that there is an inevitable tradeoff between quality and cost. Unfortunately, using such a conventional cost-and-service logic can result in too much time and energy spent on planning for saving money rather than on setting strategies to overcome budget constraints. This approach tends to ignore service value and quality, often losing sight of users. Consequently, service will be sacrificed and information users, who see a decline in library services offered to them, may turn to the alternative information resources, such as commercial vendors who offer easy, fast, and low-cost document delivery service. If this happens, the role of libraries in the information society of the future will shrink dramatically.[3] Further, as the library can no longer demonstrate a need for its services and collections, budgets will continue to be cut.

Essential to seeing beyond budgetary limitations to maximizing service is not to seek ways to save money but to analyze cost elements. Cost elements of a service can be broken down into tangible and intangible factors. Tangible factors include the cost of facilities, supplies, equipments, and computer systems. They are functional, practical, and real tools which can be quantified. When these tangible elements are analyzed wisely, staff can exploit them in the most efficient manner, which results in saving time and improving productivity.[4] Unlike tangibles, intangible factors cannot be easily or directly quantified. The analysis of intangibles presented by Leonard Berry, A. Parasuraman, and Valarie Zeithaml concluded that these consist of: reliability (the ability to perform the desired service dependably, accurately, and consistently), responsiveness (the willingness to provide prompt service), assurance (employees' knowledge, courtesy, and ability to convey trust and confidence), and empathy (the provision of caring, individualized attention to people).[5] These factors can not be evaluated by efficiency measures alone. Effectiveness of service and patron satisfaction are the important determinants, and these factors often relate directly to perceptions of the intangible factors. It is important to foster appreciation of the intangibles of quality service among staff during training, and also to evaluate staff by high quality standards.[6]

Accordingly, the manager must focus on maximizing cost tangibles and improving intra-personal intangibles which contribute to quality work. Quality service does not automatically happen with more equipment, more labor hours, or higher-cost materials. "More often than not, better quality can mean better productivity," David A. Garvin pointed out. Further, he claims that ". . . what is needed is a revolution in the way managers think about the continuum of [service] development activities. By this we do not mean a shift only in their conventional approaches to quality problems but also in their readiness to make the long-term investments in people and equipment necessary to make better [service] less expensive."[7]

The point is that rather than becoming consumed with saving money, the administration and managers of the library should work together to develop and promote service values, vision, and goals and dedicate services to achieving higher quality through an understanding of the entire service process.[8] In many cases, budget crises offer the manager opportunities to reevaluate operational procedures. The manager should be able to raise questions such as: which tasks are the most labor-intensive and time-consuming; what are new options for handling them; where are there redundancies or duplicated efforts; are staff using automated systems to their full capacities; and are old methods being used to solve new problems?

Through such a process evaluation, the access services department of the TTU Libraries created a new "Article Delivery" service without increasing costs. In this service, any article needed by faculty can be requested through the access services department without checking the holdings of the Tech Library. If the requested journal article is owned by the library, staff verify the call number, locate the journal, copy the article, and deliver it to the departmental office within 48 hours at the cost of ten cents per page. A requested journal article that is not owned by the library will automatically be processed by ILL, and fax service is promised for rush requests. A cost analysis has shown that the cost per item decreases as more items are delivered. In fact, the total cost of delivering 100 items to 40 departmental offices is no more than 50 items to the same number of department offices on campus.

Since many manual tasks of the ILL/borrowing processes have been simplified by using the ILL database management system, student assistants (SA's) in ILL no longer spend hours managing paper files and retrieving records. Instead, this time is now spent retrieving journals from the stacks and delivering materials on campus. Circulation SA's also provide back-up for photocopying articles during peaks of ILL activity. In part due to the more efficient utilization of SA's, ILL "filled request" statistics increased 30% in the first year after the introduction of Article Delivery. Further, requests for the article delivery increased 30% in three months after the service was implemented. Most important, the Article Delivery service was an extension of an existing service (ILL material delivery), which was handled without adding staff or equipment.

MANAGING CHANGE TO QUALITY SERVICE

Analyzing cost factors and re-evaluating operational procedures to maximize services can lead to change. Staff resistance to change can be a barrier to achieving larger objectives. People can feel threatened and defensive when they perceive that change would alter the stable environment that has been developed over the years. According to David A. Garvin's quality service study, dealing with change leads to inevitable disruptions within the organization.[9] Extra efforts will be needed to establish new operations and skills, and the immediate impact of these efforts is likely to be a short term reduction in productivity. New ways of operating are seldom assimilated immediately. Learning and adjusting to new operating procedures normally require a large up-front investment of time and energy. Sometimes the process can be painful.

The principles of managing change to quality service have to be institutionalized in the library in order for change to be successfully introduced. This means that top management must openly advocate quality service and work to improve the organizational culture to minimize resistance and reinforce the value of service as a long-term goal, so that middle management (the access service manager) can transform the quality concept into action. Staff must be mobilized around the concepts of quality service and user-centeredness. This process requires that:

- Job security and job satisfaction should be emphasized. The manager needs to help staff perceive change as an opportunity for improving job performance rather than as a threat to job security. Any change that will affect positions and work groups should be communicated before the change is made.
- Appropriate training programs and continuous learning opportunities should be developed for staff to improve skills and gain new expertise. The manager should encourage staff to use creativity and autonomy to develop new options to accomplish their jobs. Empowering staff in this manner can help lead to job satisfaction and increased skills. Organizing a department with narrowly defined job descriptions is counterproductive to change, because it restricts the processes of empowering workers and adapting to change.
- Quality standards must be stated before quality service can be introduced. Systematic measures of service and work performance can convey to staff what is necessary for consistent services and help develop the intangible factors so important

to quality service. Exceptional performance should be acknowledged and rewarded; it is the manager's responsibility to fulfill people's need for recognition. Also, the principle of user-centeredness should be stated as a goal of quality service.
- Teamwork should be organized for quality improvement. Teamwork means sharing information, learning skills from one another, solving problems together, and sharing the excitement of productivity and quality work that the team has produced. Employee involvement plays an important role in fostering the quality culture and is instrumental in determining how quickly plans can be implemented with minimal mistakes resistance.[10] Trust is the key to building a team environment. The more trust can be built within the team, the better and the more honest communication will be. In managing change to quality service, the access services manager must develop this trust in the work place.

It can be useful to devise an operational pattern to reflect the routine flow of work through the department. Using this pattern, the manager can sometimes determine opportunities for maximizing human resource in the department. The access services department of TTU Libraries has used computer-aided analysis (lotus 123 spreadsheet and dBase software programs) to chart hourly work flow and generate data which are plotted in tables and graphs representing daily, weekly, and monthly activities. Such analysis has insured unit supervisors and staff members adequate staffing levels to perform various tasks within the department. This can also maximize staffing flexibility. For example, at TTU the work flow analysis, combined with an analysis of demand patterns, indicated specific times when SA's could be assigned to stacks work, especially to deal with overflow periods, and when circulation and reserve SA's could be re-assigned to photocopy materials for ILL or assist with delivery services during peak periods. In addition, the flexibility of cross training has freed up fulltime staff to take on responsibilities in other areas, e.g., providing library tours and assisting with online database searches. As a result, increased workloads in each area have been handled swiftly without additional staff. New services and special projects, such as delivery services to faculty, shelf reading, and stack shifting projects have been managed with the same number of student assistant hours. Full-time staff members in the department who have been cross-trained not only develop new skills and service perspectives, but also new directions of job satisfaction, recognition, and promotion potential.

Overall, the access services manager is in a position to lead and support staff and to change work behavior. The manager should be able to use appropriate management strategies to identify barriers to change, diagnose problems, and generate and select among alternatives for change.

QUALITY SERVICE AND COMPUTER TECHNOLOGY

With the installation of an online catalog system or the upgrading of an existing computer system, constructive communication efforts must be initiated within the department to help staff facing technological change and to implement quality services for patrons. Developing effective communication channels for managing technological change can alleviate potential problems and maximize the staffs operational abilities with the new computer system.

Recently, the access services department of TTU Libraries has experienced such a change. In an effort to assist staff in adapting to the new system, several steps were undertaken before and after implementing the circulation module of the new online system. At training classes, the department head introduced the new system to staff step-by-step by drawing the structure of the circulation module and bibliographic database, outlining the steps of merging the old files of the circulation system to the new one, charting the timeline for system implementation, specifying the system functions, and preparing a reference handbook (including commands and quick references). Additionally, question-and-answer sheets were prepared to introduce the concepts of bibliographic and circulation databases and their terminology and to address the work flow issues between access services and the bibliographic control departments. Finally, a "Special Column" of the access service department's newsletter (a bi-monthly publication) has been dedicated to subjects pertaining to the online system and recognized staff expertise, efforts, and accomplishments.

In managing for the introduction of new technology, the access services manager should envision and communicate opportunities utilizing hardware, software, and network capability for achieving total quality service. This entails:

- Knowing the skills basic to understanding system analysis, database structure, and programming in order to deal with the uncertainty and to utilize the full potential of the system. Choosing suitable software and hardware from today's fast-growing computer market can be very confusing and time-consuming. To avoid dissatisfaction or confusion after the system is in place, computer skills and knowledge are crucial in evaluating and developing a computing system.[11]
- Identifying the emerging new technologies that are likely to impact information service and selecting those to be fully used for services and productivity. For instance, utilizing the VAX (the mainframe at the TTU computing system) and EtherNet (the campus network), the head of access services initiated an "Electronic Library Services" system and programmed the system onto the VAX. These electronic services allow faculty and students to communicate their needs with librarians from their homes or offices at any time of the day or night, e.g., to request ILL materials or copies of articles, to suggest purchase of new books for teaching or research, to inquire the name of the library liaison assigned to their departments, to ask for a library instruction class or library tours, or to display library hours.[12]
- Understanding the needs and demands for information and the use of information in the community. Technology is now growing to meet the demand for timely and customized information. Materials available in electronic format will ease pressures on libraries to have a large local collection of little-used, highly specialized periodicals, emphasizing, instead, access to material held by cooperating institutions. It is crucial for the manager to understand how to use and manage these newly developed

technologies in order to increase the accessibility of library resources and to enhance quality service.
- Articulating the need for restructuring the access services department to respond to patterns of work that are created by the new technology. Computer technology will continue to offer staff new options in handling library operations; therefore, new skills, responsibilities, and roles for workers will be required in the process of change. Redesigning jobs or responsibilities can be an effective approach to giving service people increased visibility in providing services.[13] This process can change the work processes and the structure of the department.

In short, the access services manager must be knowledgeable both of the technologies available and their capabilities, and of the concerns and aptitudes of the staff who will use them.

CONCLUSION

It is clear that economic and technological changes have had a profound impact on library services and have created uncertainties and future challenges for access services. The ultimate challenge for access services is not just to deliver service to users or to control costs, but rather to leverage value over cost to achieve the goal of quality service.[14] The process involves seeking new methods and developing new perspectives to capitalize on the strengths of tangible and intangible elements of the department and to meet new demands and expectations for information services. The overall objective of managing total quality service is to achieve a continuous quality improvement effort and to ensure that various service functions are executed in a consistent manner.[15] Once a quality service philosophy has been openly espoused, it can become a foundation concept of a library's service ethic and unite the efforts of various units.

In maximizing and managing quality service, the access service manager must foresee new directions and technologies of information service, attain breadth of service perspective, and envision new options for achieving total quality service and high productivity. Adopting and implementing the concept of quality service, which has been influential in various service-oriented businesses and other professional operations, can revolutionize the delivery of library services, and thus the prestige of this relatively new organizational concept in libraries.

REFERENCE NOTES

1. *Service Quality: Multi-disciplinary and multinational perspectives*, edited by Stephen W. Brown et al. (Lexington Books, MA, 1991). A good general overview of the quality service concept.
2. Amy Chang, "A Database Management System for Interlibrary Loan," *Information Technology and Libraries*, Vol. 9, No. 2 (June 1990): 135-143.
3. Richard M. Dougherty, "Library Cooperation: A Historical Perspective and a Vision for the Future," in *Advances in Library Resource Sharing*, edited by Jennifer Cargill and Diane J. Graves, Meckler, Westport, 1990.
4. Fean-Paul Flipo, "On the Strategic Implications of Tangible Elements in the Marketing of Industrial Services," In *Service quality: Multi-disciplinary and multinational perspectives*, edited by Stephen W. Brown . . . et al. (Lexington Books, MA, 1991). p. 1-18.
5. Leonard Berry, A. Parasuraman, and Valarie A. Zeithame, "A Conceptual Model of Service Quality and Its Implications for Future Research," *Journal of Marketing*, Vol. 49, No. 4 (Fall, 1985): 41-50.
6. James L. Heskett, W. Earl Sasser, Jr., and Christopher W. L. Hart, *Service Breakthrough: Changing the Rules of the Game* (New York: The Free Press, 1990), p. 115.
7. David A. Garvin, *Managing Quality: The Strategic and Competitive Edge* (New York: The Free Press, 1988), p. 85.
8. John Sculley, *Odyssey: Pepsi to Apple* (New York: Harper & Row, Pub., Inc. 1987), p. 259.
9. David Garvin, "Quality on the Line," *Harvard Business Review*, 61(5) (Sept/Oct, 1983): 65-75.
10. Will Kaydos, *Measuring Managing and Maximizing Performance* (MA: Productivity Press, 1991), p. 145-147.
11. Amy Chang and Susan L. Markar, "Guidelines for Software Quality Assurance," *Library Software 11. Review*, Vol. 9, No. 2 (March/April 1990): 75-79.
12. Amy Chang, "Developing an Electronic Information Service In An Academic Library," *College & Research Libraries News*, Vol. 52, No. 4 (April, 1991): 237-239.
13. James L. Heskett, "Lessons in the Service Sector," *Harvard Business Review* (March-April 1987): 118-126.
14. Heskett, 1990.
15. James R. White and Victor R. Dingus, "Quality Services: A New Business Partner," *Quality Progress*, V.21, No. 11 (Nov. 1987): 56-60.

Information Delivery in the Evolving Electronic Library: Traditional Resources and Technological Access

John B. Harer

SUMMARY. The emergence of the electronic library has greatly increased access to bibliographic information. While there are many new technological advances in information services, electronic delivery is still only possible in limited forms. Users often have the capability to identify information, verify its availability status, and even place an order for it electronically. Nevertheless, in most cases, it can only be delivered via conventional means. This creates a situation where a great amount of bibliographic information can be located online in real time, but acquisition of this information may be time-consuming and lead to patron frustration. Some enduring purposes of traditional access services are thus discussed in terms of their significance in an electronic library environment.

INTRODUCTION

Increasing access by whatever means should have a positive impact on the delivery of a product or service. When the Coca-

---

John Harer is Head, Circulation Division of the Sterling C. Evans Library at Texas A&M University. He holds an MLS from Clarion University and a second Master's in public administration from the University of Baltimore. He is an active member of the LAMA SASS Circulation Services Committee and the Intellectual Freedom Committee of ALA. The author thanks Rachel Robbins, University of Texas at Arlington, for her work on a previous study that led to the development of concepts in this article, and to Jay Poole, Texas A&M, for his excellent advice and moral support.

© 1992 by The Haworth Press, Inc. All rights reserved.

Cola® Company added buckpassers to vending machines, one salesman said it doubled sales virtually overnight. The buckpasser was innovative piece of technology that demonstrably increased access and, as a result, the delivery of a product. People who did not have change did not have to go away thirsty.

Will electronic access lead to the same success in the delivery of library information as a buckpasser on a Coke® machine did for that product? Obviously, the two products, information and Coca-Cola®, are very different; the complexity of the formats in which information is contained cannot necessarily be compared to the simplicity of a 12 ounce can of Coke®. Information access is affected by numerous factors, and the diversity of formats in which it is conveyed, as well as the technologies and human factors associated with its retrieval, can make delivery more or less difficult. A Coke®, on the other had, is easily manufactured and access is readily available either in retail outlets or through coin-op machines. Nevertheless, the assumption that increased access will result in more rapid delivery is one that many patrons may have, regardless if the commodity is information or a soft drink.

D. Lamont Johnson and Linda L. Carr, educators at the University of Nevada at Reno, recently voiced this very concern in an article on the electronic library:

> We get excited about the prospects of the electronic library every trip we make to our existing university library. . . . The trip from our office across campus to the library is pleasant enough, but it is the frustration we feel when we get there that starts us dreaming of a better way. Often the quest for a very routine piece of information results in a hour of fruitless searching. Our frustration level peaks when we find that the article we want has fallen between a crack: not yet on microfilm, not yet in the bound volume or missing from the periodical shelf. Our frustration boils over when, after an arduous search, we find the right shelf, the right periodical, the right volume, but the pages have been torn out![1]

The authors further projected their expectations that, in an ideal electronic information environment, there would be no need to go to the physical library building, since information will be available instantaneously, much like a Coke®. Such futuristic scenarios notwithstanding, comprehensive information access may never be entirely possible electronically, since the total intellectual property of any discipline comes in many formats, through many resources. The management of these resources remains the thrust of access services management despite the evolution of the electronic library. Attention to resource management is paramount in all libraries, even the electronic ones.

THE INFORMATION CYCLE NETWORK

Acquisition of information by library patrons is a circular process, hereafter referred to as the "Information Cycle Network" (ICN). The ICN contains three components. The first is *identification*, i.e., searching for information, using whatever means available, and identifying a source. The second component is *access*. Once the source is identified, the patron will determine its availability and location. The last component is *delivery* of the source or actual information. The circle is often completed when one source points to more information and further leads to identification of information resources.

In an idealized electronic library, it has been suggested that researchers could perform all three ICN functions at a single workstation. At present, this can be accomplished on a very limited basis by some researchers, at some institutions, for certain types of information. For example, the CARL system includes general reference tools such as *Grolier's Encyclopedia* in full-text, an article access service, UnCover, to over one million articles in 10,000 unique serial titles, and the full-text of articles from the Information Access Company's Magazine ASAP(TM) and Trade & Industry ASAP (TM) databases.[2] These systems, however, can by no means serve the needs of all patrons. It still may be a long time before the third component of the ICN, delivery, is possible for most individuals.

In the meantime, integrated library systems have vastly enhanced the patron's ability to identify and verify the availability of information. As an example, the Wilson Multi-database Product (MDAS) is an electronic periodical index available for library system such as NOTIS. The MDAS Product increases identification and access by combining the book catalog and periodical indexes, as well as providing library status and availability information. Despite these systematic enhancements to the first two components of ICN, traditional methods of delivery are still required for fulfillment of the third.

Further, there is the potential that, even where electronic means of information delivery exist, they may lead managers to be overly "bit" conscious. This can happen in two ways. First, the patron may focus attention on just those "bits" of information that are available full-text, online, to the exclusion of others that are not. Second, these "bits" may be extracted from a whole, and this piecemeal presentation of the information might give the patron a quite different perspective on the context in which it was originally presented. For example, a book might contain several "bits" (chapters, sections, etc.), but it is also a total work of intellectual property, worth acquiring and using as such.

Most library systems that exist now enhance means of identifying information and checking its availability status. Some make information available in full-text, although, even when this is the case, the information that can be retrieved electronically might still be just so many "bits" of complete resources. The present state of technology bears out the need to maintain traditional access services, especially as they relate to document delivery. Further, it can be argued that unless the book ceases to exist as an information resource, libraries can never cease to provide such services.

INFORMATION DELIVERY IN AN ELECTRONIC LIBRARY

As technology makes greater information access possible, it is vital to remember that steps must also be taken to enhance information delivery. Modern technology makes broader access and identification possible, but it also tends to raise expectations about what is easily available and what can be quickly obtained, and in that sense better technology does not necessarily mean that all elements of the ICN are better served. Through searching electronic resources, such as, for example, an Internet accessible library catalog, a patron might identify a needed source of information and verify its location and status, and in doing so develop unrealistic expectations about how and when it might actually be acquired.

It is useful to consider how the ICN worked in a traditional, non-automated library. Typically, the first step would take place when a patron identified a resource by searching the card catalog. The inadequacies of the card catalog today do not negate the fact that, at its inception, and until replaced by electronic bibliographic access, it represented a revolutionary vehicle for bibliographic identification. This technology met the needs of the first component during an era when resources came in fewer numbers and in more manageable formats than today, and is still meeting these needs in non-automated libraries.

Traditionally, the second two elements of the ICN have been handled through cataloging and circulation services, which remain critical in electronic libraries. In an early work, Brown and Bousfield instructed the profession on the essential requirements for circulation services as they saw them in the 1930s. They listed four necessary tasks: (1) contacts with patrons, (2) keeping records, (3) delivery of books from the stacks, and (4) shelving.[3] Of record keeping, they emphasized that " The keeping of loan desk records requires accuracy . . . for cards misfiled usually mean books not supplied."[4] Of shelving, they also emphasized that "Books misshelved are books lost. Accuracy in shelving is essential."[5]

In a non-automated environment, access can be gained by determining the location of the item and, if necessary, checking its availability status. Delivery would then occur when the physical item was found and used. These tasks completed the ICN, as it was conceived before the advent of electronic bibliographic access, i.e., contacts with patrons and keeping records satisfied access and verification of availability, while stacks maintenance and circulation services were the primary means of information delivery.

The present day climate for access services has made satisfying the third ICN component sometimes complex, difficult and/or frustrating for the patron. Brown and Bousfield's 1933 model, which basically dealt with providing access to and delivery of locally held resources, still provides a useful point of reference for service delivery in electronic libraries. Even if entirely electronic information delivery becomes possible in the future, the current status of information delivery is far from that ideal, and if traditional methods of information delivery are neglected, library users' needs and expectations will not be met.

It is recommended that access services managers consider the delivery of information resources from a "macro" (or holistic) perspective. The macro perspective takes into account *every* aspect of resource delivery that is possible, including accurate shelving services for those who use the library, abundant and effective photocopy services for materials with borrowing restrictions, document delivery services for appropriate clientele, and circulation services for accurate bibliographic verification and borrowing, as well as any other aspect affecting access to the building and the collection. Many of these services are entirely traditional, but can also be adapted in an electronic library.

There are three elements that must be considered in the macro perspective, and these subsume virtually all library departments and operations. The first element might be called "peripheral factors," which are all of those library functions beyond the direct control of access services managers, but which nonetheless influence or affect access. Perhaps the prime factor in this component is an accessible building. If patrons have difficulty entering the building or, more commonly, become discouraged by its complexity or have difficulties orienting themselves, then access is effectively denied. Physical plant support is also essential to maintaining an accessible building environment.

Peripheral library *services* are also vital. For example, without an accurate and effective catalog, electronic or otherwise, identification of and access to materials are seriously jeopardized, and the delivery of resources and information cannot occur. Finally, user education is vitally necessary to ensure that all patrons can maximize use of the library's services and facilities and by doing so, enhance information delivery potential. User education takes place through both formal and informal means. Formal means include workshops, classes, and tours. Informal methods can include readable pamphlets and guides and an effective sign system. These aspects of library management are not the exclusive concerns of access services (with the possible exception of signage), but should be mentioned here because of their role in maximizing access and supporting the three components of ICN.

The second element of a macro perspective to resource delivery encompasses those services and procedures that have commonly been united under the umbrella of access services, including circulation services and record keeping, shelving and shelf management, and resource security. Some key access services factors and performance issues will be discussed in the next section.

The third element comprises all alternative means of delivery of resources. When libraries opened their stacks, self-service became the predominant form of information delivery. While the patron's ability to identify, verify the status, and locate the physical material depends upon the performance of an infrastructure of the aforementioned peripheral and access services, it was nonetheless expected that the patron could successfully fulfill all three ICN components independently using the resources provided. The other main delivery alternative in a traditional service environment would be document delivery, where the patron received personal delivery of information, which had either been requested or was anticipated to be of interest.

There are certainly other traditional and non-traditional delivery alternatives. Full-text electronic delivery has already been mentioned as a developing alternative. Telefacsimile technology provides another popular alternative. Also, though not typically regarded as such, a photocopy machine is a form of information delivery technology in that it provides a means of gaining access to a resource that might otherwise not be made available to a patron. A photocopy of an article might, in fact, be preferred to the actual journal in which the article is published, since, in this format, the patron may do things with the information, such as mark or highlight passages, that are prohibited with the original source.

Finally, in addition to full-text online alternatives, various other possible forms of document delivery exist in some electronic libraries. For example, patrons can install a PC Fax board into their personal computers, which permits them to send and receive documents that can be stored in a personal computer and then printed off as a file later.[6] A relatively new service, ARIEL, has been beta tested and implemented at several research libraries. This system combines RLG applications software with a personal computer, document scanner and laser printer. Typically, articles from bound journals are scanned into the PC, transmitted over Internet to the recipient's workstation, and printed.[7] Also, as has been described previously, the CARL system has a full-text bibliographic database.[8]

By invoking the macro perspective, an access services manager can clearly see how virtually all library operations contribute to the ICN and make for successful document delivery. "Peripheral" functions especially make identification and verification possible and direct patrons to the locations of resources. Making sure that these resources are in their proper locations and controlling the conditions by which patrons use them are typically responsibilities of access services–these services can be looked upon as forms of traditional document delivery. Finally, in addition to these traditional forms, there are various alternative means and technologies used for achieving document delivery. By whatever means, however, the goal of document delivery is the same: to get needed information into the hands of the patron. Getting this done requires that the access services manager pay attention to a variety of traditional and non-traditional performance issues, which are discussed further in the next section.

CRUCIAL PERFORMANCE ISSUES IN INFORMATION RESOURCE DELIVERY

Library managers examining how document delivery occurs in their libraries can gain perspective on the complex and interacting variables of the ICN by analyzing them from a macro approach. Often, the term "document delivery" is narrowly interpreted to mean specific hand-to-hand delivery of materials. If considered in the broader context, a number of services not typically considered document delivery still accomplish the same thing: getting information to patrons. It is important that managers identify the means by which document delivery is accomplished in their libraries. Likewise, it is important to remember that document delivery is the third step of the ICN, and that achieving the other two is its prerequisite.

For access service managers, in particular, there are many functions and services essential to making it possible for patrons to move from one step in the ICN to the next, and due attention should be paid to all of these. Some of these are: maintaining the accuracy of circulation records, encouraging efficient and accurate stacks maintenance, implementing necessary security measures, and managing a viable photocopy service.

Patrons who have identified a citation to a needed resource will then wish to verify its availability. Absolute accuracy of circulation records may be an impossible ideal, although automation has greatly enhanced record-keeping capabilities. In a 1981 study, Martin reported the findings of a survey of circulation system managers that showed those with online systems were much more satisfied with the accuracy of their records than batch or manual system managers. Fully 70% of online system managers agreed that their circulation control system had very accurate circulation records, while batch managers reported a 54% satisfaction rate and manual system managers reported a 30% satisfaction rate.[9]

Still, electronic systems do not solve all record-keeping problems. In a 1987 study, Intner reported that some of the major problems reported by circulation librarians of manual systems were the lack of quick and accurate access to circulation information and failure to control chronic abuses of library privileges. She noted that "Computer systems may overcome some kinds of record errors such as transcribing numbers, names, or other data incorrectly and misfiling records, but they will not be infallible since errors in human data entry will be compounded throughout the system."[10] Also, the implementation of an online system could force reorientation, which she observed when she wrote "The effects of widespread implementation of computer systems in all types of libraries has been to highlight the need for written policies and procedures . . ."[11] Finally, automation requires that specific attention be paid to human and machine interactions. Training of staff in an automated environment is often more intensive than in a manual one, but is essential in order to minimize the human errors that can undermine system integrity. Some circulation systems are less prone to human error factors than others; for example, a system that provides audible or visual cues can alert staff to situations where special attention must be paid to a patron transaction or item record, and can potentially reduce human error factors.

Shelving is one function of access services that has not been automated. While portable scanners are sometimes being used for inventory control, the labor intensive and detail oriented tasks of shelving will likely always be done by human beings. Yet it is a crucial service for the delivery of resources, and should remain so while the book is at the center of library collections. With shelving, human error can have serious consequences, for a misshelved book is, in effect, a failure to deliver a resource. The performance issues that require attention are staff training and evaluation, shelf-reading and inventories.

Shelving performance can be relatively easily quantified. In 1933, Brown and Bousfield suggested that a book should be returned two hours after it was discharged.[12] It is doubtful that many libraries, especially the larger ones and academic libraries at the end of the term, could adhere to this performance standard. Still, such standards and performance measures can be useful and, as Sharp suggests in her study at Brigham Young University, further research should be done to determine what reasonable expectations are.[13] Library users have a right to expect timely reshelving of materials but the definition of "timely" has yet to be defined through research.

Shelf-reading is the primary way to correct errors, but as Bennett, Buxton and Capriotti have stated, it can be the most boring kind of library work.[14] Their approach to managing shelf-reading activities emphasized training and performance standards. "The success of this shelf-reading program can be attributed not to any elegant mathematical formula but rather to an understanding of human nature: People can handle even the most boring work well if the task is divided into manageable quantities of time, space and personnel."[15]

The other means for reducing errors is to perform an inventory, but as Kohl suggests, "Undertaking a traditional, complete physical inventory on any regular basis becomes almost prohibitively expensive once the collection exceeds 100,000 volumes."[16] In the private sector, an inventory is considered essential because it establishes the true assets and hence the actual net worth of the firm. Even while acknowledging the labor and time demands of such a enterprise, it is still fair to ask: is the net worth of a library collection any less valuable, not only in terms of actual cost to the institution, but also to the services available to the patron? Each organization must weigh the time and effort it would take to do an inventory against the benefits that would accrue from doing so. Also, Kohl suggests a more efficient approach is to do inventories of separate parts of the collection based on records and reports of collection use; this may prove quite valuable as a procedure for inventory of a large collection.[17]

Resource security is another basic concern for the delivery of information resources. This is hardly a new concept: the closed stack was and still is designed strictly for security. While it is inevitable that opening the stacks to the public will increase the loss of materials, doing so is critical to the delivery of information. Minimum security standards for a building with open stacks can be controlled at the exit locations. Electronic security systems are commonly used in many libraries, but they are not foolproof.[18] Fair and effective performance in security procedures should take into account the following phenomena:

- Not all "thefts" are intentional: forgetfulness and haste are common, human errors. Policies for handling patrons caught in the security system should take such factors into account.[19]
- Not all "thefts" represent a permanent loss: many items later "turn up," for whatever reasons (A distinction that may be made by users, but seldom by librarians is between items "illegally borrowed" and those actually stolen. The forum may have been taken so as to circumvent circulation restrictions, but with no real intention of being kept). A statistical analysis of the found rate of missing items can be useful for collection management decisions.

- Not all "thefts" are by library patrons: employee theft is not confined to the private sector. Security policies should address issues related to employee theft.
- Not all losses are due to thefts: mutilation is still a problem and may be more so in a library with an electronic security system.[20]

Weiss suggests prosecution as a deterrent which would help in eliminating mutilation problems.[21] Another solution is to create a smaller or restricted collection for high risk items. This is not to suggest a return to closed stacks or to hinder intellectual freedom for security purposes. Rather, the policy issue should be one of compartmentalizing collections for better supervision, rather than leaving them unattended in the open stacks. To do so should be presented as a positive, rather that negative form of information delivery.

The photocopier service is the final point of information resource delivery to be addressed here. Performance problems with this service are numerous. In particular, the causes of service interruptions should be examined. These may occur due to mechanical problems; equipment failures are common, and even when machines are operating properly, supplies need to be monitored and replenished periodically. Interruptions might also occur due to patron factors, such as long lines or confusion about the operation of the machines. Studying the causes of these interruptions can yield a great deal of pertinent information on how the machines will be used, where they can be placed for optimum effect, and what kinds of machines will best meet the library's needs.

Once the causes of interruptions have been determined, eliminating or reducing them requires policy and/or administrative action. This begins with the selection of a copy machine. With machines for public areas, "user friendliness" is an obvious, but sometimes overlooked feature. The image area of a copy machine should make it clear where the paper is to be placed, with marking for letter-size and legal-size sheets. The essential operating buttons should be conspicuous and clearly labeled—a print button, paper tray selection, number of copies, and copy darkness adjustment are all the only ones necessary. The best sources of pertinent information to consider in a library purchase decision are reviewing sources and testimonials from library users. Machine paper tray and toner capacity should be high in order to minimize maintenance interruptions: a paper tray capacity of 1000 or more sheets is preferable, as is a toner/print capacity of upwards to 100,000. Also, carefully consider if advertised features suit the library's needs. For example, many copiers have, as a major selling point, the speed of the copy made. This standard, measured in seconds, is an office-efficiency standard with little value for a public photocopy service because the seconds of time saving in a fast machine are insignificant to the minutes of time savings in machines that are more reliable. The copier that stays up and running the longest is the ideal, not one that is fast by office standards.

In each of these operations from the realm of access services, it is useful to consider the roles that they play in fulfillment of the stages of ICN when establishing performance standards. Successful performance of circulation record-keeping functions, for example, will result in accurate and effective verification of a resource's availability status. Similarly, stacks maintenance and photocopy services make materials physically available to a patron (i.e., deliver information), and should do so with a minimum of patron confusion or frustration. Performance standards for specific procedures can be measured in terms of how efficiently they contribute to the overall goal of making it possible to fulfill the discrete steps of the ICN.

CONCLUSION

Electronic technologies have revolutionized the means by which library patrons work through the processes of the Information Cycle Network. Still, many traditional operations of library services, which can best be examined at a "macro" level, remain critical. Most notable among these are document delivery services. Document delivery by whatever means, traditional or electronic, is essential to a service oriented philosophy of access management. Within this realm, many of the access services requirements noted by Brown and Bousfield in 1933 are still as crucial today as then and will remain so as long as there are collections of resources in hardcopy formats and as long as the book remains valuable in and of itself, not just for the bits of information contained within. Access services managers–and indeed library management in general–can benefit from designing services, establishing performance standards, and writing policies and procedures that link these factors to their role in helping patrons move through the tasks of the ICN. Anything short of this emphasis will doom the user and the library to frustration.

REFERENCE NOTES

1. Johnson, D. Lamont and Linda L. Carr. "Is the Electronic Library for Real?" *Education Technology.* Vol. 31, no. 4 (April, 1991) p. 24.
2. Lenzini, Rebecca T. and Ward Shaw. "Creating a New Definition of Library Cooperation: Past, Present, and Future Models." *Library Administration and Management.* Vol. 5, no. 1 (Winter, 1991) p. 38.
3. Brown, Charles Harvey and H.G. Bousfield. *Circulation Work in College and University Libraries* (Chicago: American Library Association, 1933. p. 65).
4. Ibid.
5. Ibid. p. 67.
6. Harer, John B. and Rachel H. Robbins. "A PC Fax Board Document Delivery Service: An Interim Step to Full-text Document Delivery." In *The Proceedings of the Twelfth National Online Meeting, May 7-9, 1991.* Medford, NJ.: Learned Information, c1991.
7. Jackson, May E. "Library to Library." *Wilson Library Bulletin.* Vol. 65 (April, 1991) p. 84.
8. Lenzini, op.cit., p. 38.
9. Martin, James R. "Communications: Automation and the Service Attitudes of ARL Circulation Managers." *Journal of Library Automation.* Vol. 14, no. 3 (September, 1981) p. 192.
10. Intner, Sheila. *Circulation Policy in Academic, Public and School Libraries.* N.Y.: Greenwood Press, c1987.
11. Ibid., p. 7.
12. Brown, p. 67.
13. S. Celine Sharp. "A Library Shelve's Performance Evaluation as it Related to Reshelving Accuracy." In Gregg Sapp, ed. "Access Services Management" (The Haworth Press, Inc. 1992).
14. Bennett, Margaret Johnson, David T. Buxton and Ella Capriotti. "Shelf-Reading in a Large, Open-Stack Library." *The Journal of Academic Librarianship.* Vol. 8, no. 2 (May, 1982) p. 82.
15. Ibid.

16. Kohl, David F. "High Efficiency Inventorying through Predictive Data." *The Journal of Academic Librarianship*. Vol. 8, no. 2 (May, 1982) p. 82.

17. Ibid., p. 84.

18. Richards, James H., Jr. "Missing Inaction." *The Journal of Academic Librarianship*. Vol. 5, no. 5 (November, 1979) p. 266.

19. Ibid.

20. Kesler, Elizabeth Gates. "A Campaign Against Mutilation." *The Journal of Academic Librarianship*. Vol. 3, no. 1 (March, 1977) p. 29.

21. Weiss, Dana. "Book Theft and Book Mutilation in a Large Urban University Library." *College and Research Libraries*. Vol. 65 (July, 1981) p. 345.

Access to Library Materials in Remote Storage

Claire Q. Bellanti

SUMMARY. Providing good access to library material in remote storage is the key to making the use of remote storage an acceptable option for dealing with overcrowding in libraries on prime campus land. Users' concerns with remote storage include issues such as browsability, retrieval time, and distance factors. Each of these concerns must be addressed to provide users with adequate access to stored collections. Electronic browsing can replace physical browsing. Turnaround time may be reduced with requests submitted through electronic mail, telefacsimile transmissions, and regular pickups. At the UC Southern Regional Library Facility, bibliographic access is provided by the UCLA online automated system, ORION, and the union catalog for all of the University of California, Melvyl™. The primary focus of policies and procedures at the facility is to provide quick and easy access to materials once they are stored.

INTRODUCTION

One of the most pressing collection management issues facing academic libraries today is the space crunch created by collection growth which, over a period of time, has exceeded stack space and building capacities. Many academic libraries have turned to storing books in places away from the regular stack collection. Storage may be as elaborate as that of the California State University,

---

Claire Q. Bellanti is Director of the UC Southern Regional Library Facility and Head of Access Services at the University of California, Los Angeles, CA 90024-1388. She holds an MA in history from the University of Nevada, Las Vegas and a Master's in business administration from UCLA.

© 1992 by The Haworth Press, Inc. All rights reserved.

Northridge, automated storage and retrieval system, where bins are stored in warehouse style shelving and retrieved by miniload cranes directed by computer commands. Or storage choices may be as simple as placing extra shelves in a basement of an existing campus building. Most of the literature on library storage focuses on how collections grew too big for their buildings, models by which librarians may manage the collection and select materials for storage, or descriptions of the remote facilities themselves.[1] Access to library materials in remote storage has been discussed less frequently in the literature. In the coming years, as remote storage facilities fill up and the demand for services continues to grow, the issues that will dominate the field are those related to access to the materials. This article describes a number of such issues, drawing on examples from the University of California's Southern Regional Library Facility (UC SRLF).

REMOTE STORAGE AT THE UC SOUTHERN REGIONAL LIBRARY FACILITY

The University of California operates two regional storage facilities, one in the northern part of the state and one in the south. The purpose of the UC SRLF, as indicated in its "Statement of Operating Principles," is:

> to store, preserve and provide access to low use library materials of research value in a cost effective economical manner for the libraries of the University of California. As part of an effort to foster interlibrary cooperation, participation by other segments of the library community, public and private, is accepted.[2]

The facilities use industrial style shelving, which is divided into nine and one-half foot high levels from which materials are retrieved manually. Both have their bibliographic records online in a union catalog, MELVYL™. At the end of the fiscal year 1990/91, the UC SRLF housed 2.1 million volume equivalents of stored library materials from the five southern University of California campuses: UC Irvine, UC Los Angeles, UC Riverside, UC San Diego, and UC Santa Barbara.

The building opened in October, 1987. In the first two years a large temporary staff added almost 1.5 million items. More than 300,000 items have been processed each year since the initial loading was completed. Of a staff of 21.5 Full Time Equivalents, approximately 7.5 are devoted entirely to public services, including retrieval, copying, mailing, circulation functions and on-site information and access. Another 10.5 FTE process incoming materials by searching for records in MELVYL™ and ORION, the UCLA online information system, downloading records, sorting out bibliographic problems and changing locations and shelf numbers. The remaining 3.5 FTE carry out personnel, payroll and other administrative functions. An additional 6.5 FTE in student employees shelve books and assist with processing.

While storage facilities with a similar mission as the SRLF's are becoming increasingly common, storage is not a universally popular solution to library space problems. Much of the resistance to storage may be attributed to concerns about access to these library materials. No matter how well libraries adhere to their carefully developed criteria for selection, someone is eventually going to need some of the material that has been placed in remote storage. That user has a right to expect its delivery within a reasonable time frame. Providing good access to remote collections is the key to making library storage an acceptable alternative to using expensive library space on prime campus land.

The first problem for most users is that physical browsing is not feasible in many storage facilities. Sometimes the choice of shelving, or the style of retrieval, dictates that stacks must remain closed to those who are not staff members. For example, in order to achieve high density at the SRLF, the basic plan is to shelve materials by size, in two rows deep and in accession number order. The SRLF policy allows faculty access to the stacks (no other user groups are permitted access), but browsing these stacks would be a frustrating and not very fruitful experience. Other facilities, such as the one at Harvard and those modeled after it, use industrial shelving components more than thirty feet high with mobile mechanical lifts to transport staff members to stored bins. As mentioned previously, materials at the California State University, Northridge are stored in similar bins and an automated retrieval system is used.[3] While these systems achieve high density, they do not allow for any physical browsing, which is the means of access many people prefer. Although browsable storage in industrial shelving seems to be a rare exception, Southern Illinois University chose to shelve materials in its facility in call number so as to permit browsing.[4] Call number order can sometimes be maintained when moveable compact shelving is used for storage; this type of construction is often used to maximize space use within a library. Summing up these issues, Michael Gorman notes that "It is not access that is at the root of the idea that libraries should expand on one site. It is the idea of browsing."[5]

The lack of browsability is just one access problem inherent in storing library materials in remote facilities. Others include a lack of patron awareness of the facility and difficulties related to retrieval due to time and distance factors. Still, at least for the near future, storage is a reality that cannot be escaped. Some of the methods of dealing with these problems are: electronic access, a variety of delivery services, and on-site access.

ELECTRONIC ACCESS

Electronic access to stored collections may eventually provide an alternative to the much-desired physical browsing. Whether it will depends on two factors: the level of computer literacy among the users and increasingly effective bibliographic retrieval capabilities provided by online catalogs. One recent assessment of general research behaviors and attitudes toward remote storage and technology was carried out by Wendy Lougee et al., among humanists at the University of Michigan Library. The study concluded that negative attitudes toward technology were common among this group of scholars. However, the group of

> associate professors (or those roughly 31-40 years of age) uses the library most intensively and draws upon remotely

housed collections most frequently. It is also this group that seems more inclined to try new methods of accessing bibliographic information such as library automation might afford.[6]

What is striking about this study is that within this group of younger professors there was far greater acceptance of online bibliographic sources. If this is the case, then it would imply that as older faculty members retire, there will be less resistance in the future.

In an academic library, patrons knowledgeable of appropriate search techniques can use Boolean strategies to "browse" an online catalog by subject, keyword, author, and/or title. Such electronic browsing strategies for materials in storage is most effective when complete bibliographic records are available in the database. Effective searching for materials with minimal bibliographic records often requires that those chosen have sufficiently relevant key words in their titles so that they can be retrieved. Selection is seldom so clear-cut and easy to control, however; thus a minimal record of a title does not generally do the job as well. Perhaps what would be most helpful to users would be content analysis of books in storage, although it would also be inordinately expensive with current technology. There are also cost/benefit tradeoffs to consider in full cataloging vs. minimal cataloging of little used materials.

When books are organized to achieve density rather than being shelved in a classified order, powerful searching capabilities are required to manipulate the database in ways other than the traditional subject, title, and author searches. Because the SRLF is a cooperative facility, storing materials from the five southern University of California campuses, it is likely that faculty or students at UC Irvine, for example, may wish to retrieve records only for Irvine materials stored at SRLF, or they might want to search for materials by date of publication or language. The UC online union catalog, MELVYL™, has many of these capabilities, including subject and keyword searching with Boolean logic, and it provides for limiting searches by language, campus and date (last ten years). Additionally, the SRLF uses ORION, UCLA's online information system for processing and circulation. ORION has Boolean search logic, allows for limiting searches by date, decade, media type (e.g., book, journal, audio-visual), and branch library. ORION even provides for call number searching, thus permitting electronic searching closely akin to physically browsing the stacks. These features mitigate a key concern of users by providing flexible electronic browsing.

Another benefit that the user may find with stored library material is that the loan periods can be longer than those they receive at their home campuses. Material has most often been selected for storage because it has been identified as low-use, and loans can be established for longer periods than is the case for items in a general collection. An automated circulation system can give the storage facility the ability to automatically assign loan periods by type of material and user. The SRLF uses the ORION circulation module, which has been programmed specifically for SRLF needs. In addition to allowing for variable loan periods and longer ones for certain classes of users, SRLF can track both the library to which the material was sent and any patron in the system to whom it was checked out.

A final advantage for libraries with electronic access to books in remote storage is that such access can facilitate cooperative purchases between campuses. Material of low use does not have to be duplicated on all campuses. The University of California has had a strong commitment to shared purchase arrangements, but for the most part, such purchases have been kept at one or two of the nine campuses. Declining book budgets are one of the driving forces behind a more active approach to sharing collections, and collection development librarians are discussing new roles for the regional storage facilities in shared collection development.

LOCATING AND RETRIEVING THE MATERIAL

The user who has identified a relevant bibliographic citation then needs to know how to obtain the material. In planning SRLF, the campuses designed procedures to inform the user of an item's location in storage at the earliest possible moment. In most cases, the location is listed on the MELVYL™ union catalog with the accession/shelving number. For many UC libraries MELVYL™ is the public access catalog. For others which have their own local PACs, such as Innovative Interfaces at UC San Diego and UC Irvine, the location information may be entered into the local system. When an item is deposited by UCLA, SRLF simply changes its location and adds the accession/shelving number onto the existing ORION record. To make the same changes for the other four southern campuses of the University of California, staff download the pre-existing MELVYL™ record onto a disk in a personal computer, update the record, and store it in the SRLF inventory control file in ORION. The altered record is sent back to MELVYL™ by tape. In 1990/91, SRLF staff searched for the bibliographic records of 309,699 items, of which 287,666 items were barcoded and added to the collection. The remaining items were reported as having a problem in their bibliographic records and returned to the depositing campus.

Quite frequently, the storage location is distant from users. For example, UC San Diego's books are stored in SRLF, 120 miles from San Diego. Even on campuses where library materials are placed in local storage, the distance and lack of immediate availability can be perceived as obstacles by many. Turnaround time needs to be fast and efficient for users to accept remote storage as an appropriate access alternative. For off-site locations this implies a regular, if not dedicated delivery service.

The SRLF is mandated by governing board policies to meet a 48 hour turnaround time. Currently, all requests received at SRLF by 11 a.m. on a weekday are filled and ready for pickup by the campus at 1:00 p.m. the same day. The southern UC campuses pick up their own material using a regional bus network with UCLA as the hub. Some years before the construction of SRLF, the intercampus service was set up to transport users and books for interlibrary loan, and one reason for the SRLF's location on the UCLA campus was to take advantage of this pre-existing service. The routes have expanded to include the SRLF, with daily stops by each campus bus to pick up and deliver materials (and sometimes users).

Requests for stored materials are accepted by mail, telephone, telefacsimile or through an electronic mail paging system on ORION. When using ORION, the request is transmitted instantaneously to SRLF. Anyone requesting an item while viewing it on ORION can see its current circulation status. If it is in circulation, library staff can place a hold on the material. Paging requests totaled 60,977 for 1990/91, which was approximately 3% of the total deposited. That figure also represented a 32% increase in requested items from the previous year, which compares to an 18% increase in the total number of volumes. The SRLF has only been in existence a little over four years, but the number of staff devoted to retrieval and other circulation functions has been continually increased in order to keep up with the rapid growth of requests.

To minimize patron frustrations with remote access, the process of placing requests for materials must be quick and efficient. As soon as end-users at UCLA identify a title in ORION as held at SRLF, they may send electronic mail requests directly to the facility without any further intervention. Other UC campuses with access to ORION can use this electronic paging system as well; most have separate ORION accounts for interlibrary loan. ORION is also now available to users and staff alike at other campuses through an Internet connection with MELVYL™.

Materials deposited by any campus may be sent to any requesting campus directly. (Special collections materials are an obvious exception to this procedure and are returned only to the depositing campus for protection.) This speeds up the process by eliminating ILL forms and extra physical handling. The ease of sharing stored materials among campuses may also lead to a re-examination of traditional ILL policies among the campuses.

Turnaround time may also be minimized by using telefacsimile. The SRLF fax machine transmits directly from the printed page, thus eliminating additional time photocopying for fax. Fax transmittal also compares favorably with photocopying and mail deliveries on a cost effectiveness basis. The cost elements of mailing articles include retrieval, copying, packaging, labelling and postage. For telefacsimile the elements include retrieval, transmitting and telephone line time. Fax-ed materials may not be transmitted as promptly as those mailed, but when fax transmissions are batched and sent after working hours, telephone line costs may be as inexpensive as the mail. On the other hand, telefacsimile is not always suitable for transmitting highly detailed print or half-tones. The speed of telefacsimile must be weighed against the requirement for accuracy and clarity.

Finally, on-site use is another important component of access to any library facility. In some cases, such as when a user wishes to examine long runs of a serial title, on-site use may be preferable. In addition to saving transportation costs, time, and potential damage to the material, on-site use can give the user greater control. Storage facilities must address the details of who may use the facility on-site, and what restrictions might exist in policies. For example, non-UCLA library patrons must schedule a trip to SRLF.

CONCLUSION

What will the future hold for access services and remote storage facilities? The book materials in storage are likely to be there for many years. Most storage facilities, such as SRLF, have sophisticated humidity, temperature and ultra-violet light controls and are thus designed to preserve the library materials for hundreds of years. However, some of the older facilities are beginning to reach capacity. For example both of the University of California's regional facilities were planned to be built in phases to accommodate 11 million volume equivalents. The first phase of the UC SRLF is already more than two thirds full, and SRLF Phase 2 is in the planning stages. Phase 2 of the Northern Regional Library Facility was completed in 1990. Is it feasible for universities to go on building storage facilities or might other solutions be adopted?

One popular solution to this dilemma is to consider reformatting certain library materials. Reformatting has the advantages of preserving materials that might otherwise disintegrate and reducing the space required for the remaining materials. Most commonly print media are being reformatted into microfilm or microfiche, but electronic options (both scanned images and ASCII files) are the newest technologies that might be applied to this problem. In considering these new technologies, the question of how users will gain access to the materials must be the highest priorities. Microformats have never been popular with users. They are not easy to read, not cheaply copied, and many users do not seem to be happy with the quality of copies from reader-printers. Electronic imaging and videodisc are two new technologies that seem to provide alternative to miniformats and offer great possibilities for improving access to materials in storage. With this technology, articles could be delivered directly to the end user through file transfer programs. Videodisc technology can also be a boon to preservation as it maintains, and may even enhance photographs and archival materials. But computers and videodisc players are not yet commonly owned, and many issues, such as intellectual property management, remain to be resolved. It is neither economically nor technologically possible to reformat millions of books rapidly enough to solve library space problems. For now, reformatting should be viewed as a means of enhancing access to stored materials. Improving access to library materials in remote storage, with old and new technologies, must now become one of our highest priorities.

REFERENCE NOTES

1. One exception is: Wendy P. Lougee, Mark Sandler, and Linda L. Parker, "The Humanistic Scholars Project: A Study of Attitudes and Behavior Concerning Collection Storage and Technology." *College and Research Libraries* (May, 1980): 231-240.

2. University of California, Southern Regional Library Facility, "Statement of Operating Principles" (Los Angles, 1988): 2.

3. Norman Tanis and Cindy Ventulah, "Making Space: Automated Storage and Retrieval," *Wilson Library Bulletin,* 61, (June, 1987): 25-27.

4. Kenneth G. Peterson, "New Storage Facility at Southern Illinois University," *C&RL News,* 51 (January, 1990): 39-43.

5. Michael Gorman, "A Box Where Sweets Compacted Lie: Compact, Subcompact, and Miniaturized Libraries and the Myth (?) of Browsing," *American Libraries* 15 (April 1984): 210-211.

6. Lougee et al.: 237.

ADDITIONAL SOURCES

Association of Research Libraries. Remote Storage. SPEC Kit 164. Washington, D.C.: ARL, Office of Management Studies, 1990.

Cooper, Michael D. "A Cost Comparison of Alternative Book Storage Strategies." Library Quarterly 59 (July 1989): 239-260.

Feinman, Valerie Jackson. "From Attic to Annex: The Story of an Off-Campus Storage Facility." The Serials Librarian 5 (Summer 1981): 49-57.

Kennedy, James and Stockton, Gloria. The Great Divide: Challenges in Remote Storage. Chicago: American Library Association, 1991.

Kountz, John. "Robots in the Library: Automated Storage and Retrieval Systems." Library Journal 112 (December 1987): 67-70.

McClung, Patricia. "Still Growing Strong: UCLA Library." Wilson Library Bulletin 57 (June 1983): 822-827.

The Impact of Networked Information on Access Services

Greg R. Notess

SUMMARY. The increasing number of electronic serials, books, and other documents being produced, and the opportunity for wide distribution of information over the Internet has raised new issues regarding library access to information. Few libraries currently provide access to such information sources, nor do most network users think to turn to a library to find these documents. This article concentrates on the possibilities for integrating existing networked electronic information into current library structure by exploring both the variety of electronic documents currently available on the network and the present means of access, followed by a discussion of the possibilities for providing library access and implications for access services.

INTRODUCTION

The advent of the electronic library has been proclaimed for years. While it certainly has not yet fully arrived in the mainstream of the library business, the past few years have witnessed the rise of many components of the electronic library. For example, Sony has recently introduced a portable electronic book player.[1] Of greater significance is the phenomenal potential of the vast store of information in electronic form already available on the Internet. An

---

Greg R. Notess is Reference Librarian and Assistant Professor at Montana State University. Correspondence may be addressed to the author at: the Libraries; Montana State University; Bozeman, MT 59717-0332. He may also be reached via BITNET to align@mtsunix1 or via Internet to align@maia.oscs.montana.edu.

© 1992 by The Haworth Press, Inc. All rights reserved.

ever increasing number of library catalogs are accessible on the Internet, along with many offering indexes and full text files.[2] Librarians have become more active on the networks in recent years, as has been demonstrated by the growth in the number of library oriented computer conferences and the number of subscribers.[3] United States Supreme Court opinions, position papers, weather reports, and technical reports are available and circulating on the network with ever more frequency. Electronic journals, disseminated over the networks, are increasing in number and prominence.[4] Bill Katz even includes *Psycoloquy*, a peer reviewed e-journal, as one of 1990's best ten new magazines.[5]

Even as these electronic information sources continue to multiply exponentially, they still represent the untamed frontier of information. Directories and guides are being developed, but access to this wealth of information is limited to those with network connections, navigational ability, and knowledge of the sources available. Libraries can be a positive force in exploiting this network information frontier by recognizing the wealth of materials available and providing library access and cataloging for such materials. Such a move in regard to network accessible information would impact all library departments. By investigating the types of documents available on the network, access services librarians can plan strategies for providing library access and dealing with potential problems relating to access services.

TYPES OF NETWORKED INFORMATION

While many of the varieties of information on the Internet come in simple electronic versions of a printed format, the potential of huge files and rapid transmission across continents has created some unique formats as well. A primary motivation behind a 1988 proposal for the creation of a peer-reviewed electronic journal on crop growth was that an electronic journal could include complete data sets and simulation software code, which are not included in paper journals.[6] As the Internet continues to develop and greater access becomes available, many other variations on print media and previously unforeseen formats will emerge. The following is a categorization of major, currently existing formats of networked information.

Computer Conferences: Computer conferences or electronic discussion groups are a type of "computer mediated communication" that facilitates a one to many distribution.[7] An individual can send the same message to many others. Two primary types of computer conferences are the Bitnet listserver-based discussion groups and the Usenet newsgroups.[8] Both provide a very timely means for people interested in a specific topic to exchange information and to express opinions. The listserver distributes e-mail messages to all "subscribers" for a specified list; whereas Usenet newsgroup postings are sent in their entirety to member sites, where local users read only the groups that interest them. A significant feature of both computer conference formats is that not only can these groups provide current information, but because many are archived, the archives can be searched and previous postings can be retrieved. Within the realm of access services, the CIRCPLUS listserver deals explicitly with issues related to the management and operation of a circulation or access services department.[9]

Books: Although it is awkward to read books on a computer screen, they are becoming increasingly common on the network. Sony's previously mentioned portable electronic book reader is one non-networked example. Of the various sources for electronic books on the Internet, Project Gutenberg, run by Michael Hart, is perhaps the best known. Project Gutenberg aims to have 10,000 books in electronic form by the year 2001. While only a few dozen are presently available, they include such works as Lewis Carrol's *Alice* books, *Moby Dick*, *The Federalist Papers*, and *The World Factbook*. Works in preparation include *The Oxford English Dictionary* and *Encyclopedia Britannica, 11th edition*.[10] All the Project Gutenberg "publications" bypass the copyright question since they include only works which are either non-copyrighted or for which copyright has been obtained. Technology has not yet provided the means of making electronic books as enjoyable to read as their printed counterparts, but for textual analysis or quotation searching the electronic format is a true boon to the researcher.

Reference Tools: Reference works, which have traditionally appeared as books, are often ideally suited to electronic format.

These reference works appear as databases such as (1) bibliographies, (2) directories, and (3) other miscellaneous collections of information.

1. Many bibliographies are available on the network, which is an ideal means of distribution for them. Topics range from a general Internet resources bibliography,[11] to a bibliography of the ray tracing literature,[12] to another of articles in *Information and Computation* (formerly *Information and Control*) covering the years 1982-present.[13] Subject bibliographies are available in such diverse fields as history, architecture, and physics. One subject-specific source, the Comserve mailserver, includes many bibliographies in the field of communications.[14] While most are plain ASCII text files, some are "typeset" in postscript or are designed to be imported into a database manager.

2. Some examples of directories include listings of scholars, computer conferences, and libraries available on the Internet. Campus-Wide Information Systems often include a directory feature for the local campus.[15] Comserve provides a directory of scholars in the communications field.[16] As previously mentioned, there are directories of Internet-accessible libraries, electronic serials, and computer conferences. Many of these directories are available exclusively on the network.

3. Since any type of document that could be put into machine readable form could be made available on the network, there are many miscellaneous documents available. One example is the Weather Underground from the University of Michigan. This telnet accessible service gives weather reports from around the country, current weather observations, and selected ski reports.[17] Other examples include databases of recipes and the *New Hacker's Dictionary*, a listing of computer jargon with definitions.[18] Even *Choice* book reviews are available full-text through CARL.[19]

Two recent developments provide a common interface for searching such directories and other databases. The Internet Gopher software is a client/server protocol designed to search for information on multiple hosts. This allows the user to learn one protocol for searching multiple files.[3] In a similar vein, the Wide Area Information Server (WAIS) provides a single search engine, based on the Z39.50 NISO standard, that can search multiple Internet databases.[21]

Electronic Serials: The advent of electronic serials has sparked much debate and anticipation in the library and publishing worlds. Touted as a solution to the spiraling serial price crisis, the electronic journal promises great potential for libraries.[22] There are different visions of the format of the electronic journal. Some see it simply as an electronic version of the typical paper journal, while others argue for a format which allows a faster, more interactive exchange of ideas.[23] The most ambitious electronic journal (at the time of this writing) is the forthcoming *Online Journal of Current Clinical Trials*, a joint venture between OCLC and the American Association for the Advancement of Science. This refereed journal can be viewed and printed in typeset quality (given the appropriate hardware and software) and promises publication within 24 hours of acceptance of an article.[24]

Miscellaneous: Any type of document that can be transformed into machine-readable form can be made available on the Internet. Other types of network available sources include technical reports, reprints, and software. A variety of technical reports have appeared on the network. Requests For Comment, the technical documents for network architecture and related issues, have existed only in electronic form for years. The Government Accounting Office has released reports to the network community in hopes of reaching a broader audience. Reprints of articles that appeared first in print have traversed the network. Copious amounts of public domain software for all types of operating systems and hardware platforms are available. The future potential of this resource is vast as the new forms that are created.

CURRENT ACCESS

Of all the aforementioned varieties of networked electronic information sources, few if any are available in most libraries. To retrieve networked information, there are two prerequisites: physical access to the Internet and the basic knowledge necessary to navigate the networks. Physical as first requires a computer with an Internet connection. There are a variety of options for connecting to the Internet. Most academic institutions have a connection through a mainframe in the computing center. Software now exists to turn a desk top into an Internet mode; however, there are costs. In discussions on the network, cost estimates for a full Internet connection usually end up in the five digit range. More affordable alternatives are becoming available through services such as the Colorado Supernet, the World, and Netcom, which offer services in the range of $20/month. Most academic libraries have some network connectivity, either on public or staff terminals. Some of the larger or more fortunately located public libraries are also establishing network connections. With cheaper alternatives becoming available and the recent passage of the National Research and Educational Network authorizing legislation, many libraries with no current Internet access may find it a greater possibility in the coming years.[25]

The knowledge prerequisite is another matter. The Internet has no centralized authority and is designed to function under multiple platforms. Although many of its strengths derive from this decentralization, it also means that there are multiple systems and access methods to be learned to access the wealth of electronic information. Proficiencies with a local electronic mail system, the listserver program, a newsreader program, File Transfer Protocol (FTP), telnet, and a variety of compression programs provide the basis for becoming a successful Internet traveler. While these basics may be second nature to the computer scientist, this knowledge base is complex and foreign to most library users. In addition, the "how-to" proficiency is only half of the knowledge equation: a person also needs to know what documents are available and where they might be located on the network. Currently, much of this information is obtained by word of mouth on the network or is announced on appropriate lists or to newsgroups. This situation addresses the potential role of libraries, for what is needed is some type of bibliographic control on the network.

LIBRARY ACCESS

A compelling argument for providing library access to such information is that it will he otherwise unavailable to large segments of the population. Another is that once the investment in hardware and network connectivity has been made, most of the information is available free of charge. While individual libraries can begin the work of bibliographic control, it can be hoped that federally funded research into Internet resources by OCLC may lead to some centralized cataloging.[26]

When a document is in electronic form, it can easily be stored in multiple locations or printed into hard copy. Many networked documents are available in different stages at separate locations. Cataloging decisions will need to be made regarding to which of these locations and versions the bibliographic record will refer. One possibility would be to create a catalog record for the document, serial, or database and, in place of a call number, give the nearest network location (which does not always mean nearest geographically) along with sufficient login instructions. Documents could be retrieved and stored locally, but while local storage means local control, it can cost for storage, and often library computers have little storage space available. Access from storage at other sites will be less costly, but the local library loses control over the original. If the remote site decides it needs to free up some disk space, the files could be dumped.

Physical access creates various difficulties. Two distinct user groups should be considered: the traditional walk-in user and the remote user who can dial in from a home computer. For the first group, access to resources that can retrieve and produce a readable version of the information is essential. For documents not printed and housed in the library, certain hardware will be necessary to obtain network access to the actual document. For plain ASCII text files a printer and the Internet connected microcomputer will suffice. For more complete access to forthcoming documents such as *The Online Journal of Current Clinical Trials*, a 286 PC with Windows™ 3.0, a VGA monitor, modem, and a laser printer may be necessary. Since some may prefer to download instead of or in addition to printing, 3.5" and 5.25" disk drives should be included in the hardware configuration. Even with all the hardware, the patron will need to have much more knowledge to retrieve the document than that required to read a call number and find a book on a shelf. Considering the advanced skills required, it could well be more efficient to have library staff retrieve the document. One possibility would be to have the catalog entry give the option to have the document either printed at the circulation desk or sent to an e-mail address. While software is being developed that could automate this option, in the meantime a library staff member could receive the request, obtain the document on the network, and print or e-mail it.

While no library provides full bibliographic and physical access to all the previously described networked information, some libraries are beginning to address the handling of electronic journals. Virginia Tech, for example, established a task force and a plan for cataloging selected e-journals. One great advatage of living in a networked environment is that Tech's cataloging can be viewed by anyone with an Internet connection. Notes are provided in the MARC record to alert patrons to both the network access point, such as the listserv address, and a local access point in the university's INFO system.[27]

ACCESS SERVICES ISSUES

How will such networked information sources impact access services? As with many innovations in library science, different libraries will assign responsibility to different departments, and cooperation from all library departments will be necessary to achieve fullest access to these media. One issue within access services' purview is circulation, which could be interpreted in the world of networked information as providing copies of information for a person to read at home. If the material is not copyrighted or has a license which allows unlimited copies to be produced from the electronic original, circulation departments could provide a paper or disk copy for anyone interested. One frequent complaint about electronic documents is the awkwardness of reading them on the screen. A library should be able to provide readable printouts of electronic documents to those who would like to take the document home. For those who would "read at home" on their own microcomputer's screen, facilities will also need to be provided so that users can download data to disks.

The copyright questions promise to be quite complex. In a recent article on copyright, Okerson writes that "current copyright law does not address the realities of the kind of scholarly communication increasingly available in the electronic information age."[28] The availability of more strictly copyrighted material on the network will only increase as progress is realized in managing royalty payment schemes for such materials. Fortunately, much of the material on the network now is either not copyrighted, in the public domain, or copyrighted with free distribution rights granted.

Reserve services are related to both copyright and circulation issues. Documents requested for reserve could be retrieved on the network and stored locally for the duration of the class. They could be located both in the library reserve area as a printout of acceptable quality and/or in a central library computer system, which students could access from the library or a home computer. Subdirectories could be set up for specific classes, and documents could be placed accordingly. An electronic version of a reserves list can be set up by the computing center or an individual faculty member on a central computer completely bypassing the library. While some institutions may welcome such a role for the computer center, bringing this function under the aegis of the library could allow for a systematic means of obtaining copyright owners' permission for use of certain readings and verifying that appropriate citations and copyright disclaimers exist on all the documents.

While reshelving of documents will most likely be unnecessary for electronic versions, shelf-reading, if defined as a periodic verification that documents exist at a specific cataloged location, would still be necessary in the electronic library. For documents not held on a local computer, it would be essential to periodically verify that they still exist at the designated location. For anonymous FTP documents, the path may be changed as more documents are added and new subdirectories are required, and that would require a change in the local catalog record. Even for works held in local electronic storage, periodic verification that the file has not been damaged by system failures, power surges, or accidental deletions would be a wise precaution.

Those libraries providing individual patron accounts on their computers for e-mail and other network activities could issue accounts by access services. This could become a process connected to library card registration. Accounts could be set up allowing full access to the Internet, or allowing e-mail access and limited telnet capabilities such as in the Freenet systems.[29]

As a greater number of patrons establish e-mail accounts and more documents become available electronically, document delivery services become more cost effective. As in the model mentioned earlier, for electronic documents that a user could not immediately obtain, an option could be offered that would allow the library to retrieve the document then send it to the user's e-mail address. While this might require staff time at first, programs could be set up that would retrieve the file and e-mail it to the appropriate address.

Since networked information opportunities will most likely increase the demand for traditional access services, additional staff may be required. At a minimum, staff training in the varieties of information available on the Internet and the procedures to retrieve these documents would be necessary.

CONCLUSION

While the vision of the fully electronic library continues to be extolled and developed, libraries are now beginning to address access issues for existing electronic information sources.[30] It can be expected that the public will be able to enter the library (in person or via computer) and obtain bibliographic references to networked information and receive assistance in retrieving electronic documents. A person might walk into a public library, find reference to the Weather Underground, press a key that would open a connection to this resource, browse recent weather conditions, press another key that would request a printout of current conditions for a certain state, then pick up the printout at the circulation desk, or a scholar at home might come across a reference to an article in the electronic journal *Post Modern Culture*, dial in to the library catalog, find an entry for the journal, then place a request for the electronic delivery of the article.

Access services can play a crucial role in the delivery of networked information in the evolving electronic library by investigating circulation, copyright, and reserve functions in the transmission of networked information. The sources exist; the technology exists; now is the time for librarians to take the initiative and begin to implement access to the wealth of electronic information sources on the networks.

REFERENCE NOTES

1. "Sony's Electronic Book: A New Library Format?" *Library Journal* 116 (November 15, 1991): 26.
2. There are a number of directories available, all of which are revised irregularly. See Billy Barron, *UNT's Accessing On-Line Bibliographic Databases*, available via anonymous FTP from **ftp.unt.edu** as/library/libraries.txt and Art St. George and Ron Larsen, *Internet-Accessible Library Catalogs & Databases*, available via aonymous FTP from **ariel.unm.edu** as/library /internet.library. For an electronic, hypertext directory, see Peter Scott, *Hytelnet, Version 5.0*, available via anonymous FTP from **access.usask.ca** as/hytelnet/pc/hyteln50.zip
3. See Charles W. Bailey, "Library Oriented Computer Conferences and Electronic Serials." Revised editions distributed periodically on the PACS-L mailing list from **listserv@uhupvm1**. Additions have appeared almost every month for the past year or so, and the PACS-L list itself now boasts more than 3000 subscribers.
4. Michael Strangelove and Diane Kovacs, *Directory of Electronic Journals, Newsletters and Academic Discussion Lists* (Washington: Association of Research Libraries, Office of Scientific and Academic Publishing, 1991). This work is a combination of two documents available on the network: Michael Strangelove, *Directory of Electronic Journals and Newsletters*, 1st ed. July 1991, available by sending the messages **get ejournal1 directory** and **get ejournal2 directory** to **listserv@uottawa**, and Diane K. Kovacs, *Directory of Scholarly Electronic Conferences*, 3rd rev., 1991, available via anonymous FTP from **ra.msstate.edu** in the **/pub/docs/words-1** directory, all file names beginning with **acadlist**.
5. Bill Katz, "The Ten Best Magazines of 1990," *Library Journal* 116 (April 15, 1991): 51.
6. Basil Acock, Stephen R. Heller, and Stephen L. Rawlins, "An Electronic Journal for Sharing Data on Crop Growth," in Phyllis S. Glaeser, ed., *Scientific and Technical Data in a New Era: Proceedings of the Eleventh International CODATA Conference, Karlsrühe, Federal Republic of Germany, 26-29 September 1988* (New York: Hemisphere Publishing, 1990), 308.
7. For a more detailed description of computer conferencing see Howard Rosenbaum and Gregory B. Newby "An Emerging Form of Human Communication: Computer Networking," in *ASIS '90: Proceedings of the 53rd ASIS Annual Meeting* (Medford, N.J.: Learned Information, 1990), pp. 305-306.
8. An excellent introduction to both can be found in Jonathan Kochmer,

NorthWestNet User Services Internet Resource Guide, 3rd ed. (Seattle: NorthWestNet, 1991), pp. 71-94. This document is also scheduled to be made available via anonymous FTP from **ftphost.nwnet.net** in the **nic/nwnet/userguide** subdirectory.

9. To subscribe to CIRCPLUS, send "Subscribe Circplus First_Name Last_Name" message to CIRCPLUS@idbsu.idbsu.edu.

10. Jonathan Kochmer, *North WestNet User Services Internet Resource Guide*, 3rd ed. (Seattle: NorthWestNet, 1991), pp. 99-100.

11. Gord Nickerson, *Internet-Accessible Information Resources Bibliography* (October 1991) available via anonymous FTP from **hydra.uwo.ca** (129.100.2.13) as **libsoft/intenet_biblio.txt**.

12. Richard Speer, *Cross-Indexed Guide to the Ray Tracing Literature* (July 1991); available via anonymous FTP from several sites, including **princeton.edu** (128.112.128.1), as **/pub/Graphics/Papers/speer.raytracing.bib.ps**.

13. Available via anonymous FTB from **theory.lcs.mit.edu** (18.52.0.92) as **ftp/pub/ meyer/iandc.bib**.

14. For a basic introduction to services available from Comserve send the message **Send Comserve Helpfile** to **comserve@rpiecs**.

15. For example, see Yale University's ENTERPRISE CWIS (accessible by telnet to **yalevm.ycc.yale.edu** port **300**) and New York University's INFO CWIS (accessible by telnet to **info.nyu.edu**).

16. For information on this feature send the message **Help Topics Whitepages** to **comserve@rpiecs**.

17. The Weather Underground is accessible by telnet to **hermes.merit.edu** (at the **Which host?** prompt, type umweather) and directly to **madlab.sprl.umich.edu** port **3000**

18. *The New Hacker's Dictionary* is available by anonymous FTP from **mc.lcs.mit.edu** (18.26.0.179) as **pub/jargon/jargon296.ascii**

19. *Choice* book reviews are accessible by telnet at **pac.carl.org** in menu choice 60.

20. Software for the Gopher client is available via anonymous FTP from **boombox.micro.umn.edu** in the **pub/gopher** directory. To see an example of its implementation, telnet to **anthrax.micro.umn.edu** (128.101.95.23) and login as **gophor**.

21. Richard Marlon Stein, "Browsing Through Terabytes," *Byte* 16, no. 5 (May 1991): 157-164. For a prototype WAIS system **telnet** to **quake.think.com** (192.31.181.1), login as wais.

22. For an excellent overview of possible impacts of electronic serials on serial publishing, see the recent series of articles in *College and Research Libraries*: Kenneth E. Marks, Steven P. Nielsen, Craig H. Petersen, and Peter E. Wagner, "Longitudinal Study of Scientific Journal Prices in a Research Library," *College and Research Libraries* 52 (March 1991): 125-138; Eldred Smith, "Resolving the Acquisitions Dilemma: Into the Electronic Information Environment," *College and Research Libraries* 52 (May 1991): 231-240; Paul Metz and Paul Gherman, "Serial Pricing and the Role of the Electronic Journal," *College and*

Research Libraries 52 (July 1991): 315-327; Ann Okerson, "With Feathers: Effects of Copyright and Ownership on Scholarly Publishing," *College and Research Libraries* 52 (September 1991): 425-438; and Ronald F. Dow, Karen Hunter, and G. Gregory Losier, "Commentaries on Serials Publishing," *College and Research Libraries* 52 (November 1991): 521-527.

23. Ann Okerson, "The Electronic Journal: What, Whence, and When?" *The Public-Access Computer Systems Review* 2, no. 1(1991): 9. *The Public-Access Computer Systems Review*, appropriately, is an electronic peer-reviewed journal. This article can be retrieved by sending the message **get okerson prv2n1** to **listserv@uhupvm1**.

24. Martin Wilson, "AAAS Plans Electronic Journal Venture with OCLC," *Information Today* 8 (November 1991): 19-20.

25. *High-Performance Computing Act of 1991*, 105 *Stat.* 1594 (1991). The text is also available via anonymous FTP from **nis.nsf.net** as **nsfnet/nrenbill.txt**.

26. "Internet Resources," in *Annual Review of OCLC Research: July 1990- June 1991* (Dublin, Ohio: OCLC, 1991), pp. 18-19.

27. To view the catalog records, telnet to **vtnet.cns.vt.edu** (128.173.5.4). The following e-journals are among those included: *Psycoloquy, The Public Access Computer Systems Review,* and *Electronic Journal of Communication.* For a more detailed description of the management process, see William Dougherty et al., "Report of the Task Force on the Electronic Journal" May 17,1991. (Available from Myra Hereford, University Libraries Director's Suite, Virginia Polytechnic Institute and State University, PO Box 90001, Blacksburg, VA 24062-9001, Internet: **myra@vtvm1.cc.edu**.)

28. Okerson, "With Feathers," p. 429.

29. For an example, see the Teleport option available on the Cleveland Freenet, accessible by telnet to **129.22.8.76** or **129.22.8.75** or **129.22.8.82**.

30. Brett Butler, "The Electronic Library Program," *Library Hi Tech* 9, no. 2 (1991): 21-30.

The Role of the Access Services Manager in Policy Formation

Alberta S. Bailey
Lora L. Lennertz

SUMMARY. This article describes the role of the access services manager in the formation and implementation of policies related to patron access to the library and its services. Automation of libraries has made it possible to re-think assumptions regarding levels of service provided, the ways in which these services are offered, and the development of related policies. The types of policies, factors influencing them, their development and implementation, and the expanding role of the access services manager in this process are discussed. Given the speed with which technology changes and the increase of user demands for new electronic based services, a proactive approach is needed to adequately address these and other issues in the future. The access services manager is in a unique position to provide input and support for the type of policy formation efforts required to fully address the library's response to user access issues in a changing environment.

INTRODUCTION

Academic libraries are in a period of transition from focusing budgetary resources and efforts in acquiring materials to attempting

---

Alberta S. Bailey received the MLS degree from Case Western Reserve University and is currently Head of Public Services. Lora L. Lennertz received the MLS degree from the University of Illinois and is currently Head of Circulation and Access Services. Communications to the authors may be addressed to University Libraries, University of Arkansas, Fayetteville, AR 72701-1201. BITNET ASB417@uafsysb or lennertz@uafsysb.

to connect users with the right information "just in time" to satisfy their information needs. One result of this shifting focus is the emergence of the concept of access services. Access services places the user at the center of its activities. It is through the delivery of access services that users are connected to the materials they seek. But how do we determine what levels of access to offer, and to whom? Do all users have equal access to every item in the collection and all services provided? Are these services and collections available at all times when the library is open? Can a person obtain access from a remote location? The answers to these and many other questions related to access in its various forms are determined by library policies.

When they are well thought-out and clearly written, library policies allow for the equitable distribution of services and resources. Of all library departments, access services units rely most heavily on policies in the performance of daily tasks. Typically, access services units are on the front line for explaining and enforcing library policies. Although access services departments may be configured in different ways, usually beginning with a circulation department and adding on other public or technical services units, their high degree of direct contact with users provides perhaps a library's most comprehensive view of user access problems. The access services manager thus brings a unique perspective to the policy formation process.

In exploring how policies affect access and the role of the access services manager in forming and implementing policies, it is important to look at the traditional academic library approach to policies, the factors that influence these policies, how policies are developed and implemented, and issues related to technology and electronic access.

FROM COLLECTIONS TO ACCESS

Academic libraries are struggling to cope with the economic realities of shrinking budgets, inflationary costs of materials, and the new demands and opportunities of technology. As they retool themselves in response to these factors and plan proactively for the future, traditional organization patterns and ways of providing services are being replaced by new structures and different approaches to satisfy user information needs.

One currently popular approach is to shift energies and resources from building and owning local collections to providing access and delivery of diverse information sources to the user within an acceptable time frame. De Genarro (1984) states that it should be clear to all by now that no research library can meet its users' needs solely, or even largely, from its own collections.[1] Battin (1982) reports that the projected costs of space, processing, and materials required by the traditional research library are far greater than any university can afford.[2] As the costs associated with acquiring, housing, and maintaining collections continue to increase, libraries are looking more and more to access services as a means by which to satisfy user information requests.

In addition to economic considerations, the capabilities provided by existing and emerging technologies are also contributing to a shift of emphasis from collections to access. Bibliographic access is made easier by menudriven, user-friendly online catalogs, CD-ROM databases, and services such as OCLC's FirstSearch and EPIC. Physical access to documents is available direct to users through telefacsimile and services like CARL's Uncover2, which is accessible over the Internet. As more of these options have become available, many library managers have come to believe that it is more economical to expend funds for enhancing on-demand document delivery rather than outright purchase of materials, especially in cases where the information request is non-recurring, esoteric, or out of the library's collection development scope. Studies comparing the costs of access to those associated with ownership are needed to shed further light on the economics of this issue.

Consistent with the shift in focus from collections to access is the realization that a new paradigm for the delivery of information is needed. This paradigm is represented by the concept of access services, which places the user at the center of its activities. This concept is evolving as libraries experiment with many different configurations and structures. In some libraries, this erosion has been signalled by changing the name of a department, usually circulation, to access services. In others, several public and/or technical services departments have been combined administratively under the direction of a librarian, the access services manager. Regardless of the structure, the underlying philosophical shift to the access services concept is a complicated process. Depending on the degree to which this concept is adopted and integrated throughout the organization, most areas of library service will be affected. For these reasons, it is critical to communicate this shift in focus, with all of its policy and philosophical implications, to library personnel.

Inherent to the access services concept is a user-centered approach to the delivery of information services. When a commitment is made to adopt the access services concept, it is important to review the library's mission statement, as well as the goals and policies which support it, in order to consider how all factors reflect this new focus. The most basic goal of access services has been stated fairly simply: to provide services that enable a patron to leave the library with needed materials in hand (Thierer 1983).[3] In a broader context, goals may address all factors that facilitate a patron's entry into the library and use of its collections (ACRL Library Access Task Force 1990).[4] Goals in automated libraries might additionally focus on remote or dial-in access concerns and the integration of new, technologically-based services such as CD-ROM databases, end-user products, networking, facsimile document delivery, and online catalog gateways.

Once the goals of an access services department have been established, policies describe the functional parameters that are used in measuring whether goals are met. The policies themselves do not establish a total service philosophy, but are a reflection of that philosophy (Scholtz 1991).[5] Policies serve as the basis for planning, budgeting, and providing staff guidelines for day-to-day activities. In the case of access services, the policy formation process and the resulting policies are what determine the degree to which user-centeredness is achieved. This is the subject of the next section.

LIBRARY POLICIES AND ACCESS

The level of and commitment to quality access services are expressed by library policies. The extent to which the user-centeredness of the access services concept is reflected in library policies can depend to a large degree on how the policies are formed and who has input. Once library management has adopted an access philosophy and the shift in service emphasis that it entails, it becomes crucial to review and update all policies that affect access. Since access is influenced by many factors and because the access services manager has unique and diverse contacts with patrons, it is critical for the access services manager to have a dominant role in policy formation efforts.

Studies of traditional policy formation efforts in academic libraries reveal a tendency to develop policies in reaction to specific problems (Webster 1972).[6] This approach is *reactive* and does not fully exploit the power that systematic policy formation offers as a *proactive* management tool. Implementing the access services concept is an inherently proactive approach. The process of carefully examining current policies and revising them, or formulating new ones where appropriate, is an important step in the adoption of an access services paradigm.

Policies govern most user transactions and affect their ability to identify and locate materials. Patron access issues are reflected in policies concerning patron types and services provided, identification requirements, fines and fees, borrowing periods and assistance provided by the staff. Physical access to collections involves policy issues such as material retrieval from closed stacks or remote storage, special locations of materials, signage, use of copiers and other equipment, document delivery, and handicapped access. Finally, bibliographic access issues related to policies are multi-faceted and involve the structure of catalog and database records, use of multiple catalogs and databases, and staff assigned to database maintenance activities (ACRL Library Access Task Force 1990).[7] Decisions must be made as to cataloging level, what tools to bibliographic access will be offered, how items will be classified and indexed in the online catalog and to what degree users may rely on library staff for assistance. (Bonds et. al. 1986).[8] Often, there will be tradeoffs. For example, enhancements such as boolean searching and the inclusion of journal articles within the online catalog (Pitkin 1988),[9] give the user more options, but complicate the methods of access.

To demonstrate the effect of library policies on users and their ability to find information successfully, consider a fictitious student, Jamie, who is trying to locate materials on a particular subject. Jamie does not know how to use an academic library. Once inside the library, Jamie looks around, but, finding no clear direction, approaches the first desk in sight. The student workers staffing the desk inform Jamie that this is the circulation desk and give directions to the reference desk. There is a line at the reference desk. Finally, when the reference librarian is available, Jamie is directed to the CD-ROM work station and obtains a list of citations to journal articles. Since the assignment requires that books on the subject be consulted as well, Jamie asks the librarian for further help finding books and is then directed to the online catalog. With lists of relevant articles and books in hand, Jamie searches for the physical items. Jamie finds that while most of the books and journals are located in separate collections, some of the journals cited on the list of articles are shelved with the books. Next, Jamie discovers that some of the articles needed have been ripped out of the journals, one title is available only in microform, and another volume is at the bindery. Frustration is beginning to set in. Finally, Jamie discovers that some of the materials on the lists are in the biology library across campus, one title is in off-site storage, and still others are not owned by the library. There is no doubt, at this point, that Jamie is frustrated.

What are the policy factors causing Jamie's frustration? The first factor may have been a matter of inadequate signage. If adequate signage had been available clearly identifying the reference desk and its services, as well as maps of the building layout, the referral from the circulation desk might have been unnecessary. Of the many areas affecting access, signage is often overlooked but has perhaps the greatest initial impact on access. Signage policies might address such concerns as language used in signs, their placement, and uniformity of style.

Providing access to collections has always been a primary goal of libraries. For Jamie, the methods of gaining physical access to needed materials were complex and inconsistent. There are many policy issues related to periodical access. Circumstances will vary from library to library, and there may be good reasons for considering such options as separating collections, using remote storage, collecting materials in micro formats, etc. Still, user-centeredness should be an important consideration in determining policies for where and how collections will be kept. Jamie, like many other patrons, is not particularly concerned with the underlying reasons why materials are kept in different locations or formats but wants only to locate the necessary information with the least amount of effort and resistance. According to Cipolla (1988), the user's preference regarding journal access is to find the title of an article on a given topic, find the periodical containing that title, and find the issue immediately. [10] Certainly this view is applicable to other material formats and information sources.

Jamie, like other patrons, found that some needed materials had been mutilated. Unfortunately this situation is not rare. A recent survey at Kent State University indicated that 63.7 percent of the sample population had found a periodical which was mutilated (Lilly et al. 1991).[11] Providing quality copiers for print and microform materials, purchasing popular journals in other formats, and installing security systems are all methods of reducing theft and mutilation. A policy of providing interlibrary loan for missing or mutilated materials may have been beneficial. A book or article missing from the collection is no more accessible than one that has never been acquired.

Access to services is just as important as access to collections. Jamie was fortunate to have received competent and effective reference service (although having been made to wait might reveal an underlying problem in staffing policies). So Jamie was also able to make good use of the online catalog and CD ROM resources. The scope and coverage of these resources is another policy issue. The online catalog might, for instance, have provided access to other electronic information resources (e.g., indexes, reference works, statistical sources), instructional systems, consultation systems (Bailey 1989)[12] or other collections (Griffin 1985).[13] Other services that might have benefitted Jamie are interlibrary loan or other document delivery options such as CARL, which provides facsimile transmission of requested documents (Lenzini 1991).[14] Telefacsimilie services, in particular, might have met Jamie's need to retrieve materials in time to complete the specific assignment. As

DeGenarro (1989) suggests fax can revolutionize access by making it possible to transmit journal articles quickly to remote locations.[15]

Although perhaps not relevant to Jamie's immediate needs, maximum electronic access to collections through the Internet is another area that deserves the careful consideration of library policy makers. Throughout the United States, the "wired" campus has arrived. Virtually every major higher educational institution has campus-wide networking systems installed or is in the process of deployment (Lynch 1989).[16] Once the campus network is installed, access to the Internet can usually be made available. Remote access to library catalogs provides a rich source of information for library user groups but also requires planning and policy development with consideration to current and potential users (Sloan 1986).[17] A number of libraries already provide access to their catalogs through statewide networks and/or the Internet. A 1985 study of ARL libraries indicated that of 115 libraries, 32 with OPACs already provided remote access, 21 planned to provide remote access, and 39 libraries without OPACs planned to institute remote access with the implementation of the OPAC (Jamieson and Dolan 1985).[18] Remote access provides information to a diverse clientele possessing a wide range of skill and technical expertise and providing user-centered services to such a broad group–some of whom may not even be known to the library–requires very careful planning, policy-making, and evaluating.

Policies related to existing and emerging technologies may have to address various external factors over which the library has little control. For example, most academic libraries are already connected to the university's campus network. For that reason, many of the information policy issues of the wider university community can have an impact on the library and its users. Woodsworth (1991) discusses a new trend in universities of designating a chief information officer who is responsible for overseeing all information technology on the campus.[19] As libraries become increasingly active in the networks, cooperative partnerships with computing services departments is beneficial. Unfortunately, such collaboration is not always easy to achieve (Baker 1990).[20] Finally, national policy issues might exert another level of external control over library operations, such as any related to the eventual development of the National Research and Education Network (NREN).

This discussion comes full circle with the realization that these networked information sources will be part of the near future library environment in which Jamie will work. Completing assignments such as that which brought Jamie to the library in the first place may require skills with these resources. Library policies and procedures will very likely affect the ways in which library users like Jamie gain and use these skills.

IMPLEMENTATION OF ACCESS POLICIES

Full adoption of the access services model requires that every member of the library staff understand the concept, how services and policies have changed or are changing, and how these changes will affect them. To accomplish this task, library administration must communicate reasons for and the importance of this shift in focus. As the concept is implemented, expectations of library staff as well as benefits to users should be made clear.

Library staff training is an essential component of any plan to alter service orientations, and it provides an opportunity for staff input. Staff in the units that are designated to be integrated into the new access services department must be consulted and included in the process. Full explanations as to why this new arrangement is worthwhile should be provided. Negative staff attitudes can be one of the greatest obstacles to successfully implementing access services policies. Taking these steps can help to foster positive attitudes and internalization of the new service philosophy.

It is especially important to involve those library staff who have primary responsibilities in the areas for which changes are being proposed. Input from these individuals is essential because of their valuable perspectives with regard to serving the public. When policy changes result in procedural changes, the front line staff may often be the source of practical ideas and identify unforeseen consequences of the shift. Opportunities must be allowed for two-way communications.

Positive user response is the best indicator that the library has been successful in making this change. It should not take very long for users to notice the difference when an access service philosophy is in place. Gathering and evaluating user feedback can thus be a valuable follow-up to the implementation of new policies.

THE ROLE OF THE ACCESS SERVICES MANAGER

The access services manager represents empowerment for the user when there is true commitment to the access services concept. The user-centered focus that is achieved when policies reflect the needs of the users becomes manifest when information requests are filled promptly and without the frustration experienced by Jamie. Access to the collections is the natural goal of the user and the library. Most library users want and are able to negotiate the academic library environment independently, provided that user-centered policies make it possible for them to do so. The access services manager's unique job perspective, which results from having responsibilities that overlap public and technical services, and from the nature of this person's contacts with users, can be critical in forming user-centered policies.

In the policy-making process, the access services manager can serve as the advocate of users. For example, a sometimes overlooked area in which the access services manager can provide effective input for policy-making is collection development and management. The access services department supports the work of collection management through activities in the areas of circulation, shelving, storage, and retrieval of materials. Access services managers are best able to provide library administration with information regarding patron usage patterns and data on items missing from the collection. This data has a direct bearing on physical access and availability. Further data on interlibrary loan transactions is replete with information valuable to collection development. By knowing collection use and circulation patterns, the access services manager is in an excellent position to provide input regarding policies on broad collection development issues.

Other collection management issues related to access services are preservation and security. Because the access manager has responsibilities associated with building and facilities management, it is often this person who is most familiar with the library's physical layout and environmental control and how these factors affect the condition of the general collections. Procedures for handling damaged materials, leaking roofs, and other building concerns that affect user access should be addressed in policies. Collection security matters pertaining to minimizing loss of materials through theft and mutilation and responding to security incidents are typically overseen by access services departments. Keeping statistics on loss of materials and making recommendations for replacements and withdrawals might be part of the access services manager's role.

As previously stated, adopting an access philosophy means not only maintaining locally owned materials but also filling the increased demand for physical access to the materials not available in-house, but for which bibliographic access had been obtained. Frustration might occur due to discrepancies between user expectations and library capabilities. For example, it is not unreasonable for a patron to expect that the physical text for any citation retrieved through an electronic literature search can be provided by the library, whether from its own collections or through interlibrary loan or other document delivery methods. However, it may be unreasonable for the patron to expect this information to be provided free depending on the cost incurred by the library, or within the user's acceptable frame. In the role as an advocate for the patron, the access services manager can facilitate the adoption of new technologies by addressing internal and external user access issues.

Perhaps the greatest contribution the access services manager can make in bringing the user-centered focus to policy formation is in the area of technical services, especially cataloging. Studies indicate a number of problem areas in both subject access and document availability (Whitlatch 1990).[21] For example, studies of online catalog searching at four research libraries found that 35 to 57 percent of searchers yield zero postings, while 8 to 14 per cent retrieve over 100.[22] Where such circumstances exist, it might be useful to seek input on indexing policies from several departments, not the least of which is access services. While it is not common, some access services departments have cataloging responsibilities and report to technical services.

In summary, there is no department or service in the library unaffected by the characteristic user-centeredness that is the hallmark of access services. It has, in fact, been suggested by Buckman (1988) that the concept of *access* can unify librarianship.[23] Policies should reflect this point of view. The access services manager possesses knowledge and experience gained from direct contact with patrons and is able to address the user's perspective in forming policies. This type of input must be considered in creating a balance between what is efficient for the library and what makes good sense for improving user access.

CONCLUSION

Forces of economics, technology and user expectations are causing academic libraries to shift their focus from collection building to providing access. In making this shift, many libraries are adopting the access services concept that places the user at the center of its activities. The commitment to this concept requires the designation of one person, the access services manager, to coordinate the many functions associated with access and establish appropriate policies. The access services manager becomes an advocate for the user. By adopting an access philosophy, the library is taking a proactive approach to policy formation which ensures that the access services concept is visible throughout the organization.

It is not enough however, to merely change the name of a department to "access services" in order to implement the underlying principles of the concept. It is necessary to review and revise mission statements, goals and objectives, and policies to make them consistent with this philosophy. These policies determine the degree to which users become the central focus of library activities and service orientations. To be effective, the policy formation process must include as many staff as possible since most areas of the library are affected. It is imperative that the access services manager play a dominant role in this process. When users are able to see that the library's structure and policies are developed from a user's perspective, they will recognize the important role libraries play in helping them to obtain and use information in an increasingly complex technological environment.

REFERENCE NOTES

1. Richard De Genarro. "Shifting Gears: Information Technology and the Academic Library," *Library Journal*, 109, no. 11(1984): p. 1204.
2. Patricia Battin, "Libraries, Computers, and Scholarship," *Wilson Library Journal*, 56 (April, 1982): p. 582.
3. Joyce Thierer, "Ever Hear of Access Services" in *Improving the Use of Libraries. Proceedings from the Spring Meeting of the Nebraska Library Association, College and University Section (Peru, Nebraska, April 14-15, 1983)*. Edited by Elaine A. Franco. (Lincoln: Nebraska Library Association, 1983), ERIC microfiche ED 234 817, p. 91.
4. ACRL Library Access Task Force, "ACRL Guidelines for the Preparation of Policies on Library Access," *College and Research Libraries News*, 51, no. 6 (1990): 548-553.
5. James C. Scholtz, *Video Policies and Procedures for Libraries* (Santa Barbara: ABC-CLIO, 1991): p. 265.
6. Duane Webster, "Library Policies: Analysis, Formulation and Use in Academic Institutions," *ARL Occasional Papers* 2(1972), p. 11.
7. ACRL Library Task Force, "ACRL Guidelines for the Preparation of Policies on Library Access," *College and Research Libraries News*, 51, no. 6 (1990): 548-553.
8. Kathleen Bonds et al., *Task Force on Access to Information.* (Santa Barbara: University Library, University of California, Santa Barbara, 1986), Eric microfiche ED 297 729, p. 23.
9. Gary M. Pitkin, "Access to Articles Through the Online Catalog," *American Libraries*, 19, no. 9 (1988): 769-770.
10. Wilma Reid Cipolla, "Finding a Way Out of the Serial Maze," *Library Resources & Technical Services*, 32 (1988): p. 151.
11. Roy S. Lilly, Barbara F. Schloman and Wendy Hu, "Ripoffs Revisited: Periodical Mutilation in a University Research Library," *Library & Archival Security*, 11, no. 1 (1991): 43-70.
12. Charles W. Bailey Jr., "Public Access Computer Systems: The Next Generation of Library Automation Systems," *Information Technology and Libraries*, 8, no. 2 (1989): 178-185.
13. Mary Ann Griffin, "Collection Development to Information Access: The Role of the Public Services Librarians, *RQ* 24, no.3 (Spring 1985): p. 285.
14. Rebecca Lenzini and Ward Shaw, "Creating a New Definition of Library

Cooperation: Past, Present and Future Models," *Library Administration & Management*, 5, no. 1 (1991): p. 38.

15. Richard De Genarro, "Technology & Access in an Enterprise Society," *Library Journal*, 114, no. 16 (1989): 40-43.

16. Clifford Lynch, "Linking Library Automation Systems in the Internet: Functional Requirements, Planning, and Policy Issues," *Library Hi Tech*, Issue 28, 7, no. 4 (1989): p. 7.

17. Bernard Sloan, "High Tech/Low Profile: Automation & the 'Invisible' Patron," *Library Journal* Library Computing Supplement, 111, no. 18 (1986): LC4, 6.

18. Alexis J. Jamieson and M. Elizabeth Dolan, *University Library Experience with Remote Access to Online Catalogs*. (1985) ERIC microfiche ED 267 805, p. 6-7.

19. Anne Woodsworth, *Patterns and Options for Managing Information Technology on Campus* (Chicago: ALA, 1991), p. 20-42.

20. Shirley K. Baker, "Are the Intentions Honorable? Some Critical Questions about Library-Computer Center Cooperation" in *Convergence: Proceedings of the Second National Conference of the Library and Information Technology Association, October 2-6, 1988*, Boston, edited by Michael Gorman (Chicago: American Library Association, 1990), p. 245-249.

21. Jo Bell Whitlatch, "Access Services" in *Academic Libraries: Research Perspectives*, edited by Mary Jo Lynch (Chicago: ALA, 1990), p. 67-105.

22. Karen Markey, "Integrating the Machine-Readable LCSU into Online Catalogs," *Information Technology & Libraries*, 7, (September, 1988): 299-312.

23. Michael K. Buckman, *Library Services in Theory and Content*, 2nd ed., (New York: Pergamon Press Inc., 1988).

Changing Circulation Policies at an ARL Library: The Impact of Peer Institution Survey Data on the Process

Merri A. Hartse
Daniel R. Lee

SUMMARY. This article examines the technique of using peer institution data as a basis for forming and proposing changes in circulation policies at an ARL Library. Peer institutions for the University of Arizona Library were surveyed in respect to their circulation policies. The data were compared to other academic library circulation policy surveys and used to recommend specific changes in the graduate loan period, the fines structure, telephone renewals and fees for non-university borrowers. The process of using peer institution data focused discussion and proved to be an effective catalyst for changing policies. Most important, it was a process considered relevant by library and campus administrators.

INTRODUCTION

Among the several roles of an access services manager are those of implementing, monitoring, and enforcing circulation policies. These roles serve both to provide effective access to the library's

---

Merri A. Hartse, MA, is Circulation Librarian, University of Illinois at Urbana-Champaign, 203 Library, 1408 W. Gregory Dr., Urbana, IL 61801.
Daniel R. Lee, MLS, is Assistant Circulation Librarian, Yale University, P.O. Box 1603A, Yale Station, New Haven, CT 06520.

© 1992 by The Haworth Press, Inc. All rights reserved.

collections to as large a clientele as possible and to provide effective protection of those collections for the library's future clientele. This dialectic has a direct impact on public relations in that they define precisely how a patron may use the library. Policies intended to insure access to the entire library community, past and present, might actually restrict the level and type of access available to a particular individual.

Unfortunately, circulation policies are often maintained purely by inertia. They are adopted at one stage in a library's development as a response to certain conditions, and then preserved through periods of change, both superficial and fundamental, in the way the library is used. They are maintained even though no one can quite remember why such rules were established; even though no one can explain the rationale behind them to the patron with a question about a particular policy; and despite staffing, workflow and technological changes which the existing policies do not address or can not accommodate.

At the loan department at the University of Arizona Library several factors, such as continued growth of the university and library community as a whole, new technologies, and the arrival of a new department head, came together in the spring semester of 1988 to break the inertia and suggest certain changes in circulation policies. The library administration had begun a series of discussions on longstanding procedures and policies generally regarded as "sacred cows," but which could be re-examined under these new circumstances. The loan department recommended possible policy changes concerning the fixed graduate due date, telephone renewals, the fines structure, and charging borrower's fees to non-primary users for consideration.

Members of the department recognized that more information was needed to justify and gain approval for any proposed policy change. It was further realized that appropriate and acceptable data upon which to base policy changes could be difficult to obtain. Seeking a means for gathering data that would (1) provide administrators with the information required to form fair and effective policies, and (2) be considered relevant by library administrators, the loan department decided to undertake a survey of its 16 peer institutions concerning circulation policies.[1] Peer surveys were being done at higher administrative levels to determine such things as market criteria for job salaries and campus funding levels, and these surveys were considered a valid measure for drawing comparisons not only for the library administration, but for the university administration as well. This article describes the use of data gathered from this peer survey in formulating and proposing changes to policies in these areas at an academic research library.

THE PROCESS

The survey conducted by the loan department covered four areas: renewals, charging non-university patrons for borrower cards, fines, and graduate student and faculty loan periods (see Figure 1). Questionnaires were sent to the library's 16 peer institutions. Thirteen were returned for an 81% return rate. The survey data aided staff in forming proposals for new policies in all four areas. The process worked a bit differently in each policy area, but in all cases the technique of using peer institution data lent validity and justification to the process.

Graduate loan periods: At the University of Arizona, books loaned to graduate students were all due on a single day at the end of the semester. This was convenient for graduate students, but it also created problems. On one hand, it was a date that was easy to remember and could be publicized readily. However, it created a tremendous end-of-the-semester bottleneck for library staff faced with discharging and shelving thousands of items over a very short period of time. This in turn required a shift in service emphasis, such as suspending in-house pickup of material in favor of discharging, sorting and re-shelving the barrage of returned books. Often such a shift resulted in the overall reduction of services provided for the library community as a whole, an unwelcome example of circulation policies having a negative impact on library public relations.

Buckland's 1969 study at several British Universities demonstrated that patrons tend to wait until the due date to return items to the library "and that this pattern emerges regardless of the length of the official loan period, the status of the borrower or the subject

FIGURE 1 CIRCULATION

1. Do you use an automated circulation system? ___ Yes ___ No
   Vendor _____ Years Installed _____
2. What is your annual circulation? _____

A. Renewals

3. How many renewals is each borrower category allowed?
   Indicate number or write "unlimited," if that is the case.
   undergraduates _____ non-university
   graduates _____ faculty _____ staff _____
4. Do you allow overdue books to be renewed? ___ Yes ___ No
5. Do you allow renewals in any situation other than when
   the patron is present with books in hand?
   ___ Yes ___ No

Skip to question 17 if you answered "no."

6. Do you allow renewals if the patron is present but the
   books are not?
   ___ Yes ___ No
7. Do you allow BULK renewal of all items on a patron's
   record when the items are not in hand at the check out
   site:
   ___ Yes ___ No
8. Do you allow renewal requests over the phone:
   ___ Yes ___ No

Skip to question 17 if you answered "no."

9. Do you allow phone renewals for all borrower categories?
   ___ Yes ___ No

10. If no, list which categories are allowed phone renewals?

11. What are your operating procedures for phone renewals?
    ____ Have a telephone near a terminal and keep the patron on the phone while doing the actual renewing?
    ____ Tape record all such requests and do the actual renewing at some later time?
    ____ Other (please explain)

12. Patrons can use telephone renewals to:
    ____ either renew individual items or all items (except for those with special conditions)
    ____ renew all items only (except for those) with special conditions)

13. How do you handle informing a patron if a particular book cannot be renewed for a specific reason?

14. What problems, if any do you have with the way you are currently doing telephone renewals?

15. What advantages, if any, do you see in the way you are currently doing telephone renewals?

16. Do you have any data or perceptions to share indicating that Telephone renewals have an impact on the length of time ____ books are kept out.

FIGURE 1 (continued)

B. Charges for Non-Primary Users.
For questions 17-20 primary users are defined as the students, faculty, and staff of the college or university.

17. Do you charge primary users for borrowers' cards?
    ___ Yes ___ No
18. Do you allow non-primary users borrowing privileges?
    ___ Yes ___ No

Skip to question 21 if you answered "no."

19. Do you charge non-primary users for their borrower's cards?
    ___ Yes ___ No
20. How much do you charge $ _____ per _____ (time period)

C. Fines

21. Do you levy fines for overdue materials ___ Yes ___ No

Skip to question 31 if you answered "no."

22. For what types of materials do you levy fines? Check as many as apply.
    ___ all normal loans ___ overdue special loans (e.g., reference items, ___ overdue recalled loans ___ overdue reserve loans periodicals, etc.)
23. For which classifications of borrowers do you levy fines? Check as many as apply.
    ___ all normal loans ___ graduates ___ faculty ___ staff
    ___ non-university

24. Do you have a minimum level of fines accrual at which borrower privileges are revoked or suspended?
_____ Yes _____ No

25. If you answered "yes," what is that level? $ _____
26. At what rate do fines accrue for overdue regular loans?
    $ _____ per _____
27. At what rate do fines accrue for overdue recalled loans?
28. At what rate do dines accrue for overdue reserve loans?
29. At what rate do fines accrue for overdue special (e.g., reference, periodicals, etc.) loans?
30. What is the maximum overdue fine that can be applied to a book.
31. What do you charge to replace a book (list Processing fee separately if one is applied)?
    $ _____ (replacement) _____ (processing fee)

D. Graduate/Faculty Loan Periods

32. What is your regular loan period for graduate students?
33. What is your regular loan period for faculty?
34. Do you have a single date when all books checked out to certain borrowers are due?
Stop here if you answered "no" and proceed to the end.

35. Which categories of borrowers have a single due date?
    _____ graduate students _____ staff
    _____ faculty
    _____ undergraduates _____ other (please identify)

FIGURE 1 (continued)

36. What is the single date on which all materials are due?
 _____ end of the quarter _____ end of the academic year
 _____ end of the semester _____ other (please identify)
37. Approximately how long does it take to reshelve after all _____ materials are returned on or around a single due date?

 _____ 1-2 weeks _____ 3-4 months
 _____ 3-4 weeks _____ more than 4 months
 _____ 2 months _____ comments

THANK YOU FOR TAKING THE TIME TO COMPLETE THIS SURVEY WE WOULD APPRECIATE YOUR NAME AND PHONE NUMBER SO THAT WE MAY CONTACT YOU IF ANY QUESTIONS ARISE.
Name: _____ Telephone No. _____
Institution: _____
 _____ I would like to receive a copy of the results.

matter of the books borrowed."[2] Buckland argued that not only would changing to a revolving date mitigate such problems as the end-of-the-semester bottleneck, but it would also allow staff to continue in-house stacks maintenance activities such as pick-ups, thus improving access for all library patrons.

Survey findings showed that only 38% (five institutions) of the peer respondents had a single due date for a specific class of borrowers. All five had such a date for faculty; only three also had such a date for graduate students.

As University of Arizona Library administrators were already familiar with the extraordinary burden the graduate due date placed on the staff, the survey data provided additional impetus to have the fixed date eliminated. Although users were not formally surveyed as part of the process, graduate students and faculty had frequently voiced complaints to library administrators and staff about the chaotic stacks maintenance problems that occurred at each semester's end. Discussion then focused on an appropriate loan period for staggered graduate student due dates. The peer survey yielded some interesting patterns: 54% (seven of the responding libraries) had graduate loan periods ranging from two to four months. Only 15% (two libraries) provided a six month loan period (see Figure 2).

Considering the survey results, as well as recognizing that a four month loan period would provide a close equivalent to a semester, the library decided on that as an appropriate loan period. Library-wide discussion took place at Librarian's Council, a group of representatives from every department of the library, including branch libraries, which makes recommendations to the library administration. Once approved by the library administration the change from a fixed graduate due date to a revolving four month loan period was smooth. Flyers were distributed to graduate advisors in all academic units, bookmarks were placed in books borrowed by graduate students for a semester before the change took effect, and the campus newspaper ran a feature story on the change. Adjustment by both patrons and staff required about a semester. Graduate students were pleased to continue receiving the equivalent of a semester loan and staff no longer faced overwhelming library conditions at the semester's end.

FIGURE 2

Graduate Student Loan Periods

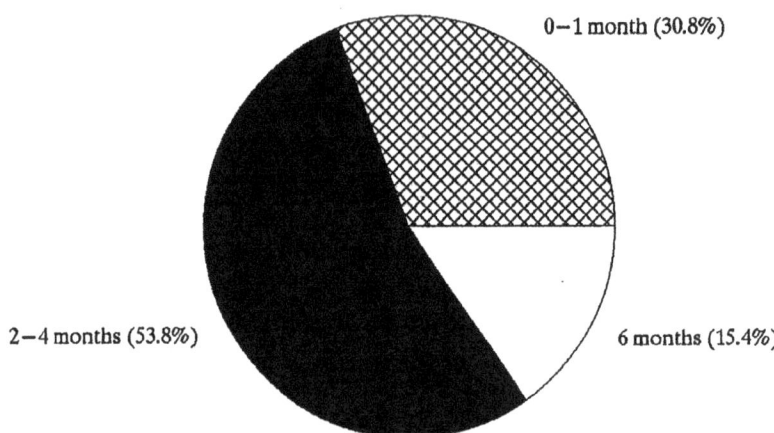

Fines: The loan department proposed two changes to the library's fines structure: (1) lower the ceiling for overdue books from $25 to $10, but make it non-negotiable, and (2) adjust the default book replacement cost to reflect current book prices. Overdue fines accrued at 25 cents per day with a cap of $25. However, it was a longstanding practice for fines office staff to negotiate fines for patrons who chose to appeal. It was felt this practice was unfair to patrons who did not complain. Overdue fines needed to be applied in a more equitable manner. Also, for the past nine years the library had charged only $25 plus a $10 processing fee to replace a lost book. During that time the average cost of a North American monograph, excluding the processing fee, had risen to $40.61.[3]

The libraries surveyed had devised a variety of fines schedules. All sites levied fines for overdue materials. Some had a flat rate, some had a per day rate, and one had a flat rate for the first few days followed by a per day rate (see Figure 3).

FIGURE 3

Overdue Fines

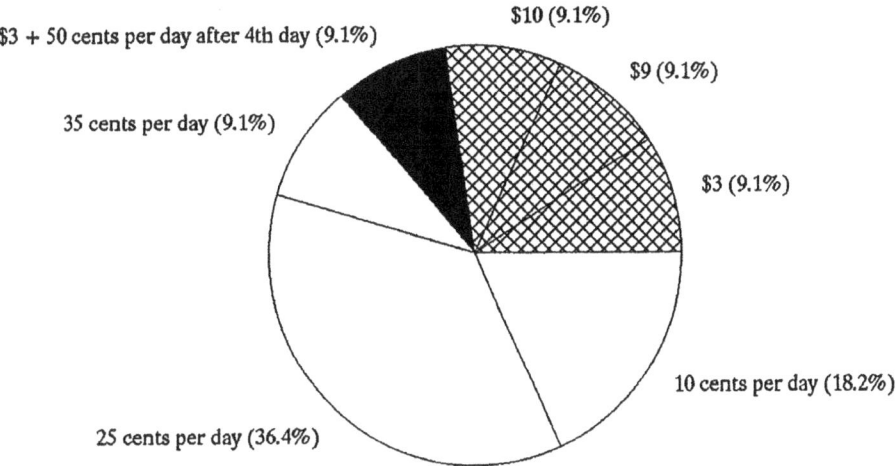

Surprisingly, 69% of the peer respondents charged faculty overdue fines (one did so only for recalled items). This practice is both supported and refuted by earlier studies. Gherman et al. reported in 1973 that 81% of ARL libraries surveyed imposed overdue fines on faculty.[4] However, in a more recent survey of 43 academic libraries, DuBois found that 69% do not fine faculty members.[5]

Other survey data showed that peer libraries charged a variety of replacement costs. The most common charging structure was based on the average cost of the book per subject area. The second most common structure was to assess the current *Books in Print* price or a default cost if the item in question was not current. One library charged the *Books in Print* cost or five cents per page. One reported replacement costs of $38-$66, depending on the publication date of the book. Processing fees ranged from zero to $15.

The survey data were used to demonstrate that the proposed changes were consistent with fines structures used by peers. After discussions which involved staff throughout the library, library administrators accepted the proposed changes. Public relations strategies similar to those used for the new graduate student loan period were also implemented.

Renewals: Telephone renewals were not allowed at the University of Arizona, but had been considered for some time. The loan department had favored such a move, as it was expected to relieve some of the congestion at the service desk, and, more important, to satisfy informal, but frequent requests for such a service from borrowers. Sixty-nine per cent of the respondents allowed for some sort of phone renewal, although one library did so only for patrons with disabilities. This result is considerably higher than the 41% reported by DuBois, suggesting, perhaps, that more libraries are expanding services to meet the needs of patrons who conduct their library business from remote locations.[6]

Unlimited renewals were granted by 77% of the responding institutions, which compares to the findings of Dubois's study in which 85% of academic libraries surveyed allowed unlimited renewals regardless of the method of renewal.[7]

All nine of the peer libraries which responded as allowing phone renewals used a dedicated phone line and held the patron on the line while a staff member performed the renewal at a terminal. Snags or problems could be dealt with while the patron was still on the line. While analyzing the peer survey data, loan department staff also examined the telephone renewal procedures of the other major academic library in the state, Arizona State University in Tempe, which had developed an innovative phone renewal program using an answering machine to record patron requests for book renewals. There a student employee processed the tapes at a convenient time and renewed the items. Postcards were sent to patrons who had materials which could not be renewed for various policy reasons, such as when the patron had an expired borrowing record or if an item had been recalled. While such a service obviously has its merits, the loan staff felt strongly that they would prefer to deal with renewal problems while they had a patron on the line.

One survey question asked respondents to list perceived advantages and disadvantages in the way they currently handle telephone renewals. Respondents were asked to provide any available data to substantiate their perceptions. Two libraries found the feature to be too popular and thus too time-consuming. One library reported that a lack of proper training sometimes prevented library personnel from informing the patrons of problems with their renewals. One library limited the number of renewals per phone call to five, which caused some patron dissatisfaction. Only one library expressed concern over renewing items that in fact were lost.

Generally the advantages expressed were patron convenience and good public relations. Two libraries reported that phone renewals reduced lines at the circulation desk. Several libraries also reported that phone renewals reduced the number of notices sent, and reduced the quantity of books turned in at the end of a semester.

Based on these findings a team of loan department staff members was assigned to develop a draft telephone renewal proposal. The team reviewed details of the recommended proposal and alternative procedures. The proposal basically called for the implementation of a telephone renewal service which applied many of the same policies currently in place for renewing materials in person. For example, unlimited renewals would be offered and books that were overdue or had been recalled could not be renewed. The service would be handled centrally at the main loan desk and would require the installation of a phone line. The loan department proposed that existing staff would handle the service, as it was expected that fewer staff would be needed to renew books for patrons at the desk. Developments were reported regularly at department meetings and input accepted from all loan staff. Some policies were dictated by the limits of the Geac circulation system in use. For example, Geac requires that renewals be done by either a single command encompassing all of a patron's current charges (bulk renewing) or by individually entering each item barcode number. A menu listing items to be selected for renewing is not available. Therefore, a decision was made that only bulk renewals could be done over the phone as it would be impractical for patrons to read the barcode numbers of the items they wished to renew.

Once a basic policy was fleshed out, an informal meeting was called with representatives from all the circulating sites (e.g., maps department, media center, and the music library). The policy was reviewed and it was explained that any material, such as scores, sound recordings or maps could be excluded from the renewal process if a particular library unit did not wish to participate in the service. A final proposal was completed and presented at meetings of department heads from the various public services units where much discussion ensued. Once the public services division felt comfortable with the policy it was presented to Librarian's Council. In general, it was felt that a telephone renewal service would reduce lines at the circulation desk, assist in the preservation of the collection (patrons would not be required to haul books back and forth to the library simply to renew them) and it would provide a convenience requested by patrons. Some unit heads wanted to limit the number of times material could be renewed in an effort to minimize potential abuse by patrons who may renew materials they have lost or damaged. Library administration was concerned that telephone renewals would lead to patrons keeping materials longer than necessary and thus would ultimately reduce the number of books on the shelves available for browsing. No data existed to support or refute such a claim. So, although the proposal ultimately received unanimous support from all divisions, the university librarian turned down the recommendation.

Although telephone renewals were not implemented, the process yielded positive results. The loan department formally aired the issue of telephone renewals and gained support from other library departments. A better understanding developed in the library system about telephone renewals. Most important, as with all the policy change proposals, the needs of library users were properly conveyed to the administration.

Charges for non-primary users: As a state-funded institution the University of Arizona Library provides borrowing privileges to residents of the state, 18 years and older. The loan department was responsible for issuing cards, free of charge, to state residents. Loan staff had long felt that some type of borrower's fee for this group was appropriate as it was difficult to apply any sanctions against non-university borrowers who did not return materials. Fees collected could be used to off-set book losses. The survey results showed that 46% of the respondents charged fees to non-university patrons for borrowing privileges. None charged their university-affiliated clientele. Charges averaged $40 per year with a range from $15-$100. One site charged a one-time $10 deposit.

This particular set of data was not immediately used to propose changes. After a period of two years, during which the telephone renewal issue was discussed and the graduate student loan period and the fines structure were each revamped, attention returned to changing non-primary clientele for borrowers' cards. Based partly on the survey results library administrators felt comfortable adopting a one-time $10 processing fee for non-university borrowers' cards. The fees collected remained in library accounts and were used to bolster the book replacement fund.

CONCLUSION

Several elements came together that allowed the loan department staff at the University of Arizona Library an opportunity to propose fundamental changes in circulation policies. The peer institution data that were gathered had a significant impact on the process. Not only did this data aid the staff in developing sound proposals, but administrators clearly felt more comfortable endorsing most of the proposed changes knowing that they were in line with policies elsewhere. As DuBois concluded in his survey findings "it was useful to know that lending rules in force already or being recommended for adoption did not represent an aberration from the norm for other academic libraries."[8] In the Arizona experience, most of the proposals forthcoming from the peer data process were accepted; one was not. Nevertheless, throughout the process peer survey data was viewed as valuable evidence in support of each proposal and proved to be an effective catalyst for changing circulation policies.

REFERENCE NOTES

1. The Association of American Universities (AAU) Data Exchange Group develops the list of peer institutions in which the University of Arizona is automatically included. The university has no voice in the selection process. This particular peer list is based on such factors as the number of Ph.D programs, number of degrees awarded, number of students, research rating designation, and land grant status. The University of Arizona's peer institutions are the University of Maryland, Ohio State University, University of Minnesota, the University of

Iowa, Michigan State University, the University of Illinois at Urbana-Champaign, University of North Carolina, University of Virginia, University of Texas, University of California, Berkeley, Purdue University, University of Missouri, University of Florida, Penn State University, University of Washington, and the University of Colorado.

2. Michael Buckland, *Book Availability and the Library User.* (New York: Pergamon Press Inc., 1975): 138.

3. *The Bowker Annual Library and Book Trade Almanac, 36th Edition 1991.* (New Providence, NJ: R.R. Bowker, 1991): 429.

4. Paul Gherman et al., "Faculty Loan Regulations in ARL Academic Libraries." ERIC ED 082792 (Detroit, Michigan: University Libraries, Wayne State University, 1973).

5. Henry J. DuBois, "From Leniency to Lockout: Circulation Policies at Forty-Three Academic Libraries," *College & Research Libraries News* 11 (December 1986): 700. Also, for a discussion of circulation policies at a broad range of academic libraries, see Intner, Sheila S., *Circulation Policy in Academic, Public and School Libraries.* (New York: Greenwood Press, 1987): 16-64.

6. DuBois, 700.

7. DuBois, 700.

8. DuBois, 702.

Traditional Access to the Library via Telephone Service: A Case Study

Tammy Nickelson Dearie
Alice J. Perez

SUMMARY. Telephone reference service at the University of California, San Diego's Central Library had become problematic in recent years due to increased volume of patron demand, both in-person and on the telephone. In order to meet the demand the library established a separate information desk service which became the first line of service for incoming telephone callers. Staff at the information desk screened callers and transferred appropriate reference calls to the reference desk. In 1991 the information and reference desk staff conducted a survey to see how well this arrangement was meeting the needs of their primary patrons. The survey results provided the departments with valuable information that has helped them to take new directions to better serve the needs of the primary patrons.

INTRODUCTION

Telephone access to the University of California, San Diego Central Library's reference service had become increasingly difficult for the primary clientele (UCSD faculty, staff and students) and for non-affiliated users (local community, state and private

---

Tammy Nickelson Dearie is Acting Head of the Access Services Department, and Alice J. Perez is Coordinator/Reference Desk and Collection Librarian of the Research Services Department in the Central Library, University of California, San Diego, 9500 Gilman Drive, La Jolla, CA 92093-0175.

© 1992 by The Haworth Press, Inc. All rights reserved.

college students, high school students, and the general public). The reference phone, which automatically rolled over to an answering machine after three rings, was seldom answered or always busy. The message on the answering machine informed callers that the reference librarian was busy serving in-person patrons and could not answer calls; please call back. The reference desk, many times triple staffed, was unable to serve in-person patrons and answer the ever ringing phone at the same time. Surveys of the literature identified many trends in dealing with similar problems elsewhere, such as offering separate telephone services, providing electronic reference services and even curtailing all telephone service. The majority of articles advocated the trend toward separate information desk services, which are designed to screen callers and in-person patrons.[1] In many instances, libraries implemented information desks as a pilot project or as experimental services, which immediately became established service points after the testing period.[2,3]

During 1989 and 1990, the library underwent a strategic planning process to develop a new mission statement, goals and objectives. Part of the library's mission was to provide a "library without walls." This term was used to identify a new service philosophy and provide direction for the development of new supporting services. In 1990, using the "library without walls" concept, the access services department, in conjunction with the research services department, implemented an information desk service to screen incoming callers, both in-person and on the telephone. All incoming calls to the library's main information number were answered by the information desk staff. These staff members answered directional, holdings questions and basic informational questions and transferred true reference calls to the reference desk, to the appropriate UCSD library (one of the eight campus libraries), or to another department. Typical directional and holdings questions might have been "where is the government documents collection?" or "do you own this book?" Basic information questions might pertain to a library policy or procedure. Information desk staff were given criteria for identifying questions that required use of reference tools (other than the library catalogs) or which were otherwise out-of-scope. These would then be forwarded to the reference desk. If the reference librarian could not answer the phone, the call would roll over to an answering machine which would tell the caller that the reference desk was busy. Many times the information desk staff would keep the caller on the line until they could get through to the reference desk or would give them the reference desk's unlisted number to call directly.

Even with this configuration, the research services department was concerned that too many of the calls, especially from the primary clientele, were still being unanswered. In 1991, in an ongoing effort to evaluate the telephone service, a survey of the Central University Library information and reference desk activities was conducted in order to assess the need to provide extended telephone service, determine what sort of service was being provided, and most important, who constituted the clientele of these services. Library management believed that telephone service to the primary clientele within the context of the "library without walls" should be comparable to other remote access options currently offered, such as dial-in catalog links, a campus information system, circulation services by telephone, electronic requesting and delivery of library items and electronic access to library departments, services or librarians.

The survey was conducted during the third week (April 15-April 21,1991) and eighth week (May 20-May 26, 1991) of the spring quarter; these were selected on the assumption that, during a ten week quarter, they would provide the best representation of the work flow at both the information and the reference desks. The hours of the survey were from 9 a.m.-9 p.m., Monday-Thursday; 9 a.m.-5 p.m. on Friday; 10 a.m.-4 p.m. on Saturday; and noon-6 p.m. on Sunday. Although the information desk is open longer hours than the reference desk, the survey was limited to hours when both desks were open.

Two distinct forms were used-one for the information desk, the other for the reference desk. Both forms included columns along a horizontal axis which indicated patron types: "UCSD" (student, faculty, staff), "Non-UCSD" (includes Friends of the Library, Extension students), and "No Response/Neglected to Ask" (unidentified either because the patron refused to identify his affiliation or the reference provider failed to ask the patron to identify his/her affiliation).

The information desk form (Figure 1) had along a vertical axis categories for "Type of Question," (which included sections for "Direction," "Holdings," and "Information") and "Origin of Call" (which included sections for "Call Forwarded to Reference Desk-Unanswered," and "Call Forwarded to Other Branch/Location"). At the information desk, directional questions were defined as "where is" type questions and holding questions such as "do you own this item?" Informational questions related to basic facts, such as library hours. Ready reference questions would be transferred to the reference desk and not counted at the information desk (Figure 1).

The reference desk form (Figure 2) included categories for "Type of Question," (which included sections for "Holdings," "Information," and "Search"), "Origin of Call," (which included sections for "Call Forwarded from Information Desk," "Call Directed to Reference Desk," and "Call Forwarded From Other Branch/Location") and "Call Unanswered." Holdings and information questions were defined essentially the same as at the information desk. (These types of questions would come to the reference desk only when the patron called directly there, bypassing the information desk.) Ready reference questions were counted as information questions. Search questions were identified as complex reference questions that involved the use of several reference sources.

When receiving a call, the patron was told that a survey was being conducted to improve services, then asked: "Can you tell me which category you fit into, UCSD or non-UCSD?" If the patron answered "UCSD," the information provider asked the following question for further verification: "What is your affiliation with UCSD?" While this information was not recorded, the question was asked in order to sift out those non-UCSD users who may have viewed the initial question as a barrier to service and so responded inappropriately. In any case, at the end of each call, the person was thanked for his/her response.

The following sections report the results of the survey by the categories and sections within those categories.

INFORMATION DESK STATISTICS

There were two sections to the information desk statistics form. One listed the number of incoming calls answered at the information desk by type of caller and type of question. All of the calls coming into the information desk were answered. The second section listed the calls transferred to the reference desk or other library service desk by type of caller and type of question. Not all of the transferred calls could be answered. Throughout the survey the totals tabulated for the "No Response/Neglected to Ask" category were so insignificant they are not specifically discussed in this report, even though they are shown on the charts.

Type of Question (Calls Answered at Information Desk): The total number of questions asked at the information desk was 616 (Figure 3). The most frequent type was the "Holdings" question, 310 (50%). Of those questions, 38% were from UCSD patrons, and 57% were from non-UCSD patrons. The second most asked was the "Information" question at 241 (39%), with 39% from UCSD patrons and 54% from non-UCSD patrons. The third most asked was the "Direction" question at 65 (11%), with 35% from UCSD patrons and 60% from non-UCSD patrons.

Type of Caller (Calls Answered at Information Desk): Of the 616 total questions asked at the information desk, 237 (38%) were asked by UCSD patrons, and 346 (56%) were asked by non-UCSD patrons (Figure 4). In all categories, except "Information" questions, the number of calls by non-UCSD patrons was higher.

Origin of Call: (Calls Transferred from the Information Desk): The second section of the survey form tabulated the number of calls that were forwarded to other service desks (Figure 5). "Calls Forwarded to the Central Library Reference Desk Unanswered" was the highest number, 176 (55%), while 144 (45%) went to other service desks, which include the circulation desk, documents desk and branch libraries. At all of the service points, other than the reference desk, calls were answered directly; there was no answering machine during regular service hours.

Of the 176 calls forwarded to the reference desk and unanswered, 62% were from non-UCSD patrons and 34% were from

FIGURE 1

**TELEPHONE SURVEY
INFORMATION DESK**

Date _____

Time _____

"We are conducting a telephone survey to improve our reference service. Can you tell me which catagory you fit into, UCSD or Non-UCSD?" If the patron answers "UCSD", ask the following question for further verification: "What is your affiliation with UCSD?" While we are not tracking subcategories of UCSD users, we want to ask this question in order to sift out those non-UCSD users who view the initial question as a barrier to service and so respond inappropriately. In any case, please thank the person for her/his response. You may have to ask the patron an additional question to determine origin of call.

Type of Question	UCSD (student, faculty, staff)	Non-UCSD (includes Friends of the Library, Extension Students)	No response/ Neglected to ask
Direction			
Holdings			
Information			

Origin of Call	UCSD (student, faculty, staff)	Non-UCSD (includes Friends of the Library, Extension Students)	No response/ Neglected to ask
Call forwarded to Reference Desk - Answered			
Call forwarded to Reference Desk - Unanswered			
Call forwarded to other branch/ location			

FIGURE 2

TELEPHONE SURVEY
REFERENCE DESK

Date _____

Time _____

"We are conducting a telephone survey to improve our reference service. Can you tell me which category you fit into, UCSD or Non-UCSD?" If the patron answers "UCSD", ask the following question for further verification: "What is your affiliation with UCSD?" While we are not tracking subcategories of UCSD users, we want to ask this question in order to sift out those non-UCSD users who view the initial question as a barrier to service and so respond inappropriately. In any case, please thank the person for her/his response. You may have to ask the patron an additional question to determine origin of call.

Type of Question	UCSD (student, faculty, staff)	Non-UCSD (includes Friends of the Library, Extension Students)	No response/ Neglected to ask
Holdings			
Information			
Search			

Origin of Call	UCSD (student, faculty, staff)	Non-UCSD (includes Friends of the Library, Extension Students)	No response/ Neglected to ask
Call forwarded from Information Desk			
Call direct to Reference Desk			
Call forwarded from other branch/location			

Call unanswered

FIGURE 3

Information Desk: Type of Question

Type of Question	UCSD	Non-UCSD	No response/ Neglected to ask	Totals
Direction	23 / 35%	39 / 60%	3 / 5%	65
Holdings	119 / 38%	176 / 57%	15 / 5%	310
Information	95 / 39%	131 / 54%	15 / 6%	241
				616

FIGURE 4

Information Desk: Type of Caller

Type of Question	UCSD	Non-UCSD	No response/ Neglected to ask	
Direction	23 / 9%	39 / 11%	3 / 9%	
Holdings	119 / 50%	176 / 51%	15 / 45%	
Information	95 / 40%	131 / 38%	15 / 45%	
Totals	237	346	33	616

FIGURE 5

Information Desk: Origin of Calls

Origin of Call	UCSD	Non-UCSD	No response/ Neglected to ask	Totals
Call forwarded to Reference desk-Unanswered	59/34%	110/62%	7/4%	176
Call forwarded to other branch/ location	80/56%	59/41%	5/3%	144
				320

UCSD patrons. Even more surprising was the number of calls from UCSD patrons (56%), which were transferred to other service desks, versus the number of calls from non-UCSD patrons (41%). The staff had assumed that the UCSD patrons would be more informed about the branch libraries.

Type of Caller (Calls Transferred from the Information Desk): Under "Origin of Call," the number of calls that were forwarded from the information desk was 320 (Figure 6). The totals for type of callers in this section were very close. Of the 320 calls, 139 (43%) were received from UCSD patrons, and 169 (53%) were received from non-UCSD patrons.

Of the 139 calls received from UCSD patrons, 59 (42%) were "Calls Forwarded to the Reference Desk-Unanswered," and 80 (58%) were "Calls Forwarded to other Branches/Locations." "Calls received from non-UCSD patrons" were 169, with 110 (65%) "Calls Forwarded to the Reference Desk-Unanswered" and 59 (35%) "Calls Forwarded to other Branches/Locations."

REFERENCE DESK STATISTICS

The reference desk statistics form was also divided into two sections; one section tabulated the number of calls answered at the reference desk by type of caller and type of question. The second

FIGURE 6

Information Desk: Type of Caller

Origin of Call	UCSD	Non-UCSD	No response/ Neglected to ask	
Call forwarded to Reference desk- Unanswered	59/42%	110/65%	7/58%	
Call forwarded to other branch/ location	80/58%	59/35%	5/42%	
Totals	139	169	12	320

section tabulated the origin of the calls coming into the reference desk, either forwarded calls or direct calls. Also counted were the number of calls that went unanswered during the survey period.

Type of Question: Figure 7 tabulates the total number of questions asked at the reference desk. Of the 244 questions asked, the most frequent type asked was the "Information" question at 133 (55%) followed by the "Search" question at 67 (27%), and the "Holdings" question at 44 (18%). Non-UCSD patrons had a higher percentage in all three categories under "Type of Question" (Holdings, Information, Search) tabulated at the reference desk.

Type of Caller: Of the 244 questions asked, 85 (35%) were asked by UCSD patrons, and 156 (64%) were asked by non-UCSD patrons. The number of questions telephoned to the reference desk by non-UCSD patrons constitutes the majority of calls and is significantly higher than the number of questions from UCSD patrons. As Figure 8 shows, almost 60% of the questions asked by UCSD patrons were "Information" questions. Just over half of the questions asked by non-UCSD patrons were Information" questions.

For both UCSD and Non-UCSD patrons, the smallest percentage of questions were "Holdings" questions, a little over one-fourth of the questions were "Search" questions, and the majority of the

FIGURE 7

Reference Desk: Type of Question

Type of Question	UCSD	Non-UCSD	No response/ Neglected to ask	Totals
Holdings	13/30%	31/70%	0/	44
Information	50/38%	82/61%	1/.7%	133
Search	22/33%	43/64%	2/.3%	67
				244

questions were "Information" questions. This indicates that the information desk staff were indeed transferring appropriate "Reference" telephone calls.

Origin of Call: Under "Origin of Call" (Figure 9), the total number of calls answered at the reference desk was 239, six less than 244 (the total number under "Type of Question"). The assumption is that six tallies were not reported. The most frequent number of calls to the reference desk, 151 (63%), were forwarded from the information desk. The second most frequent calls, 79 (33%) came directly to the reference desk, and third were calls which were forwarded from other branches/locations, 9 (4%). Thus, most reference desk calls were being transferred from the information desk, where they had been screened.

Of the 151 "Calls Forwarded from the Information Desk," 46 (30%) were from UCSD patrons, and 104 (69%) were from non-UCSD patrons. The number of "Calls Forwarded from the Information Desk" received from non-UCSD patrons was over twice the number of calls received from UCSD patrons.

Of the 79 "Calls Direct to the Reference Desk," 34 (43%) were

FIGURE 8

Reference Desk: Type of Caller

Type of Question	UCSD	Non-UCSD	No response/ Neglected to ask	
Holdings	13/15%	31/20%	0/	
Information	50/59%	82/52.5%	1/.33%	
Search	22/26%	43/27.5%	2/.66%	
Totals	85	156	3	244

FIGURE 9

Reference Desk: Origin of Call

Origin of Call	UCSD	Non-UCSD	No response/ Neglected to ask	Totals
Call forwarded from Info Desk	46/30%	104/69%	1/.006%	151
Call direct to Reference Desk	34/43%	39/49%	6/8%	79
Call forwarded from other branch/location	2/22%	7/78%	0/	9
				239

from UCSD patrons, and 39 (49%) were from non-UCSD patrons. The reference desk telephone number is not listed in the UCSD telephone directory, nor is it generally given out to the public unless the information desk has attempted three transfers to the reference desk and has received a busy signal or the telephone call is long distance. In these situations, the information desk will give the patron the direct telephone number to the reference desk.

Type of Caller: Under "Origin of Call" (Figure 10) the total number of calls was 239. Of those, 82 (34%) were from UCSD patrons, and 150 (63%) were from non-UCSD patrons.

Calls Unanswered (At the Reference Desk): The reference providers were asked to record tallies for those telephone calls which went unanswered due to the fact that they were helping an in-person patron and were unable to answer the telephone. The total number of "Calls Unanswered" at the reference desk was 191. The total number of unanswered "Calls Forwarded to the Reference Desk" recorded by the information desk was 176. The remaining 15 unanswered calls may have come in as direct calls to the reference desk. Of these 176 calls, the information desk tabulated 59 (34%) were from UCSD patrons, and 110 (62%) were from non-UCSD patrons. The number of calls received from non-UCSD patrons is significantly higher than those from UCSD patrons.

FIGURE 10

Reference Desk: Type of Caller

Origin of Call	UCSD	Non-UCSD	No Response/Neglected to Ask	
Call Forwarded from Info Desk	46/56%	104/69%	1/14%	
Call Direct to Reference Desk	34/42%	39/26%	6/83%	
Call Forwarded from Other Branch	2/2%	7/5%	0/0%	
Totals	82	150	7	239

However, about one third of these unanswered calls were from UCSD patrons, our primary clientele.

CONCLUSION

For each category reported by both the reference and information desks, statistics for non-UCSD patrons were higher than those for UCSD patrons. Still, during the two-week period the survey was conducted, 59 out of the 176 calls that were forwarded to the reference desk and unanswered were from UCSD patrons, the library's primary clientele. This was 34% of the total number of calls unanswered, a percentage considered to be quite high by library management. This group was thus identified as being that for which new access options were needed. Options that were discussed ran the gamut of expanding the current service, establishing a separate telephone reference service, investigating the possibility of purchasing an automatic call sequencer (a call management system which answers calls and places callers on hold), providing increased electronic access to reference services, encouraging UCSD patrons to call subject bibliographers directly, publicizing the undergraduate library's reference service, creating an electronic "reference mailbox" available through InfoPath (the library's campus information system), or a combination of various options.

Increasing the number of staff at the reference desk to handle more of the unanswered telephone calls, or establishing a separate telephone reference service would require additional staffing and funding. To do so would doubtless serve the primary clientele, but it would equally improve service to non-UCSD patrons as well. Although the library has made a commitment to serving non-UCSD patrons, budget cuts have made it impossible to expand service to this group. The number of non-UCSD patrons continues to grow, is becoming increasingly pervasive in the library and has the ability to appropriate more of our primary user services. It was decided that it would be more useful to focus on ways of providing expanded reference service to UCSD patrons. After consideration was given to all factors, it was recommended that the library begin to implement several of the options that had been identified. This library has begun with a plan to purchase an automatic call sequencer and has also re-allocated certain staff to the reference desk, where their designated primary responsibility is telephone service. The other options are under discussion and will be incorporated into future service goals.

At the present time, the information desk is still the first point of contact for the patron calling the library. The information desk screens the calls and answers "Directional" and "Holdings" questions, and only transfers those callers who need actual reference assistance. Our existing telephone service policy does not discriminate between UCSD and non-UCSD patrons; consequently, our primary clientele is limited in their access to telephone service. Therefore, it was further recommended that if the methods implemented to date prove unsuccessful, the option of screening callers for UCSD status would be considered. The screening of callers could be especially useful during midterms and finals and during periods of disruption caused by the construction of a new library addition.

Although these initiatives may not fulfill all of our primary clients' needs, nor probably those needs of our secondary clientele, they attempt to provide service through a traditional avenue, the telephone, in an era of campus information systems, electronic mail, voice mail and other technological advances and expand the library's "library without walls" concept. The success of this concept requires that patrons be able to conduct certain basic types of library business through all of these venues. It seems likely, however, that contacting the library via telephone is likely to remain the preferred means for a number of patrons.

REFERENCE NOTES

1. Kleiner, Jane P. "Information Desk: the Library's Gateway to Service." *College and Research Libraries 29* (November 1968): 496-501.

2. Larson, Joyce and others. *Enhancing Reference Service in a Subject-Divided Library: The Role of an Information Desk*. Committee Report, Central Missouri State University, Jan 1989. ED 305 937.

3. Williams, Karen. *Implementing an Information Desk: Avenues Toward Increased Quality of Reference and Loan Services. Summary and Evaluation of the Desk Experiment*, 1987, Paper presented at the Annual Poster Session of the American Library Association (6th annual conference, San Francisco, CA June 22-29, 1987). ED 290 496.

Planning for Success: Documenting Workflow in the Circulation Department

Brenda Cameron-Miller

SUMMARY. Planning is essential for circulation and access service managers so they can maximize public access to library materials, establish service priorities, identify what resources are necessary to maintain service levels, and provide staff with clear performance expectations. This article describes two tools, used at Vancouver Community Library, that enable the manager to document workflow: performance standards and time surveys. Together, these two provide a general picture of how the department meets its public service goals. With limited resources available to them, circulation and access services managers must plan to increase efficiency, or fail to meet their public obligations.

INTRODUCTION

The cost of administering the circulation department is a matter of importance to the department head. Every branch of the service, each detail of procedure, should be weighed to see whether it is worth its cost in time, effort, and money, and to judge its relative importance in the whole scheme of work. If the expense is disproportionate, the department head must devise an alternate procedure.[1]

Although Jennie Flexner wrote these words in 1927, they remain relevant to circulation and access services managers today. Appro-

---

Brenda Cameron-Miller is Circulation Librarian at Vancouver Community Library, 1007 E. Mill Plain Blvd., Vancouver, WA 98663.

© 1992 by The Haworth Press, Inc. All rights reserved.

priate allocation of resources allows staff to maximize public access to library materials and information. Unfortunately, many find that as the volume of work increases, time available to plan ways to meet this workload decreases. Nevertheless, placing emphasis on planning enables a manager to set service priorities, improve procedures, and identify when additional resources are needed to maintain current service levels. Planning also allows a manager to set and communicate clear performance expectations to staff.

Documenting workflow in the circulation department allows a manager to monitor and control the expenditure of resources. Although many managers are unable to regularly dedicate time exclusively to planning, they may find that the statistics and information they routinely gather can provide a solid basis for planning and improving workflow. The objectives of the planning process should be to define service areas and levels and document how much time and money are spent on each. With this information, the manager can set priorities and eliminate unnecessary tasks. Furthermore, the same information can be used as a supervisory tool to help set performance standards, provide the basis for meaningful appraisals, support budget requests and/or allocate resources to meet service priorities. The aim of this article is to describe simple, practical techniques by which a public library manager can analyze workflow in a circulation department.

Documentation should be a high priority in public libraries where resources are often scarce and stretching the budget to cover staffing, materials and facilities is a daily exercise. The manager of any public service department has an obligation to guarantee that public money is being spent effectively to provide the best possible service. For example, a recent article in *Public Libraries* emphasized the importance of determining programming costs in children's services as a factor in planning how time should be spent. It concludes:

> Time is the one common denominator in all of library work and it gives us our service orientation and mission. The alternative to measuring and budgeting hours is to risk the squandering of many of them. We can never have enough time, yet we can try to spend what we have by design and not default.[2]

The allocation of staff time in the circulation department directly affects the public's access to books and materials in libraries. The first step in documenting workflow is to examine how time is spent on various tasks. A manager needs to be able to clearly define what tasks and procedures are performed on a routine basis, and how much time is devoted to each. Production standards and time surveys can provide useful data toward this end. After routines are clearly defined, a manager can determine if changes need to be made to increase productivity and efficiency in the department.

Many public libraries use production standards primarily as a means of evaluating and motivating staff. In the context of this article, production standards are defined as "specific, measurable statements of what is required for a job to be performed at certain identified levels."[3] In other words, how fast and how much. Routine, repetitious tasks such as shelving or data entry are ideal candidates for assessing via performance standards. There are many articles and books available on supervision of staff in libraries; however, there is relatively little written about quantitative productivity standards. Martell writes:

> As an example, librarians rarely use the word 'productivity' except in its most pejorative sense. To talk about the number of books cataloged per hour by a cataloger is to move outside of accepted professional norms. The concept is not accepted culturally. There have been discussions about standards, but these relate to what should be done and how, not to how many.[4]

Although this statement concerns measuring professional performance, it might well be extended to the issue of setting standards for clerical tasks. The simple techniques described in the following section have proven effective for setting standards in a medium-sized public library environment.

THE ESTABLISHMENT OF PERFORMANCE STANDARDS

The Fort Vancouver Regional Library, a three county public library system in Washington state, has developed performance standards for a variety of clerical tasks. While specific expectations vary for a given routine from branch to branch, each outlet used the same methods in setting standards. For example, each branch's standard for shelving reflects its unique physical layout, volume of business, and method of processing returned books. Performance standards are an integral part of the training process for new staff and are, consequently, more of an issue in larger branches with higher staff turnover.

Shelving provides perhaps the most straightforward example to illustrate the process by which standards are established in every circulation department of each branch. The four basic steps in the process of setting standards are (1) documentation, (2) data collection, (3) implementation, and (4) review. Staff at all levels should be involved with this process, especially those whose performance will be measured by the standards. They will be more likely to accept a productivity measure if they participated in determining it.

At the start of the process, the supervisor defines and documents the steps taken to complete a given task. These processes are described in a procedures manual and are demonstrated as part of training new staff. In order to be valid, it is crucial that the factors being measured are clearly stated. With shelving, for example, issues that must be addressed include: will the shelving standard involve time spent loading and putting a truck of books in order or only shelving them; are staff timed for meeting the standard during the course of their regular duties or are they timed during a special test period, etc. Whatever decisions are made in regard to these questions, the manager must make sure standards are consistently measured and applied. At the Vancouver Community Library, shelving standards do not include putting the truck in order and are expressed in terms of the actual time spent shelving an average number of books; the data is collected daily. Further, the standards vary according to what part of the collection the book is shelved in, i.e., there are different shelving requirements for non-fiction, fiction, biographies, juvenile fiction, and picture books. An average number of books per shelf on a book truck was determined for each area by counting and averaging the number of books on at least 20 trucks. It was found, for example, there are 35 non-fiction books on a typical shelf, and a book truck may have one to six shelves of books. Staff are expected to reshelve books accurately and correct any obvious errors they happen to find. Additional time is allocated for more intensive shelf reading. These procedures are written down, and each new page is trained to shelve accordingly.

During the standards setting period, staff collect data for each truck of books they shelve. As each truck of returned books is loaded, it is tagged with a form which includes spaces for recording: (1) the date the truck was loaded; (2) the date and amount of time taken to slip (check in) the truck; and (3) the date and amount of time taken to shelve the truck. There is a space for comments, and pages routinely record when they have had excessive interruptions while shelving. After the truck is shelved, the slips are dropped in a basket and collected at the end of each day.

Initially, the shelving performance standard was determined after one month of data collection. The Vancouver Community Library has 12 pages who work a combined total of 336 hours per week. As a group, they shelved approximately 1000 trucks of books each month. When the data were analyzed, the figures were divided into three groups: pages with less than three months experience, those with three to six months experience, and those with over six months work experience. This was done because clerical staff were expected to meet the stated performance standards by six months in order to pass probation. For each page, the average amount of time to shelve a truck in each area was recorded. It was found that the pages with the least seniority had the lowest averages. However, there was no appreciable difference in the rates between the other two groups.

The standard was set based on the performance of the pages who had at least three months of work experience. Performance rates for these workers fell within a narrow range (within around four minutes from fastest to slowest per-shelf rates); the standard was established at the lower end of the range, representing the minimum acceptable performance. Periodically, the standards are reviewed, especially when the procedures for shelving are changed, in order to reaffirm their validity.

In addition to being used in staff evaluations, performance standards are also a useful basis for estimating the amount of time it takes to accomplish a particular task. If, for instance, circulation increased by 2000 books per week, the manager could calculate, based on the existing standard, how much additional time would be required to handle the increased workload, estimate the backlog that would be created, and allocate staff time appropriately. Standards developed for other aspects of circulation work can be similarly applied. At Vancouver, standards have been established for such additional tasks as checkins, processing manual records, and data entry for overdues. Finally, standards can be used as a tool for allocating staff resources even if they are not directly linked to performance expectations. For example, the expectation is that a staff member can do 150 checkouts/hour. Although staff are not timed or evaluated according to this standard, management uses it to monitor the volume of business at the counter and to assign additional staff if demand exceeds that rate.

TIME SURVEY

Obviously, many tasks within the circulation department can not easily be documented by standards. Further, some routines and services may be performed in unison–for example, cards may be filed by a person who is also watching the counter–and these types of interactions can be elusive when assessing work flow. A time survey is a useful tool for documenting and understanding workflow in these areas. A time survey examines data collected over a limited period about how time is being used on various tasks within the department. Time survey data should expand, not duplicate, that collected for performance standards.

Output Measures for Public Libraries provide some excellent and practical advice on data collection and evaluation. This source clearly suggests that meaningful data can be obtained only through careful, consistent collection techniques, beginning with a clear definition of what is being counted and how. All staff must "count the same things, in the same way," and "the data are only as good as the people collecting them." The less intrusive the methods for collecting data, the more meaningful will be the information that is derived. "The more that people are aware of the measurement, the more likely they are to be on their best [rather than their usual] behavior."[5]

The simplest way to conduct a time survey is to give staff a form on which to record their daily activities during a sampling period. At Vancouver Community Library this is mandated by the head of public services and done yearly during a two week period. It is important that everybody in the department participates, including the supervisors. The form can be divided into two columns; one headed TIME and the other TASK. Essentially staff are asked to keep a diary of their work day. Staff keep data on "actual" time expenditures per-task, and are also asked to use this to extrapolate "typical" time/task figures. The manager needs to determine how detailed and time consuming all tasks are, then create reasonable priorities. For example, the manager must decide whether it is more important to know how much overall time is spent working at the circulation desk or how much time is being spent for each circulation transaction. Once collected, the data can then be tallied and used in evaluating job descriptions and for planning. This is accomplished by listing each task being done in the department followed by the amount of time actually spent on each one. Some tasks may be directly linked to the volume of business in the department. Circulation and shelving volume, for instance, tend to go up or down in relation to one another. Other tasks may have a fixed amount of time spent on them each week, such as shelf reading, daily cleanup of the library, or processing new magazines. Special projects or assignments must also be included in the time survey. For example, the Clark County bookmobile spends ten days at the county fair each summer, and circulation department staff were assigned to work there instead of their usual assignments. Extraordinary commitments of staff and time such as this must be accounted for. The time surveys may confirm or contradict assumptions a supervisor has about how time is spent in the department. Either way, time surveys give detailed reports on how time is being spent by task and by individuals within the circulation department.

This process can yield information on the cost efficiency of the department, as well as provide a basis for budgeting. If, for example, the study shows that the volume of work exceeds the staff's capabilities, the data gathered on the degree of this shortfall lend support for increased budgetary and staffing requests. Performance standards might also be used in this process. As routines are examined, ways to increase efficiency may become evident. For example, time studies indicate optimum times during the day when shelf reading can be done, or how much staff time the manager can afford to dedicate to this task and still provide counter service priorities. Having a clear picture of what it takes to do the work will assist in setting priorities and organizing the work to meet public service goals.

CONCLUSION

The steps outlined in this article allow a manager to obtain a basic, general picture of the way work flows through the department. These work flow patterns can then be documented as procedures, and the task of writing them down often reveals ways to increase productivity. This then becomes a planning process, which can empower the manager. Problems turn into solutions, and ways to overcome barriers might be identified which can result in crafting a better library environment for patrons and staff. Cummins and Condin stated that: "The library's ability to make a successful transition to an efficient, integrated workplace depends on the strength of its efforts at productivity improvement. Increased productivity is a necessity of our time, and the manner in which we choose to participate will have far-reaching implications."[6] Circulation and access services managers must recognize the value of planning as a means of increasing efficiency in order to continue to provide high quality public service. As indicated in Flexner's opening quote, this is one of the enduring goals of library services.

REFERENCE NOTES

1. Jennie M. Flexner, *Circulation Work in Public Libraries* (Chicago: American Library Association, 1927), p. 257.
2. Laurie R. Mielke, "Sermon on the Amount: Costing Out Children's Services," *Public Libraries* (September/October 1991): 279-282.

3. "Developing Job Standards: Tell Employees What You Want." *Supervisor's Bulletin for Administration and Office Support Groups*, Number 837 (November 30,1990): 2.

4. Charles Martell, "Achieving High Performance in Library Work," *Library Trends* 38 (Summer 1989): 84.

5. Nancy A. Van House, Mary Jo Lynch, Charles R. McClure, Douglas L. Zweizig and Eleanor Jo Rodger, *Output Measures for Public Libraries* (Chicago and London: American Library Association): 15-16.

6. Thompson R. Cummins and Micki Carden, "Productivity Efforts in Public Libraries," *Public Libraries* (Winter 1987): 142.

A Library Shelver's Performance Evaluation as It Relates to Reshelving Accuracy

S. Celine Sharp

SUMMARY. Shelving is an important task in the work flow of the library. Books must be quickly and accurately reshelved in the stacks for optimum patron usage. The Brigham Young University shelving study had three purposes: (1) determine if shelving speed influences the accuracy with which books are returned to the shelves, (2) determine if the day of the week influences accuracy, and (3) determine if the length of a shelver's employment influences accuracy. Call numbers were written down from the shelver's cart after it was sorted. Later, after the shelver left for the day, each call number was checked and marked as shelved correctly, shelved incorrectly, or not found in the stacks. All test results on data revealed no interaction among the variables. The data provides some evidence, however, which suggests that job standards and evaluation may be the interacting variables with accuracy percents. Further data is needed to fully study these relationships.

INTRODUCTION

Reshelving materials is a vital aspect of providing good library service. Materials inaccurately or not promptly shelved are virtually lost to the patron and the library collection. Most shelvers are

---

S. Celine Sharp is Assistant Circulation Dept. Head at Brigham Young University. The university's address is 3083 HBLL BYU, Provo, UT 84602. This article is based upon research submitted in a paper to the School of Library and Information Sciences, BYU, September 1989. The author gratefully acknowledges H. Gill Hilton for his technical assistance.

© 1992 by The Haworth Press, Inc. All rights reserved.

student workers whose reliability may be questionable or whose understanding of the classification system might not be perfect. This research evaluates the performance of student shelvers in an ARL library.

Several factors could be studied in determining what influences the quality of work completed by a shelver. For this project three variables were tested in relation to how each influenced accuracy percents: shelving speed, day of the week and level of experience (length of time employed as a shelver).

A BRIEF REVIEW OF THE LITERATURE

Historically the literature on shelving tasks has addressed three areas: (1) book collection arrangement, (2) shelver training methods, and (3) production standards. Research is lacking on the relationship of a shelver's performance and the accuracy level of the books reshelved in the stacks.

Book Collection Arrangement: The arrangement of books on the shelves is important in among books accessible to patrons and staff. The two most common arrangements are: (1) each book has its permanent location in a specific spot on a given shelf; or (2) each book has a location relative to the rest of the collection according to its classification. The fixed location method is limited to closed stack areas such as rare book collections and storage areas. Relative location is most commonly used in open stacks.[1]

The shelving arrangement affects ease of reshelving. The first method consists of arranging books alphabetically by title within the subject classification. The second calls for arranging books, using Cutter numbers, within a broad subject classification. Research indicates that the Cutter number arrangement is most likely to avoid confusion and cause less careless shelving.[2]

Training Techniques: Proper training is vital for new shelvers. They must understand the routines of their library and have a clear understanding of the call number system(s) used in order to be efficient workers.

One efficient and effective training technique involves the use of audiovisuals. This type of program is typically divided into several units, each covering a different aspect of training. The student watches a slide presentation for each unit, while following a script. At different stages in the program, there are stop points at which the employee's understanding of information and call number systems can be tested. Another advantage of the slide/script presentation is that it can be used individually or for group instruction. Feedback from employees trained with methods of this type is positive and supervisors are freed to do other things.[3]

Student shelvers at Brigham Young are trained with a variety of techniques. During the first few days on the job, a shelver reads an orientation manual and a manual explaining the Dewey and Library of Congress classifications systems. Each manual has a worksheet that is filled out, reviewing important concepts. Alter completion of the manuals, the new employee sorts cards with sample call numbers from both the Dewey and LC systems. Shelvers then spend a minimum of two days shelf reading before any new tasks are introduced.

Shelvers are then paired up with a student supervisor and shown how to complete pick-ups, sort, shelve, etc. After eight days, the student reads a third manual and comply a worksheet which reviews shelving standards, accuracy expectations, and general shelving procedures. At this point, the stacks manager also verbally reviews things learned and gives a first report on the shelver's accuracy percent (accuracy evaluations were added to the training program alter this study).

Production Standards: Attention to performance measures and standards is on the rise in access services. To quote Hannabus:

> We undertake measurement of performance because we want to examine the ends for which we carry out the service and the means by which we meet (or fail to meet) those ends.[4]

Setting production standards in shelving is essential, especially for new shelvers. Standards serve as guidelines for trainees, provide criteria for evaluation, and encourage constant production. A standard rate for sorting call numbers is 150 books in 25 minutes. Similarly, without undue emotional or physical stress, shelvers should be able to reshelve 150 books in 50 minutes.[5]

While historical research in these three areas is informative and provides useful perspective for this study, little arch was found on the specific subject of shelving and related factors. Congruent with this study, however, at Melville Library at SUNY, Stony Brook, a simple method for checking shelving accuracy was being developed. Kendrick records a 91 percent accuracy rate there and reports adding a performance check program as useful, undisruptive to patrons and only a minor disruption for staff. He poses the questions of who is making the mistakes in shelving and how can mistakes be reduced?[6] This study has expanded on these questions and hopes to provide a useful model for libraries to implement in their own performance evaluation.

METHODOLOGY

This study was based on three hypotheses. It was expected that each shelver has an optimum shelving speed, beyond which percentages of books shelved accurately will begin to decline. Second, it was also assumed that the weekend backlog makes the first two days of the week more stressful, and as a result, accuracy will suffer. Third, it was hypothesized that alter a length of time, a shelver will experience "burn out" and become less conscientious about shelving accurately.

The study was limited to circulation library shelvers in the Harold B. Lee Library at Brigham Young University. The library's collection is near 3,000,000 volumes. Approximately 30 student workers are employed as shelvers, each shelving close to 1,000 books weekly (these figures will vary according to the time of year). No shelving is done on Saturday, and the library is closed to students on Sunday. Shelving of books in both Dewey and LC was tested. Documents, Asian materials, sampler room, learning resource center, and reference collections are not handled in the circulation area and were not included in the study.

The study was conducted in two phases, each covering a five week period. The first phase was done during the "peak" time of fall semester, 1988, which runs from the second week of November through the second week of December. The week of the

Thanksgiving holiday was excluded because employees were not required to work. The second phase was done during a slower period of winter semester, 1989, running from the second week of February through the second week of March. No attempt was made to determine the relationship of the variables according to age, sex, race, or the area of the library where a shelver works.

The following terms and roles were defined for the project: a *library shelver* is a student employee who shelves books. Tasks of shelving include gathering books off "yellow" shelves (in-house sorting areas) and those returned by patrons, sorting them by call number, loading them onto a book truck and replacing them in the stacks. A shelver is also responsible for straightening, shifting and shelf reading.

Shelving speed is the rate at which a person reshelves books. For this study, speed was calculated by dividing the number of books shelved by the number of hours and minutes spent shelving them. For example, John shelves 338 books in 1 hour and 15 minutes. His speed is figured by dividing 338 by 1.25 which gives a speed of 270 books shelved per hour. The shelving speed is based upon self-reported activity logs turned in at the end of the day by all student shelvers. The time listed reflects just that amount of time taken to shelve a book truck. Time spent sorting or doing other activities is not counted in shelving speed. These figures were rounded to the nearest 15 minutes.

Accuracy percent represents those books found correctly shelved in the stacks expressed as a percentage of all books shelved. It was found by dividing the number of books shelved correctly by the total number of books reshelved.

A *tracer* is a student employee who searches the stacks for lost books. For this study, tracers were used to record the call numbers of selected books on a shelver's sorted cart. The tracer then checked the library stacks to see how accurately the employee had shelved the selected books.

Initially it was assumed that during the study Lee Library shelvers were not aware of the research in process. Before the second phase, however, they were told that accuracy checks were being done periodically for employment evaluation. Each worker had completed the same training program when hired and was tested for knowledge of the classification systems before beginning to sort and shelve. It was also assumed that shelvers had generally similar performance trends, and that no one person's performance would bias the random sampling selection.

Tracers used in this study were former shelvers, still familiar with the stacks and shelving routines and accurate with the call number systems. Under most conditions, tracers checked call numbers within one to three hours after the shelver finished a shift, limiting the possibility of patrons browsing and misplacing or removing books.

Timing of the study was important. New shelvers are hired each semester as needed to handle the increased use of the library. Because the study involved shelvers of varying employment lengths, it was crucial to begin gathering data within days after new employees were hired. For the first five week phase of the study, data collection began the second week of November. Likewise, in the second phase, new shelvers began work the first week of February, and data gathering started the second week of that month. Thirty shelvers were employed by the circulation department at the beginning of each data collection phase. The BYU Department of Statistics, which helped plan the design of the study, determined that data were needed on fifteen employees in order to have a valid sample. Five groups were established according to level of experience. Group one consisted of those employed from 0-4 weeks; group two, those employed from 5-8 weeks; group three, those employed from 9-16 weeks; group four, those employed from 17-32 weeks; and, group five, anyone employed over 32 weeks. All student employee names were written on a piece of paper, and three names were drawn from each group to make up the sample. Each shelver chosen was assigned a number within the group for ease of recording information. This method of selection was consistent for both data collection phases in the study.

After the first week of phase one, a problem arose with shelver #1 in group three. Her accuracy was only 60% and, after consultation with the statistician, it was agreed that she had to be told about the problem. The library could not afford to allow this unacceptable performance to continue even though talking to her would bias the study. An additional name was chosen from group three and added to the sample; thus, four shelvers were tested in group three during all but the first week of phase one.

The information gathered for each shelver included day of the week, week of the study, level of experience, number of books checked each time, number of errors each time, number of books not found, total number of books shelved that day, and total time spent shelving. Results were recorded daily on a log sheet (see Appendix A).

Data were collected using 5 x 5 Latin Square (Table 1) which controls for day to day and week to week variations in order to properly measure any differences among levels of experience.

The number in the cells on Table 1 indicates the level of a shelver's experience. Group one represents the least experienced and group five the most experienced, according to the established criteria. Every group was tested one day each week. For example, on Wednesday of week four, the shelvers in experience level two were evaluated. Before phase two began, a new Latin Square was randomize to change the order of collecting data during the second part of the study.

Each day of the study, a tracer was assigned to collect data from each of the three shelvers. The tracer's responsibility was to record thirty call numbers selected at random from those books shelved by each employee during his/her shift. Two methods were devised for getting the call numbers. The first was a "setup" situation. If it could be predetermined which books the employee would be shelving when s/he came to work, the tracer would copy down call numbers from books found on the sorting shelves. This method was only used when no other shelvers were in the sorting area. Most often the second method was used, which entailed copying call numbers down from books found on carts after shelvers had sorted their carts and were in the stacks reshelving. In order to

TABLE 1. Data collection schedule by experience level and day of the week

Day	Week 1	Week 2	Week 3	Week 4	Week 5
Mon	3	5	1	4	2
Tue	2	4	5	3	1
Wed	1	3	4	2	5
Thu	4	1	2	5	3
Fri	5	2	3	1	4

maintain the security of the test, the tracer needed to remain as inconspicuous as possible. When the shelver was down an aisle with books, the tracer would randomly write down as many call numbers as possible before the shelver returned for another stack of books. When the shelver returned, the tracer would have to be out of sight. Once the employee had resumed shelving, the tracer would continue to record numbers.

Getting the numbers was difficult and, at times, stressful. Therefore, no absolute rules were given for recording call numbers. Numbers were written down at random. The tracer was instructed to record as many of the thirty desired call numbers as possible during the shelver's shift. Tracers were told, however, to try to get a variety of numbers when possible. For example, since periodicals are relatively easy to shelve, the selected numbers should not all be periodicals. In addition, call numbers are found on the face of books with narrow spines. These are more difficult to shelve, and some should be included in each group. Books from various areas on the shelver's assigned floor should be chosen.

In order to assure consistency, one tracer was assigned to do all of the accuracy checks and data recording. Within one to three hours after shelvers had finished their shift, the list of call numbers was taken to the stacks and checked. By checking call numbers as soon as possible after being reshelved, patron browsing and misplacement of books was limited. Each call number was marked as either correctly "shelved," "incorrectly shelved," or "not found."

At the conclusion of the fifth week, a preliminary analysis was made before beginning phase two. The method of collecting data was determined effective and remained the same. However, additions were made hoping to provide useful information. When checking for accuracy, the tracers frequently noticed that a large number of call numbers were not found on the shelves at all. Several possible reasons could account for this. The shelver could have badly misshelved them, but this was considered highly unlikely because the tracer did a thorough job looking for each call number. If it was not in the correct place, the tracer would look on the shelf above and below and on either side. Another possibility is that a patron could have retrieved the book between the time the shelver replaced it and when the tracer was able to check for accuracy. Also, sometimes shelvers will find a book out of order on their cart, a mistake made when sorting. In order to save time, they have been instructed that if the book cannot be shelved on the aisle where they are working they should put the book on a yellow shelf to be collected and shelved later. If this book happened to be on the list being checked, it would not be found. Another possibility is that some shelvers may just "dump" books. Finally, another problem with books not found, and the one deemed most likely, was human error. Tracers were under pressure when recording numbers and may have misread and recorded call numbers incorrectly. It was decided that those books not found should not be counted against the shelver. They were recorded as "not found" books and subtracted out of the total before calculating accuracy percents.

The large number of "not found" books was a concern, and during the second phase, tracers were instructed to write down numbers as carefully as possible. Also, on each list of call numbers, the tracer wrote down if the numbers were taken from a "set-up" situation or off a cart in the stacks. The theory was that a tracer should be under less stress when taking call numbers off the sorting shelves and, on these lists, there would be fewer missing books.

During the second phase, additional information was recorded about the type of errors made. Each time a book was found misshelved, the tracer would make a written note next to the call number indicating what type of shelving mistake was made. This was added to the study hoping to isolate specific patterns of mistakes, but no statistical analysis was intended at this time.

The accuracy mean from phase one was only 93%, and the Circulation Department management was not satisfied with this level. Before phase two began, a meeting was held with all shelvers, followed by individual interviews. At this meeting, the problems of misshelved books were discussed, and suggestions for improvement were made. Tips were given on shelving quickly, yet accurately. Employees were told that a new policy required 97% accuracy for employment continuation. When interviewed, shelvers were told their current individual accuracy percents and encouraged to improve if below the standard. They were not told that a test was being done. Throughout the second phase, all employees were regularly reminded about the accuracy policy.

After collecting the data and entering it on the daily log sheets, a data list file was created. The data file was set up with a column assigned to each of the following: day of the week, week of the study, experience level, shelver number within experience level, number of books monitored that time, number of errors that time, total number of books shelved that day, time spent in shelving that day, and books not found.

Each row in the data file represented one shelver for one day of one week. After creating the file, means, analysis of variance, and analysis of covariance tests were used for analysis of the data. These analyses were performed by using PROC GLM (Procedures in General Linear Models) in SAS User's Guide (Statistical Analysis System).[7] Log sheets for each phase were separated and analyzed individually as well as the two phases analyzed against each other. The dependent variable in each case was accuracy, with independent variables of day of the week, level of experience, and shelving speed. All tests were run at a .05 level of significance.

DISCUSSION OF FINDINGS

During phase one, a total of 21,763 books were shelved by the subjects being studied. Of that total, 1841 call numbers (8.45% of the total number) were checked for shelving accuracy. Of the call numbers checked, 1671 were "shelved correctly," while ninety-eight were "shelved incorrectly" and seventy-two were "not found." Nine data rows were missing due to employee illness or because no shelving was performed that day.

Figures for phase two were similar. A total of 19,228 books were shelved, of which 1898 call numbers were tested (9.8% of the total). In this case, 1735 books were shelved correctly, and seventy-seven books were inaccurately shelved while 86 were not found. There were seven rows of missing data.

The results of anova tests using accuracy as the dependent variable and day of the week and level of experience as the independent variables are shown in Tables 2 and 3. The tests for differences in accuracy means among days of the week for phase one shows a P-value of .48. The same test in phase two had a P-value .94. Test for differences in accuracy means among levels of experience indicate P-values of .45 and .99.

Table 4 shows the means test results of accuracy percents and shelving speed for both phases. The total shelving average for phase one was 253 books per hour, while the accuracy mean was 93.6. Phase two totals, were a 230 shelving speed and 95.6 accuracy rate. The data from each phase were combined, and an analysis of covariance test was run, with speed as the covariate. Results are

TABLE 2. Anova test for phase one dependent variable: Accuracy

SOURCE	DF	M.S.	F VALUE	PR > F
DAYS	4	.0093	0.87	0.4880
EXP LEVEL	4	.0099	0.93	0.4521

DF - Degrees of freedom
M.S. - Mean square
P-value - Statistical test of significance

TABLE 3. Anova test for phase two dependent variable: Accuracy

SOURCE	DF	M.S.	F VALUE	PR > F
DAYS	4	.0006	0.18	0.9470
EXP LEVEL	4	.0002	0.06	0.9933

TABLE 4. Means of accuracy percents and shelving speeds

PHASE	N	ACCURACY	SPEED
1	71	0.9369	253.16
2	67	0.9564	230.95

shown in Table 5. The relatively large P-value of .26 on the test for speed indicates no linear relationship between accuracy and speed. Phase one and two combined totals for day of the week yielded a P-value of .71. The combined value for experience level was .62. Thus, accuracy was not influenced by either day of the week or level of experience.

The means test results in Table 6 were broken down by phase, according to day of the week, indicating accuracy percent and shelving speed averages. Likewise, Table 7 is broken down by phase, according to level of experience, then by accuracy and speed means. It is evident that accuracy percents for phase one in both categories of day of the week and level of experience were inconsistent. There appears to be no pattern of development throughout the week when accuracy is best. The span of accuracy changes among days was 6%. Among the experience levels, the variation was also 6%. It was expected that Monday would have

TABLE 5. Analysis of covariance, combined phases covariate: Speed

SOURCE	DF	M.S.	F VALUE	PR > F
SPEED	1	.0022	1.25	0.2667
DAYS	4	.0037	0.52	0.7187
EXP LEVEL	4	.0047	0.66	0.6225

TABLE 6. Shelving and accuracy means test by phase and day of the week

PHASE	DAYS	N	ACCURACY	SPEED
1	1	12	.9213	266.82
1	2	14	.9606	256.50
1	3	16	.9457	250.78
1	4	15	.8992	250.36
1	5	14	.9567	243.85
2	1	10	.9684	221.37
2	2	15	.9511	223.44
2	3	15	.9591	229.24
2	4	13	.9587	228.80
2	5	14	.9485	249.57

TABLE 7. Shelving and accuracy means test by phase and experience level

PHASE	EXP	N	ACCURACY	SPEED
1	1	15	.9609	219.90
1	2	14	.9177	231.83
1	3	16	.9056	217.56
1	4	14	.9595	296.87
1	5	12	.9446	316.11
2	1	13	.9509	167.39
2	2	13	.9569	204.01
2	3	12	.9595	269.79
2	4	14	.9587	228.51
2	5	15	.9561	280.61

the worst accuracy rate due to pressure to shelve quickly because of the weekend backlog. However, the results show that Thursday (.89) has the lowest accuracy percent. The means shown in Table 7 for level of experience during phase one indicate that the newest employees are most accurate (.96).

Phase two results in both tables show a much more consistent pattern of accuracy percents in relation to the variables. The variation of accuracy from day to day is only 2%. Even more consistent is the fact that accuracy varies only .9% within the experience levels.

CONCLUSION

This study shows no statistically significant relationship between shelving speed and the accuracy with which a shelver returns books to the shelves. In addition, the day of the week and level of experience of the shelver had no relationship to shelving accuracy. Operationally, however, the differences observed during the two testing periods may be useful. Accuracy percentages for day of the week, during phase one, ranged from 89.9 to 96. Phase two figures were much more consistent throughout the week, ranging from 94.8 to 96.8. The results for level of experience were similar. Accuracy percents among the five experience levels ranged from 90.5 to 96 during phase one. In comparison, phase two showed extreme consistency ranging from only 95 to 95.9. The most meaningful correlation may be that of shelving speed and accuracy. The mean speed for phase two dropped 23 books per hour, while accuracy rose 2%. Though this percent is small, it is numerically large in terms of the increased number of books shelved correctly each week in the library.

This study does not propose that shelvers should be asked to reduce their shelving speeds until a 100% accuracy rate is achieved or that shelvers should be restricted as to how fast they can shelve. But, the evidence does suggest a difference between the results of the two phases that needs to be examined. Since the same data collection methods were used in both phases of the study, the most likely factors that might account for the differences were the general meeting held with employees, at which training tips on shelving more accurately were given, and the subsequent individual interviews conducted to discuss the accuracy policy.

Standards are an important part of any job. Employees must know what is expected of them for optimum performance, thus enabling job continuance and satisfaction. Library service depends heavily on quick and accurate reshelving of materials. Since no statistical relationship was shown between speed and accuracy, but an apparent improvement did result during phase two, after calling shelvers' attention to expected performance standards, it can be inferred that a library might benefit from having a stated minimum shelving speed requirement and a specified accuracy percent. Accuracy checks could be done on shelvers often so problems can be corrected as they arise. The BYU experience indicates that it is effective for the Stacks Manager to impress on each employee's mind the importance of accurate shelving. One aim here would be to increase a shelver's sense of commitment to excellence in the library. In turn, this should increase the quality of work.

The methods used in this study could be implemented to determine what kinds of mistakes affect a shelver's accuracy, and then to work on improving areas of weakness. During phase two of the study, the tracer kept track of all subjects and their individual mistakes when materials were incorrectly shelved. This provided the BYU Stacks Manager with the information needed to go back to the individuals and help them improve on accuracy. Keeping track of why books are misplaced can also be useful in writing training manuals or explaining general principles of shelving accurately during group meetings.

As this study continued it became apparent that there is a wide range of factors possibly involved in the accuracy of library shelvers. Still needed are data from a third phase of this study. Now that circulation shelvers have been aware of the accuracy policy for three years, a third phase would provide more evidence about the relationship between speed and accuracy. Without actually gathering data it appears, from informal observation, that both speeds and accuracy percents are increasing.

The amount of "not found" books remains a concern. Further research should be done tracking down these books. This task would not be easy, but may be necessary in determining a complete accuracy picture.

A final possible area for future study could be to consider how such things as job security pressure, personality traits and individual work ethic affect shelving accuracy. Information about majors, personal habits, grade point, hobbies, interests, past work experience, etc., could be gathered on shelvers over a period of time. This data would then be compared to the shelver's accuracy percents and overall job performance. From this it may be helpful in determining what types of individuals are best suited for library shelving.

It is the author's hope that this study can be replicated in other library environments to see if these findings can be generalized and aid with setting up library shelving standards.

REFERENCE NOTES

1. William H. Jesse, *Shelf Work in Libraries* (Chicago:American Library Association, 1952), p. 3.
2. Dokun Fadiran, "Classification and Shelving of Periodicals in Academic Libraries in Nigeria," *The Serials Librarian,* Vol. 13 (September 1987): 107-111.
3. Kathi Kaempf, "Training and Supervision of Library Shelvers," (Los Angeles: University of Southern California, Norris Medical Library, 1975), p. 6, ERIC, ED 112886.
4. Stuart Hanabus, "The Importance of Performance Measures," *Library Review,* Vol. 36 (Winter 1987): p. 248-53.

5. Nathan Smith, "For Student Assistants-Programmed Training," *Utah Libraries*, Vol. 133 (Fall 1971): p. 13-15.

6. Curtis L. Kendrick, "Performance Measures of Shelving Accuracy," *Journal of Academic Librarianship* vol 17, no. 1 (March 1991): 16-18.

7. SAS Institute Inc., *SAS User's Guide: Statistics, Version 5 Edition* (Cary, NC: SAS Institute Inc., 1985).

APPENDIX A

WEEK # - Date

MONDAY- group 1

	bks chkd	errors	bks shlvd	time
NOT				
Shelver #1				
Shelver #2				
Shelver #3				

TUESDAY- group 3

Shelver #1
Shelver #2
Shelver #3

WEDNESDAY- group 4

Shelver #1
Shelver #2
Shelver #3

THURSDAY- group 2

Shelver #1
Shelver #2
Shelver #3

FRIDAY- group 5

Shelver #1
Shelver #2
Shelver #3

Measuring and Managing Circulation Activity Using Circulation Rates

Matthew S. Moore

SUMMARY. This paper examines the circulation rate, the measure of items checked out per unit time, as a more accurate and useful yardstick of circulation activity than monthly volume. The article defines formulas for calculating circulation rates including items/day and items/hour for libraries open different days and hours. Circulation rates can be applied to individual libraries, systems, and categories of materials. Also examined is the utility of the circulation rate as a work load standard to guide staffing for checkout and shelving.

INTRODUCTION

George S. Bonn stated humorously the common idea of the utility of yearly or monthly circulation volume measurements when he wrote: "Gross circulation statistics are useful for comparisons, for example with figures for different years or for different libraries, and they tend to be used to demonstrate to higher authorities how well the library is serving its clientele."[1] Implicit is that gross circulation statistics are of uncertain value, and rightly so: what skeptical higher authorities and circulation managers may not understand is that yearly or monthly volumes are unreliable when compared because of the varying number of days a library is open in different months or years. If a library circulates 10,000 books

---

Matthew S. Moore is Circulation Manager, Clearwater Public Library, 100 N. Osceola Ave., Clearwater, FL 34615.

during its 25 open days in January and another 10,000 books for 20 days open in February, then circulation was obviously "busier" during the shorter February–although the monthly totals reported remain the same. For a manager concerned with the rate at which work flows across the circulation desk, monthly volumes may give only part of the picture. As a useful way to quantify circulation activity, the circulation rate, which is the monthly volume divided by the number of days open, can be a viable alternative to using the standard "gross circulation statistics."

In a similarly deceptive way, peaks and valleys of circulation may he distorted by graphs of monthly circulation volumes. For instance, January and February would he graphed as equal volumes: the peak of activity in February would be truncated to January's level. Further, any calculation made using monthly volumes, such as a trendline, might he distorted to the extent that the two months measured different time periods. Figure 1 illustrates the contrast between volumes and circulation rates, showing that peak volume and peak circulation activity occur at different times of the year. During FY90-91 for the Clearwater Public Library System, the peak volume occurred in July, yet the peak activity occurred in February. In November, February, and September, volume fell but the circulation rate increased; by contrast in March volume increased while the circulation rate decreased. For these months, a manager might report either an increase or a decrease in activity.

Other librarians have been concerned with comparing statistics for disparate months and have employed several different strategies for equalizing data. A proposal in Nancy Van House's *Output Measures for Public Libraries, 2nd edition,* contains the inchoate idea for a circulation rate. In a section on materials use measures, the authors include as "Further Possibilities" that librarians "measure circulation per hour that the library is open." They note such a measurement might be "especially useful for comparing branches" as an alternative to circulation per capita. Only one measurement is defined, circulation per hour per year, calculated by dividing annual circulation by annual hours open.[2] The same proposal is made for academic libraries.[3] It should be noted that the authors of these works are searching for useful general output measures, not

FIGURE 1

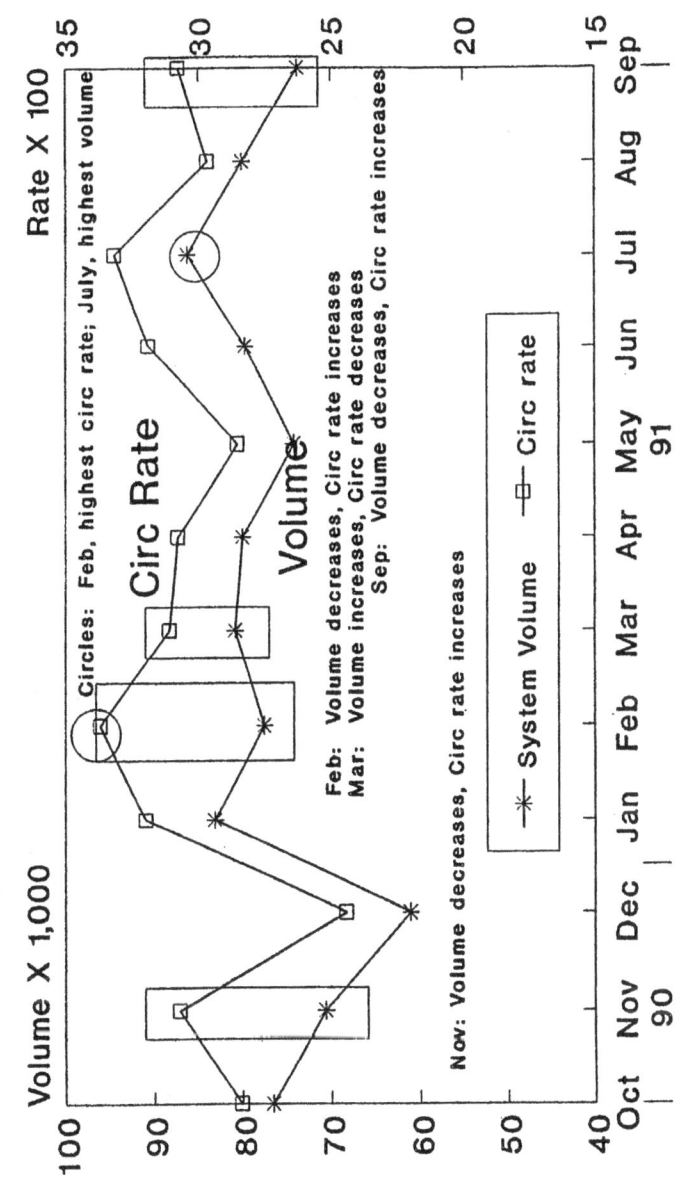

for a tool to measure circulation desk work rates, one of the best uses for circulation rates.

In her general review article "Output Measures in Libraries," Van House surveys numerous kinds of measurement models. The article's silence concerning the circulation rate recommended in *Output Measures for Public Libraries* and elsewhere suggests that this measurement remains an unexplored area.[4] Nevertheless, potentially valuable applications of circulation rates may help solve some measurement problems faced by circulation managers and other librarian. In a study of loan periods, Michael K. Buckland in *Book Availability and the Library User* employs percentages of total materials borrowed as his yardstick to compare effects of policies. He avoids the problem of the varied numbers of days in months by comparing one college term to the same term the next year, yet acknowledges differences in term lengths by noting, "the Autumn Term was nine weeks and the Spring Term was eleven weeks instead of the normal ten."[5] These methods–comparing like terms from one year to the next and using percentages–offer the manager acceptable tools for some studies, but those strategies have a drawback for work management studies. If in addition to measuring the success of the policy change, we were concerned with the effect on the circulation desk activities, then we find that percentages can mask a doubling of the work load from one year to the next. Buckland's chart of results shows that the volume of circulation increased 102-131% in one year.[6] Percentages of circulating volumes are calculated by the formula $\% = V_{part}/V_{whole}$ so that the effects of varying numbers of days in months or terms are not compensated in the formula; for example, in the initial illustration in which a library circulated the same number of books in January and February, both months would show the same percentages of the total volume of the year, although in February the library was more active at the circulation desk. In Buckland's study, the percentages of materials checked out over the two summer terms closely parallel each other; however, for the ten-week summer terms, if we assume the library was open 70 days, then the circulation rate for 1967-1968 was 183 items/day while the next year for the Summer Term the circulation rate was 454 items/day. Although the percentages of borrowing in each term remained stable, the workload more than doubled. Percentages based on volumes do not offer the manager the same kind of information as circulation rates.

Circulation rates may offer more precise information on the impact of decision-making on circulation. Buckland, for instance, graphs the effects of changing a loan policy by measuring time against annual borrowing.[7] Although his overall point is made clearly with volumes and his conclusions are sound, more precise measurements might have been made with circulation rates. The college he studied was open a different number of days each year, by as much as two weeks or more. For the Clearwater Library System, where the average annual circulation rate is above 3,000 items/day, a week would make a difference in circulation of 18,000 items and two weeks 36,000 items. Similar studies where the results are not so blatant might yield information to more precise numbers. In fact, Buckland notes that computer-aided systems will permit "a wide variety of complex analysis with far less effort than manual analysis."[8]

Paul B. Kantor in his exploration of the "vitality" of a collection calls for using the "average daily circulation" to estimate the number of books in circulation.[9] Interested in other areas, he does not explore "average daily circulation," but implicit in his discussion is deriving an items/day rate. Although his call for a circulation rate is a small aside in the overall article, it may be asked what daily circulation rate is needed. Circulation rates vary at Clearwater for the system by as much as 900 items/day from month to month, so that using that rate in a equation may require the yearly item/day rate.

Traditional monthly volume measures may be used to develop a *rate of activity* as a measurement for comparison. That rate of activity avoids the problem of measuring over different lengths of time and allows us to employ comparable units with which to understand changes in circulation activity. In brief, such a uniform *Circulation Rate* is a measure of activity per unit time, as $R = V/T$, where Rate equals Volume divided by Time. If Volume is measured in items checked out and if Time is a set number of days or hours, then this formula yields items checked out/day, or items/hour. The formula is a tool for measuring circulation rates during different time periods, and because the derived rates measure circulation activity with the same units, they invite comparisons. The circulation rate is an attempt to shape some of the numbers into something that will provide an insight into circulation activities.

It is possible to define several related circulation rates. A circulation rate that measures items checked out/day in a month is the most understandable and most useful. With a item/day rate, a manager might measure activity each month of the year and compare and contrast to find the truly busiest times and the developing trends. In addition, one can calculate down to items/hour when needed, for instance when comparing rates for libraries with different evening hours–in such a study, the library open the longest hours might have the greatest volume, yet not have the highest or busiest circulation rate. At the opposite scale, a items/day average throughout a year may prove useful for forecasting long range trends.

VISUALIZING AND USING CIRCULATION RATES

Some may find the circ rate more meaningful than raw volume in that they might find it difficult to visualize the difference between a circulated volume of 86,392 books and 57,361 books, except perhaps as a big pile or a condensed bar graph. Circ rate, however, is visualized as how many books are checked out on average, per day, or per hour. It might be easier to visualize the difference between those same numbers rendered as 1,000 books/day and 750 books/day, or 100 books/hour and 75 books/hour.

A circ rate is an average rate, not an absolute, so that it is subject to all of the problems associated with comparing averages. The average rate may never really occur: a grade point average does not mean you always get that grade, nor does averaging 65 miles/hour mean you weren't speeding. If books are checked out in a boom and bust cycle at the circ desk, the average rate may be misleading. On the other hand, to the extent that the rate reflects accurately what is happening, it can be used to assess the work rate, or average "busyness," at a circulation desk, or to compare work rates at different libraries. Circ rates in themselves do not "prove" anything, but are tools with which one can measure activity to suggest trends and needs.

A suggestion in *Academic Library Performance* asks librarians to look at "Circulation for specific parts of the collection (e.g., by classification or shelving location or type of material)."[10] The circulation rate formula may be employed to track the rate at which nonfiction, paperbacks, or videos circulate-anything one wishes to count consistently-at a branch or system-wide. Once rates with the same units are calculated, they may be used to compare categories from branch to branch, or from month to month. Figure 2 is an example illustrating a month's circulation rates activity, which allows a manager to study the effects of merchandising those categories and to observe the degree of growth or loss irrespective of its cause.

Circulation rates might provide information in various managerial situations. For example, a manager might wish to study what effect on circulation might result from increased stocking of books at one branch compared to another which has different hours. Another might wish to find the effects of dividing a videotape collection currently at one branch between two branches, which have different hours of operation. Still another might want to study the effect of opening a library on Sundays-will the circulation increase or only spread out over a longer week? Circulation rates can offer a tool that will yield more accurate measurements for comparisons than monthly volumes in these situations. Because circulation rates give comparable terms, they might clarify trends and seasonal variations in circulation that monthly volumes may obscure. And of course computer-generated numbers may be linked into spreadsheets, or used with Harvard Graphics. As a caveat, circulation rates may produce their own distortions when comparing libraries opened different hours during the day. A day for one library may mean eight hours open, for another ten hours. This problem will be discussed below.

CALCULATING WITH THE RATE FORMULA

Calculating circulation rates is generally a simple operation: to calculate the average daily rate over a month for a single library

FIGURE 2

Circulation Totals Monthly, in items checked out							
Month	Days	MAIN	EAST	CSIDE	BEACH	GWOOD	SYSTEM
Aug91	27	27,590	28,433	20,691	2,068	1,312	80,094
Sep91	24	25,197	26,248	19,009	1,911	1,430	73,795
Oct91	27	27,625	27,236	19,114	2,290	1,580	77,845
YTD							
Circulation Rates Monthly, in items/day							
Aug91		1,022	1,053	766	77	49	2,966
Sep91		1,050	1,094	792	80	60	3,075
Oct91		1,023	1,009	708	85	59	2,883
Circulation: Totals; Rates; Change from last month, from last year							
27		Main	East	Cside	Beach	GWood	System
Fiction Total		7217	7032	5066	1127	466	20,908
Fiction Rate		267	260	188	42	17	774
Change: month/yr		+2/+14	-9/-7	-2/+3	+2/-9	-3/-5	-9/-4
Children Total		5479	6339	5168	50	577	17,613
Children Rate		203	235	191	2	21	652
Change: month/yr		+10/+27	-3/-30	-33/+8	0/-2	0/-5	-39/+16
Nonfict Total		7546	5594	4832	409	319	18,700
Nonfict Rate		279	207	179	15	12	693
Change: month/yr		-19/+23	-14/-6	-15/+32	0/-3	+1/+1	-41/+47
VHS Total		4563	5258	2331	2	3	12,157
VHS Rate		169	195	86	0	0	450
Change: month/yr		-9/+39	-18/+21	-22/+3	0/0	0/0	-50/+47
Paperbk Total		2654	2518	1646	701	160	7,679
Paperbk Rate		98	93	61	26	6	284
Change: month/yr		-10/+13	-13/-24	-11/-22	+3/+4	+1/-6	-31/-44
Cat 0 Total		166	495	71	1	55	788
Cat 0 Rate		6	18	6	0	2	29

open the same hours each day, one needs the number of items circulated in the month and the number of days opened that month:

$R = V/T$, Circ Rate equals Volume divided by Time in days.

If at County Library, V = 28,438 items checked out in January; and T = 26 days opened (of ten hours each); then R_{Jan} = 1,094 items checked/10 hr day in January. This rate can be visualized as 1,094 books checked out each day open, or by simple division by 10 hours per day, 109 books checked out each hour (or even 1.8 books/minute).

Further, suppose City Library checked out 27,350 items in January, but was closed on a holiday, so was opened 25 days. In addition, City Library stayed open on a 9-5 schedule, an 8-hour day. City Library's circ rate is 30,675 items/25 days, or 1,094 items/day. However, the 1,094 items/day at City library is not comparable to the 1,094 at County Library, because of the different hours open. Because City Library was opened an 8 hour day, its items/hour rate is 137 books/hour compared to County Library's 109 books/hour.

Essentially, the calculation of the circulation rate is straightforward, plugging the volume and number of days open into the formula. But those rates may have variable meanings to the "day," whether 8 hours, 10 hours, or whatever. It is important to be consistent. If a number of libraries are open the same hours, then calculating comparable circulation rates is a straightforward use of the formula. Parallel rates may be derived for any number of libraries by using the Circ Rate formula: R_1; R_2; R_3. . . .

A *system rate* may be tallied, a useful figure for a municipal or county system, or a college with multiple libraries. The system rate may be found by either of two methods. To find R_{sys}, add $R_1 + R_2 + R_3$. . . . The resulting system rate will tell one how many books/day were checked out system-wide.

A second, simpler method of calculating a system circulation rate involves dividing the total system circulation by the number of days open. To be clear concerning the time unit, T in this case is the number of days any one library is open, since all are open the same number of days. R_{sys} = System Volume/T, where Total Volume is the total number of items circulated by all the libraries:

$$R_{sys} = V_{sys}/T_{\text{days open during month}}$$

As an example, consider $R_1 = 1,094$ items/day (from above); for R_2, let $V_{Jan} = 27,686$ items checked out, and $T = 26$ days (of 10 hours), so $R_2 = 1,065$ items/day. $R_{sys} = R_1 + R_2 = 2,159$ items/day. Or using $R_{sys} = V_{sys}/T = (V_1 + V_2)/T = 56,125$ items/26 days $= 2,159$ items/day. Each method produces the same system rate and may serve as a check, if needed.

It is mathematically more interesting to compare two or more libraries open the same hours but a different number of days. One can calculate an individual circulation rate for each library according to the circulation rate formula–using the different number of days each is open. These rates will give an accurate idea of the work rate at each library. A difficulty lies in finding a *system rate*. The two individual rates cannot be simply added together, because the libraries are open different numbers of days. For instance, if over a ten day period, Alpha Library is open only one day and circulates 1,000 books, its rate is 1,000 items/day; if Beta Library is open all ten days and circulates 20,000 books, its rate is 2,000 items/day. But to conclude that the system rate is 3,000 items/day (by adding $R_A + R_B$) is an absurdity because that approximate rate only occurs the first day; the second through the tenth day only about 2,000 items/day circulate. So the average daily circulation over the ten day measured period is much lower than 3,000 items/day–and is somewhere between 2,000 and 3,000 items/day.

The solution to finding a *system rate* for libraries open different numbers of days is to proportion one of the library's rates to the other; as a rule of thumb, change the one with the shorter number of days to match the one with the longer number of days, according to the following method:

$$R_{\text{adjusted}} = (R_s)(T_s)/T_1 \text{ or } = V_s/T_1, \text{ where } s = \text{shorter}, 1 = \text{longer}.$$

This formula produces numbers with the same units, which can be added to give a system circulation rate. One word of caution: The adjusted rate of the shorter opened library is an "as if" average, as if the library were open the same hours as the longer one. The greater the differential between the number of days open, the greater the distortion for that library's actual work rate.

A simpler, more direct method of arriving at the system rate for two or more libraries open different numbers of days is by dividing the monthly combined total of items circulated by the number of days of the longest opened library:

$$R_{sys} = V_{sys\ total}/T_{longest}$$

For example, let us use the numbers calculated above for Alpha and Beta Libraries: R_{sys} = 21,000 items total/10 days opened = 2,100 items/day for the average daily rate over ten days.[11] The system rate, however, will be an accurate average rate of books checked out per day, although the actual rate on any day may be much higher on some and much lower on others. The utility of this system rate lies in deriving a simple, overall number for multiple libraries. Such a rate may be used to compare overall circulation activity from month to month.

The next level, which allows comparisons between two or more libraries open different hours and numbers of days, is the determination of hourly rates. If, however, the difference between the hourly and daily rates is not great, one might treat the rates as if they were the same–with great caution–using the method above to proportion one library to another. In such a case, it is necessary to calculate a few rates to check to see how much distortion is created and if it is tolerable.

When needed or helpful, hourly rates can be easily determined. To calculate hourly rates directly, follow generally the same method for daily rates, except include the number of hours open each month:

$$R_h = V/Hours\ open\ per\ month$$

This formula yields items checked out per hour. Hours, like days, can be proportioned to arrive at a system rate in items/hour. Suppose there are two libraries on a college campus open different days and hours per month, and as a manager you need an accurate idea of the work rate at each library. Suppose Founder's Library circulates 40,456 items in July and was opened 250 hours, while Benefactor's Branch circulated 30,987 items but was opened only 200 hours. Does the level of activity call for shifting a student aide from one to the other?

$$R_f = 40{,}456 \text{ items}/250 \text{ hours} = 162 \text{ items/hour}.$$
$$R_b = 30{,}987 \text{ items}/200 \text{ hours} = 155 \text{ items/hour}.$$

The work rate at the circulation desk for checkout is only a 7 item/hour difference, virtually equal.

The same concerns about comparing monthly volumes apply for yearly volumes: libraries usually are not open exactly the same number of days each year, and a difference of a few days can mean may thousands of circulations, even tens of thousands. It is possible and practical to calculate and compare yearly rates in the same manner as monthly rates.

At the end of a year, using the circulation rate formula, one may divide the total number of items checked out per year by the number of days (or hours) opened during the year to yield an average daily checkout rate throughout the year:

$$R_{year} = V_{year}/T_{\text{days open in a year}}$$

Because the number of days opened during each year may vary, the circulation rate offers a more accurate idea of activity than volume, and rates can be compared year to year where raw volumes may be misleading. For example, in FY88-89, the year's volume for the Clearwater Public Library System was 890,183 items checked out in 301 days, while the next year FY89-90, the system volume was 879,851 items in 298 days. It seems that circulation activity decreased in FY89-90, since the difference in volumes suggests a drop of $-10{,}332$ items; however, being open three days fewer in FY89-90 had a effect:

$$R_{88\text{-}89} = 890{,}183 \text{ items}/301 \text{ days} = 2{,}957 \text{ items/day}$$
$$R_{89\text{-}90} = 879{,}851 \text{ items}/298 \text{ days} = 2{,}953 \text{ items/day}$$

The difference between rates suggests that circulation fell only 4 items/day system-wide, a negligible difference. The volume difference of 10,332 items occurred almost entirely because of the three fewer days opened. Note that the average 89-90 rate of 2,953 items/day multiplied by three days gives 8,859 items as the projected loss for being closed three days. Compared to the gross difference of −10,332 items, the difference between the actual count and the loss from being closed is −1,473 items, less than a day's circulation, suggesting that concern generated by a drop in volume might be misplaced.

CREATING INFORMATION

Rates can be used to produce practical information, usually by comparing or contrasting. A simple and productive use for rates is to create graphs of items/day for each month throughout the year. Such graphs have been produced at the Clearwater Public Library since going online in 1985 and reveal one or two surprises. For instance, it was commonly believed that circulation slowed during the summer months compared to the winter season, during which population doubles because of the arrival of winter residents and tourists. Graphs of monthly circ rates reveal summer slowdown as a counter-intuitive myth: circulation rates climb, but not because there are more people–there are fewer–but because the item/person rate climbs with the high check-out per person of children's books and of videotapes. Traffic at the circulation desk feels slower because some children check out stacks of books during the summer months, so there are fewer people arriving at the desk, compared to the many people during winter who only check out a few items each. Door counts show a thousand fewer people enter the branch libraries during July than in January. Figure 1 shows the peaks of activity in July contrasted to January and February.

Graphs over several years reveal a cyclical rhythm for Clearwater's Beach Library. Charted over six years, the rates are twice as high during January through March as during summer, June through August. Inspection of records shows that the Beach Library, little used by children, serves a comparatively older adult population. Its circulation configuration follows that of the tourist season or the "snow birds," who reside in the area only during the winter. Such knowledge allows possible allocation of monies for collection development away from children's materials into adult fiction and adult paperbacks. The circulation rates might be the basis for shifting staff to and from the library to meet the peak periods. Figure 3 shows the cyclical rhythm of circulation at the Clearwater Beach Library.

Graphing rates reveals that in December there occurs a drop in circulation. Analysis of the December dip through week by week tracking shows this occurs entirely within the week before and the week after Christmas, probably a school vacation phenomenon combined with the holiday press of shopping and visiting. As with summer circulation, videotape use rises, perhaps with the leisure time, perhaps with purchase of new tape-playing machines. The December dip is clearly seen in Figure 4.

Additional information may be derived from existing studies to compare with figures managers have on hand. For instance, Allen Kent's *Use of Library Materials: The University of Pittsburgh Study* develops "measures for determining the extent to which library materials . . . are used, and the full cost of such use."[12] Although circulation rates were not part of this study, the authors offer projected "usage statistics" for various campus libraries based on sampling circulation. The figures cited for "Projected Yearly Use" are given together with the hours open per trimester.[13] One can easily calculate the number of hours open per year for each college library, and using the formula derive a circulation rate for each library. For instance, usage ranges from a low of 0.6 items/hour in the Computer Science Library to a high of 5.4 items/hour at the Life Sciences Library. The intent here is to suggest that the manager can convert existing studies for comparisons to his or her own library and derive comparable measures despite differing days or hours opened; further, this particular study suggests that if actual total counts are unavailable samples may provide useful statistics.

In a related area, statistics gathered yearly by state libraries and others that list total circulations and hours open also may be converted to circulation rates for comparisons that are perhaps more meaningful to circulation managers than circulations per capita.

FIGURE 3

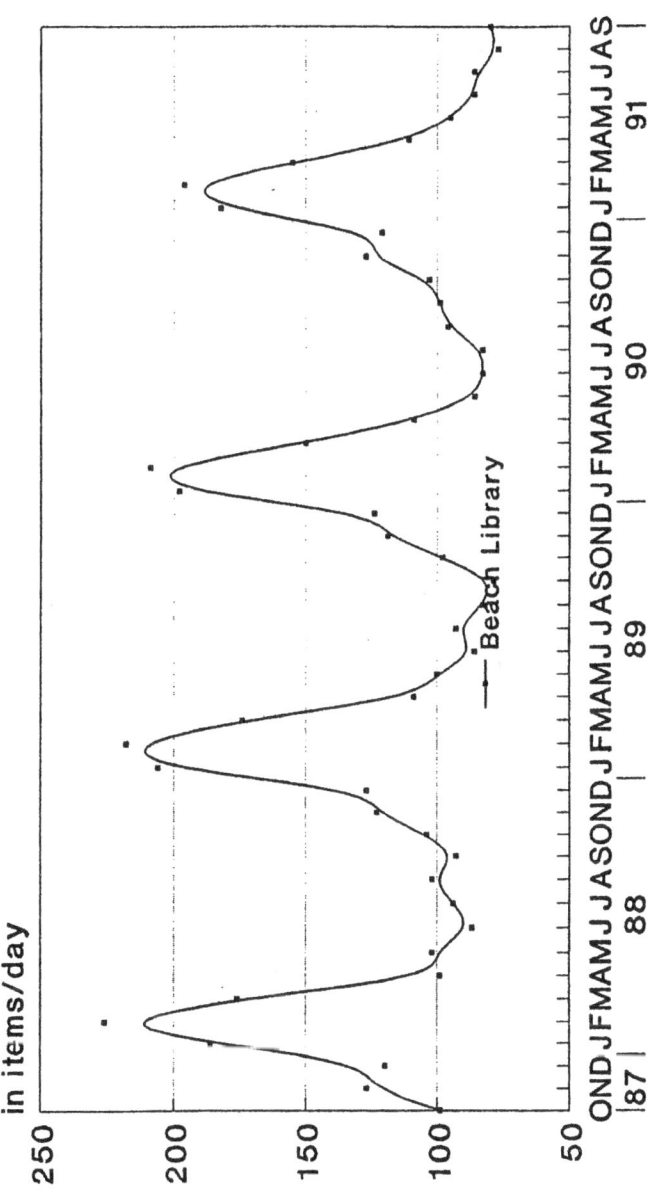

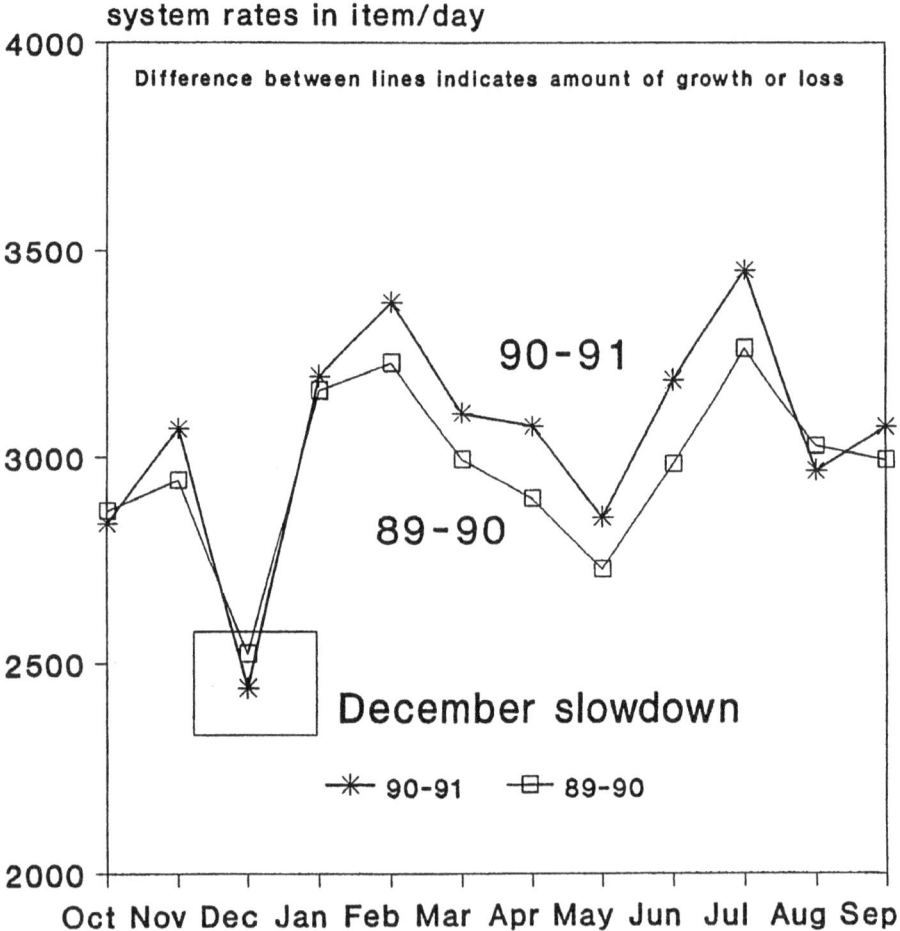

FIGURE 4

Circulation rates may provide additional meaning to some previous studies. For example, in 1975 Virginia E. Yagello and Gerry Guthrie published a study on the effect on user satisfaction of shortening the circulation period from three weeks to one week in a physics library.[14] The loan period of high use items was shortened and circulation compared in a period of three months, April through June, 1973, to the same period in 1974. A 20% increase in charges by students was the most significant result of the change.

In such a study with a relatively small volume of usage, a difference in days and hours open during the studied months *might* have made a measurable difference in the results. Let us assume that the physics library was opened 91 days in each of the periods studied as well as the same hours each day. The circulation rate for student charges was 12.2 books/day in 1973 for a three-week loan period and 14.7 books/day in 1974 for the one-week loan period. The increase brought about by the change of loan period was 2.5 books/day, which is a 20% increase. A further look at renewal statistics, which the authors note "increased markedly" as "expected," shows that in 1973 the renewal rate was 4.0 books/day for the three-week loan, but in 1974 the renewal rate rose sharply to 14.0 books/day, a substantial 250% increase.[15] Perhaps an additional conclusion that may be reached from the same data is that a latent but powerful message in the data is that the greatest effect of shortening the loan period is to increase renewal rates dramatically. This is not to suggest that the authors' conclusions are incorrect, but that they may be incomplete. The data seem to show both that user satisfaction increased slightly in terms of the greater number of individual checkouts and that another kind of user satisfaction decreased as demonstrated by the great increase in renewals (assuming that those students who renewed materials would not have had to do so under the previous system).

In terms of work rates, the shortening of the loan period increased the work activity (i.e., checkouts plus renewals) from 16.2 items/day to 28.6 items/day in order to increase checkout of 2.5 items/day to more students. At this rate, if the library was ten times busier its work rate of 162 items/day would increase to 286 items/day in order to increase checkouts to 25 items/day. If it was

100 times larger, the rates would increase from 1,620 items/day to 2,860 items/day in order to allow 250 more checkouts per day. The work rate would increase 76% for a customer satisfaction increase of 20%. Analysis of the data in this study suggests effects beyond the desired result, provides an additional perspective to the issue, and may make policy changes such as providing duplicates of high demand items more appealing or more cost effective. The reanalysis of the data in terms of circulation rates perhaps offers a tool to clarify the meaning of data and possibly to suggest additional or corrective inferences from data.

Just as changing circulation loan periods affects work rates, so too may changing the hours open affect work rates. A manager might find that lengthening hours decreased the circulation rate per hour as some library users shift their library use to later hours. Staffing needs may thus be affected; similarly, shortening hours may intensify circulation, so that the work rate at the circulation desk increases.

In consonance with the suggestion in *Measuring Academic Library Performance* that circulation be tracked for segments of the collection or by shelving areas, Clearwater Library defined a number of categories reflecting efforts to merchandise the collection to the public and to track growth or loss. Utilizing circulation rates for this purpose allows a accurate comparative analysis of categories of circulated materials. At Clearwater, all materials are assigned statistical category numbers, which are gathered into general categories of Fiction (adult material in any format except videotapes, which have a shorter circulation period), Children's (fiction and nonfiction in any format except videotapes), Nonfiction (adult material in any format except videotapes), Browsing Paperbacks (adult-fiction and nonfiction, browsing collection only), Videotapes and a small group of non-categorized items called Category 0. Statistical records reveal that since 1985 the Fiction category circulates fastest, followed by Nonfiction, Children's, Videotapes, Paperbacks, and Category 0. Nonfiction circulation, which at academic libraries may have the highest circulation, surges during the winter or school season at Clearwater, but falls precipitously with the beginning of summer, when Children's circulation rises. Figure 5 contrasts Nonfiction and Children's circulation rates, monthly. Data are collected for each branch and the main library, so that

FIGURE 5

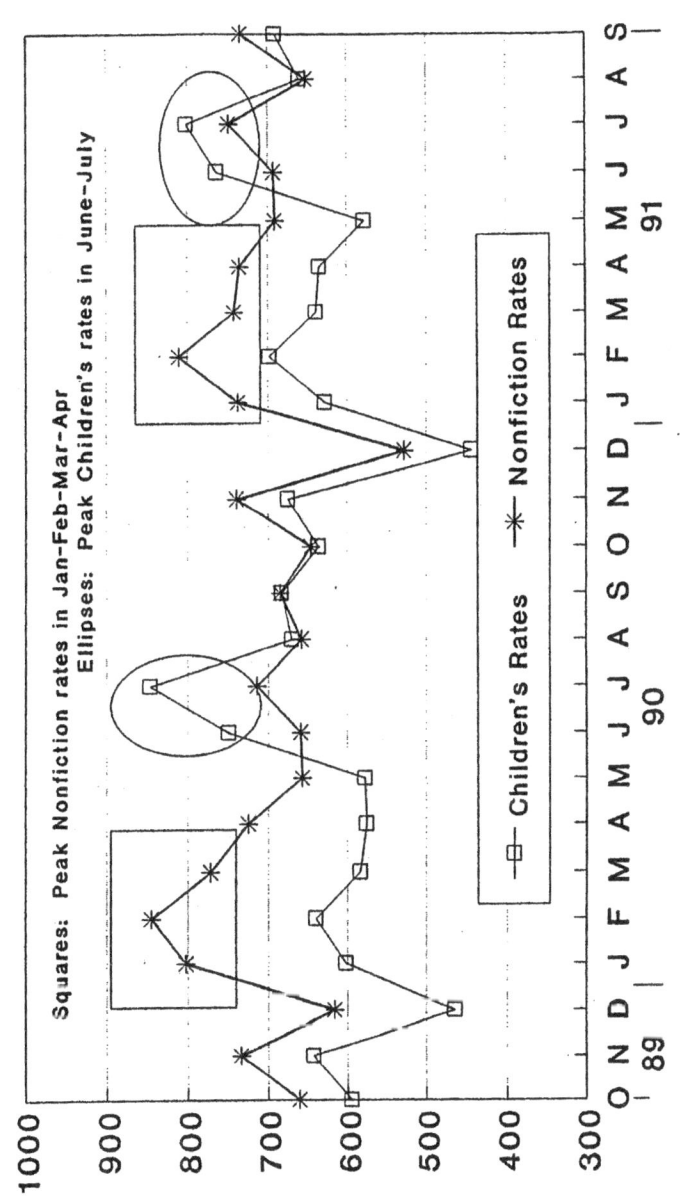

comparison and contrasts may be made in each category from branch to branch or summarized to show how the system as a whole circulates each category.

Various studies of circulation patterns break down overall circulation into its parts, such as Buckland does when studying loan periods and examining circulation of such categories as "History of the Americas," "Chemistry, and "Linguistics." [16] A further use of circulation rates might be to compare the circulation of science books from a science library compared to those from a science room at a central campus library that duplicates or overlaps the collection. Because circulation rates allow comparison of libraries with different opening hours and days, one can determine the comparative rates for the purpose of allocating staff.

Circulation rates allow a manager to track work flow through growth or decline and possibly to adjust hours between libraries. A manager can use circulation rates to decide whether or not the daily or hourly work loads are equitable among libraries or at desks, and use knowledge of the work rates, along with other factors, to consider how best to allocate staff. Much of this analysis draws from the realm of observational studies. For example, my estimate from observations at the Clearwater County Library circulation desks indicates that, without creating lines, one person can scan barcodes for checkout up to 100 items/hour, or about 800 items/day for 8 hours. Above 60 items/hour, or 1 item/minute, a second person is needed for rush periods or if the desk is assigned other work in addition to checkout, such as renewals by telephone or issuing library cards. Above 800 items/day, almost certainly two people are necessary to provide service without delays; for instance, if the rate reaches 1,000 items/day, which is 125 items/hour for 8 hours or 2 items/minute, then two people each handle about 1 item/minute. Here it is helpful to calculate standard deviations for monthly circulation rates in order to consider the extremes of work flow.

Circulation rates may also offer the access services manager some insight in allocating staff for shelving. When the book return rate is direct in proportion to the checkout rate, one may be able to let checkout rates be an index of the work rate expected for shelving; however, if there is a return at the end of the semester loan period or there is a high in-library use, a check-in rate may be found as well by the same methods. If returned books are not to pile up in the library and if a manager holds to the principle that work coming in should equal work going out–here meaning the amount of books returned in a day should be shelved within 24 hours–then at a basic level, *the shelving rate must equal the circulation rate.* If a library averages 800 items/day checked out over a month, or 1200 items/day, then the shelving rate must match those rates in order for work to be cleared within a day and not cause a backlog.

One can calculate a shelving rate by practical observation. If during a month, X number of shelvers are able to just keep up with the book returns, then the work rate for the shelvers is the circulation rate. Suppose five shelvers working 10 hours each week in a library open six days per week are just able to keep up with returned books during a month with a circulation rate of 1000 items/day. Then each week the five shelvers work 50 hours to shelve 6,000 books. The shelving rate for the five is 1,000 books/day; however, for a hourly rate per worker, one takes the total shelving hours per week divided into the weekly total to find 6,000 volumes/50 hours = 120 books/hour, or 2 books/minute, as an average shelving rate. If the shelvers work equally well, then each shelves 1,200 books/week, or 200/day. If the circulation rate increases to 12,000 books/day, then the manager needs one extra shelver; if the circulation rate decreases to 800 books/day, then the manager can assign one person to do other tasks.

Lastly, a final application might be the calculation of trendlines. Again volumes may be deceptive because of the different number of days in months; using rates may create a more reliable slope to a trendline. Figure 6 is an exaggerated example of trendlines calculated with volumes and circulation rates to illustrate the difference. For the period January through March 1990, a trendline calculated with circulation rates shows declining activity, but a trendline calculated with volumes shows increasing numbers.

CONCLUSION

Some final observations from several years of tracking circulation rates may be of general interest. Because circulation rates can

FIGURE 6

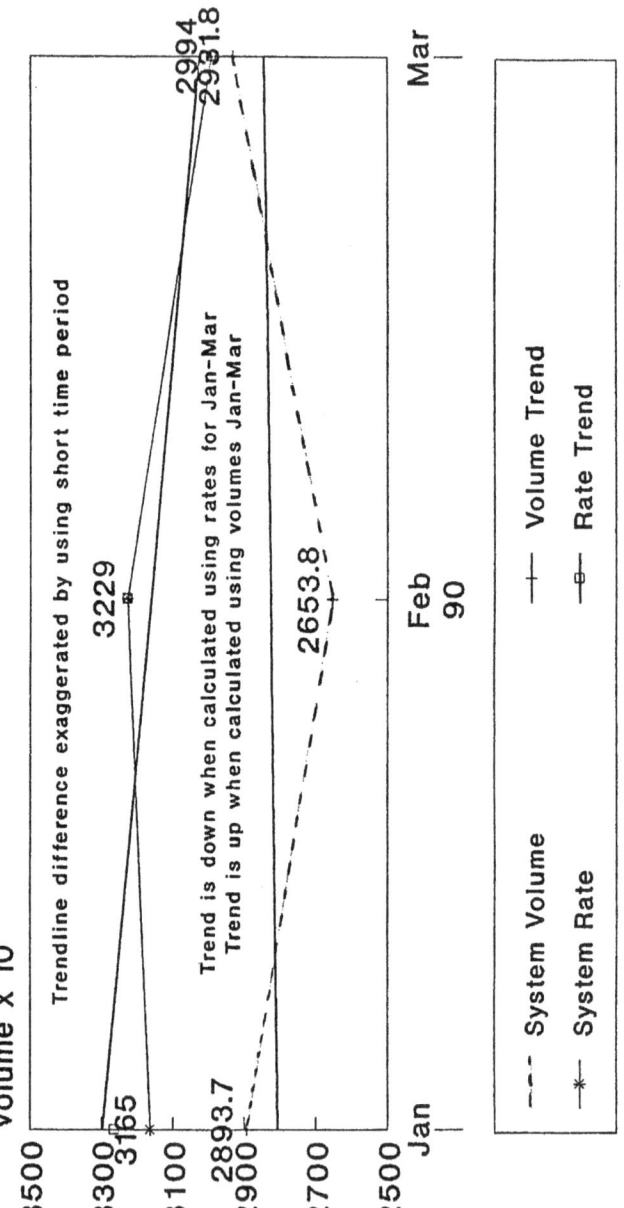

measure changes in use patterns, a manager may be able to check the effects of policy changes on circulation. In practice, however, a policy about which there is much debate may have little or no measurable effect on circulation rate.

Programming, for instance, may draw large crowds of people to the library at one time and may or may not be accompanied by check-out of large numbers. If the desired result of programming is to increase circulation in a large library, the results may be disappointing in that averaged over a month the net effect of the programs might result in no noticeable increase in overall circulation rates. Such programs as children's story times may affect a daily rate, for instance, as large numbers of children's books are checked out on Wednesday mornings and may build habits that support circulation–but the absence of such programs may only spread the same circulation over a week rather than concentrate it in a day. Further, often the programming is done at a time of greatest circulation activity so that increase caused by programming is obscured by the general expected increase in activity.

Only very large trends affect circulation rates–to increase a rate by one book/day means either one new person must check out twenty-five books or more once during the month, or twenty-five new patrons must check out one book each day. (And no prior patron may cease using the library or take less than usual). It is extremely difficult for librarians to do anything that would create such a situation–and to increase a circulation rate by ten books/day calls for one new or current patron to check out 250 books, or 250 new or current patrons to each check out one. The kind of very large social activities that affect circulation rates are beyond the control of librarians–seasons, school terms, population trends. The kind of thing that librarians perhaps can control that affect circulation rates are budgets, building new branches, and setting hours and loan periods. Circulation rates demonstrate that only large sustained changes in patterns affect overall circulation.

That caveat aside, however, circulation rates can be very versatile tools for monitoring collection use over periods of time, for examining patterns of circulation in categories of materials, and for allocating resources and predicting workloads. By studying circulation rates, the access services manager can obtain useful perspective on departmental operations and, most important, compensate for distortions and misrepresentations that are so frequently inherent in volume rate measurements.

REFERENCE NOTES

1. George S. Bonn, "Evaluation of the Collection," *Library Trends* 22:272 (January 1974).
2. Nancy A. Van House et al., *Output Measures for Public Libraries: A Manual of Standardized Procedures*, 2nd ed. (Chicago: American Library Association, 1987), p. 44.
3. Nancy Van House et al., *Measuring Academic Library Performance: A Practical Approach* (Chicago: American Library Association, 1990), p. 55.
4. Nancy Van House, "Output Measures in Libraries," *Library Trends* 38:44 (Fall, 1989).
5. Michael K. Buckland, *Book Availability and the Library User* (New York: Pergamon Press Inc, 1975), p. 122.
6. Ibid., p. 122.
7. Ibid., p. 121.
8. Ibid., p. 119.
9. Paul B. Kantor, "Vitality: An Indirect Measure of Relevance," *Collection Management* 2:2:92 (Spring 1978).
10. VanHouse, *Academic Library Performance* p. 55.
11. Derivation of the rate formula: What is the average circulation rate of two libraries over the longer number of days open? Let $R_1 = V_1/T_1$ and $R_2 = V_2/T_2$.

$$(R_{sys})(T_2) = (R_1)(T_1) + (R_2)(T_2)$$

$$R_{sys} = \frac{R_1 T_1 + R_2 T_2}{T_2}$$

Since $R = V/T$, then $R_{sys} = \dfrac{\dfrac{V_1}{T_1} T_1 + \dfrac{V_2}{T_2} T_2}{T_2}$

$R_{sys} = \dfrac{V_1 + V_2}{T_2}$ or, rearranged $R_{sys} = \dfrac{V_1}{T_2} + R_2$, so $R_1 = \dfrac{V_1}{T_2}$

12. Allen Kent et al., *Use of Library Materials: The University of Pittsburgh Study* (New York: Marcel Dekker, Inc., 1979, p. 1.
13. Ibid., p. 216-17.
14. Virginia E. Yagello and Gerry Guthrie, "The Effect of Reduced Loan Periods on High Use Items," *College & Research Libraries* 36:411-14 (Sept. 1975).
15. Ibid., p. 413.
16. Buckland, p. 90.

Triage Assessment and Management Measures for Access Services

Barry Brown

SUMMARY. Most libraries record a wide variety of numerical measures and descriptive statistics in an attempt to measure the use of their collections and services and to track any changes in those patterns. Nevertheless, if this information has no practical applications, then the entire data collection process is of little utility. In this article, the concept of triage management (which separates tasks into categories of "can wait," "hopeless," and "urgent") and the use of descriptive statistics are discussed in terms of how they relate to various functions of access services. Examples of the use of simple numerical measures to better manage changing patterns of work loads between areas of access services are examined from the University of Montana, Mansfield Library.

INTRODUCTION

Most libraries record a wide variety of numerical measures and descriptive statistics in an attempt to measure the use of their collections and services and to track any changes in those patterns. All too often this quantitative record remains unanalyzed and unused for management decisions or strategic planning. Annual reports are replete with data collected from a variety of sources, but if this information has no practical applications the entire data collection process is of little use. There is a large pool of literature devoted

---

Barry Brown is Access Services Coordinator and Science Librarian at the University of Montana, Mansfield Library, in Missoula, MT.

to library research methods and the use of statistics by librarians (e.g., Dougherty and Heinritz 1982;[1] Swisher and McClure 1984;[2] Lancaster 1988;[3] Vasi 1989[4]), and on the evaluation and measurement of library services (e.g., Lancaster 1977,[5] Murphy 1990,[6] Van House et al. 1990[7]). Several authors (Budd 1982;[8] Christensen 1988[9]) caution against the use of poorly constructed statistics and warn that quantitative studies should be done thoroughly or not at all, and that this process takes quite a lot of time.

With the advent of automated library systems, reports of all kinds are routinely generated at daily, monthly, or yearly intervals. Every system is different but most provide statistical reports on various types of transactions, and some provide special reports such as purchase alerts for items in high demand or missing. Some systems come with pre-programmed batch reports but also allow custom configured reports on almost any variable or combination of variables. This plethora of information can help provide a detailed snapshot of the activities within access services.

However, despite an abundance of papers and books on this topic, there is a paucity of information on using simple descriptive statistics and evaluative measures to manage an access services department or its components. Evaluation and measurement should be linked to goal setting, decision making and the allocation of resources. Access services are integrally related to the use of library materials. Therefore the effectiveness of access services can be measured and evaluated, to a large extent, by the careful analysis of statistics about use and reports on user activities.

Patron use statistics may also provide a glimpse into the unique nature of access services operations. These services involve a very high degree of public contact in situations of varying degrees of complexity. Providing services to patrons will generally be given a higher priority than the clerical tasks of the department and further, certain types of patrons services will have higher priorities than others. Statistics can yield useful information on how these priorities are being met and how staff can best be used to assure they will be met.

A concept that is frequently applied in access services, whether consciously or not, is that of "triage." Triage is a term originally used for battlefield assessment of the wounded, and later to all emergency medical screening of patients. Cases needing attention, under this principle, are separated into three categories: (1) the superficially wounded (can wait to treat); (2) the mortally wounded (hopeless to treat); and (3) the critical but treatable (urgent treatment needed). This concept has been borrowed and applied to various other fields such as social welfare, education, and librarianship.

Intner (1987)[10] applied the concept to handling cataloging backlogs, and Naito (1991)[11] described the use of triage in library management and concluded that it was a highly effective method for prioritizing problems in need of attention and for decision making. The essence of triage can be further applied to the daily/weekly prioritization of memos, meetings and requests. When faced with a seemingly endless and ever increasing volume of work, which is compounded by a fixed amount of time, staff, or resources, the practice of separating tasks into categories of "can wait," "hopeless," and "urgent" offers a powerful means of prioritizing one's schedule and the needs of various areas under one's supervision.

In the following sections, the concept of triage management and the use of descriptive statistics will be discussed in terms of how they relate to various functions of access services. Every institution has its own unique environment, particular priorities, and special needs. Triage can provide a method of reassessing conflicting priorities. Examples are given from the University of Montana, Mansfield Library, to demonstrate the use of simple numerical measures to better manage changing patterns of work loads in access service areas.

CIRCULATION AND STACK MAINTENANCE

In addition to their primary functions of circulating materials and maintaining the stacks, most circulation departments also perform a variety of extraneous tasks and duties (e.g., checking out typewriters, checking out keys to rooms, etc.). Keeping a list of every task or duty done in an area can be one step toward comprehensively documenting the scope of those duties (as well as building evidence against the routine addition of further duties). This list of duties is a qualitative measure that can be converted to a quantitative measure by estimating the time needed to accomplish each task and the frequency with which each task is done. Dougherty and Heinritz (1982)[12] give procedures for work sampling and time studies. With this information, the access services manager can gain a better understanding of the department's workflow, and establish limits of how many tasks can be handled without interfering with primary operations.

The area of stack maintenance, for example, is critical for making materials available to patrons and should be monitored statistically. Many helpful techniques for sampling the collection and determining various shelving statistics (e.g., lost books) are given by Hubbard (1981).[13] Instead of methodically shelf reading the entire collection, Kohl (1982)[14] describes the approach of periodically performing random samples of stack subgroups to determine those areas most in need of it. A technique for predicting future shelving needs using a computer software spreadsheet program is reported by Wallace (1990).[15] Accuracy and speed of shelving by student workers should be stressed through tests given during hiring, training and evaluations (Schabo and Breuer 1989;[16] Sharp 1992[17]). Such studies and techniques might provide background information for the creation of daily prioritized lists of stack maintenance tasks (i.e., reshelving, shelf reading, shifting), which can be left for student workers by a stack supervisor. These lists, which should require initialing by students to indicate what they have done, can provide a method of monitoring productivity. Developing performance standards for various tasks would also be useful.

An example of triage management for this area might be: (1) urgent, critically wounded but treatable: end of academic session reshelving (2) hopeless, mortally wounded: lack of adequate shelf space which requires major shifting of the collection; and (3) can wait, superficially wounded: routine shelf reading.

RESERVE

The processing of materials for reserve is similar to the cataloging and processing functions within technical services. The question of prioritizing the processing order of materials can be critical once the academic session has started. Processing in a simple chronological order (i.e., in order of date the materials or requests were dropped off) is not always the optimal strategy. There may be "emergency requests" (e.g., when an instructor's textbook has not come in yet at the campus bookstore) for special rush processing. Considerations include: some materials are easier to process than others (e.g., library books versus personal xerographic copies, which require copyright approval); some requests are easier to fulfill than others (e.g., all materials dropped off versus recall requests for checked out items or copy requests for articles); some instructors drop off large numbers of items (even though only a few are needed right away) while others bring materials on a staggered basis or only have a few items on reserve; and some courses have hundreds of students (all wanting to know where the material is that was assigned in class) while others have only a few. Meeting the needs of the largest number of users while remaining fair and abiding by stated policies can be a formidable challenge.

An example of triage management for this area might be: (1) urgent, critically wounded but treatable: processing rush requests; (2) hopeless, mortally wounded: full service for reserve requests (e.g., pulling all materials, copying all requests, etc.); and (3) can wait, superficially wounded: adding library materials to the permanent reserve collection.

INTERLIBRARY LOAN (ILL)

The philosophy of most academic libraries, for a variety of reasons, now emphasizes access over ownership. This places a burden on ILL. If interlibrary loan requests continue to increase year after year, then just as the cost of serials inflation has to be dealt with each year either by cutting titles or allotting additional funds to cover the costs of maintaining existing subscriptions, so too must ILL staffing and funding be increased or services cut. One study (Costello and Duffy 1991)[18] analyzing ILL transactions for New York colleges and universities, showed that, contrary to what might be intuitively believed, the bigger the library collection the more a library borrows, and the number of serial subscriptions has little to do with the amount of ILL activity.

Technological factors which contribute to increased ILL requests include access to the following: CD-ROM databases (Moore, 1990[19] found that installing CD-ROM databases had a significant impact on ILL transactions); locally mounted online databases (with the introduction of Wilson databases on their OPAC, Gyeszly and Allen, 1991[20] showed an increase in both ILL and in-house journal use); subsidized online searching; Internet-accessible library catalogs and databases; OPAC gateways to other library catalogs and databases; and new document delivery services (e.g., digitized FAX over the Internet such as ARIEL). Other factors might be increased student enrollment and/or new graduate programs. Providing additional staff and funding to deal with increases in ILL transactions is the most positive way to react. Arguments can be made that every dollar put into ILL and document delivery is more efficiently spent than by putting it into acquiring materials that may or may not ever be used (Shaughnessy 1991).[21] Budgets represent a library's philosophy in action, and the debate over access versus ownership is still evolving at most institutions.

Some positive ways to react to an increase in ILL requests which do not involve permanent staffing increases include the following: (1) Provide an automated, networked ILL office for tracking requests. Relatively few automated systems currently have ILL modules, so this objective is usually accomplished through a custom programmed software package. Wessling 1989[22] describes the benefits of a software program for ILL file management, statistics, and collection development. One difficulty can be getting the custom program to interface with the local automated library system and/or the bibliographic utility. (2) Choose CD-ROM databases that provide a message online indicating whether a journal is held by the library, or make available a paper list of titles at the workstation. (3) Provide lists of journals from libraries in the same town or area. (4) Review the list of journals frequently requested for which the library does not have current subscriptions and decide whether it is more cost effective to subscribe to those journals or to rely on ILL and document delivery services. This involves balancing the cost of the journal plus associated costs (e.g., ordering, cataloging, processing, shelving, and binding), against the cost of ILL and limited access for users. (5) Educate users about the institutional costs of ILL. (6) Screen requests at the reference desk (i.e., determine if the material is in the library, or if other materials owned would satisfy the user's need).

If a positive response to increased ILL requests is not possible, then explicit negative responses are preferable over none. Trying to maintain the status quo when an ILL office is already at its limit creates a natural degradation in service as borrowing time increases and more users tie up precious staff time with requests for status checks and rush service. Methods of purposely reducing requests (i.e., negative measures) include the following: (1) exclude certain types of materials from ILL, such as books available from libraries in the area or "recreational reading" materials; (2) charge for "rush service"; (3) implement upfront charges for borrowing monographs or serial articles (e.g., $1.00 per book, $0.10 per photocopied page, etc). This should be done judiciously, however, since billing tasks can be labor intensive and sometimes not cost effective.

An example of triage management for this area might be: (1) urgent, critically wounded but treatable: rush requests for primary clientele with immediate deadlines; (2) hopeless, mortally wounded: full service for ILL requests, especially when materials are owned locally at other nearby libraries or already owned by the library but temporarily unavailable) and (3) can wait, superficially wounded: using the automated library system to track all ILL requests (without a specific ILL module that interacts with bibliographic utilities this is not fully possible).

COPY SERVICE

The goal of copy service is usually to provide service to library users and prevent theft, mutilation, and vandalism of the collection. All too often however, copy service is expected to break even financially and at the same time subsidize all internal copying. Identifying internal expenses can be important when examining the performance of copy service and justifying its budget. There is a temptation to use net profits from any area of the library for necessary expenses elsewhere. It is advisable however, to keep copy service profits for equipment upgrades and maintenance, as well as ancillary expenses such as advertising. Competition from copy businesses on and off campuses presents a unique problem for those library copy services expected to pay for themselves or turn a profit.

Centralization (all machines in one area) vs. decentralization (all machines throughout building with vendacards) is an important issue that must be uniquely analyzed in each environment. The former has the virtue of being simple to manage, while the latter might be more convenient for patrons. Traffic patterns throughout the building might also be considered.

Scheduling copy service staff is another vital issue. There are often spurts in the demand for services. It can often happen that, if three workers are scheduled at the same time, they might be idle 40 minutes out of an hour. On the other hand, if one person is scheduled, s/he might have a manageable workload for 40 minutes but be unable to keep up with the demand for the other 20 minutes in the hour. One option is to schedule the number of workers needed for the busiest time during a shift, but assign other work to them during slower periods. The other option is to schedule for the slowest time during a shift. If the latter option is used, the busy worker must be able to prioritize the customers and doing so, the principles of triage can be used at the copy service counter. People with work to drop off and pick up later and those who wish to pick up work already done should be handled expeditiously and moved out quickly. Procedures must make this possible. For example, the users should not have to fill out extensive paperwork. The emphasis should be on meeting the needs of those who need to have work done immediately. To do so, policy issues might take effect. Any work of over ten pages, for example, may be deferred until later. Workers need to clearly communicate policies and procedures to the people waiting in line.

OTHER STAFFING ISSUES

A method for maximizing effectiveness of the supervision of all areas within access services is to create "counter supervisor positions." Counter supervisors are usually staff members, but could be student supervisors, who are cross trained in all areas and are available for assistance at all the service counters. Ideally, the major functions of these positions are training, supervising, and directing workflow of other workers, as well as solving problems, overriding automated system blocks, and interpreting policies at the service counters. Designating a particular counter supervisor for every hour the library is open provides continuity and allows other staff to concentrate on tasks away from the counter. Counter supervisors might also keep a complaint log, which can serve as a relative record of the numbers and types of misunderstandings or problems that have occurred at the counter. It can also provide information to consider when revising or revaluating policies.

One way to develop the largest staff within budgetary constraints is to use more student workers than classified staff, and, at some institutions, to use more work study students. Several reports have appeared in the library literature about the value of using student workers as supervisors (Fuller 1990;[23] Nagel and Molloy 1991[24]), although, at some institutions, especially unionized ones, there may be restraints on changing the staff to student ratio. Keeping student workers busy can occasionally prove challenging at service counters. Supervisors can cross train students for certain tasks, such as sorting books or loading trucks, which can be done during slower times. Also, rather than scheduling too many workers at the beginning of an academic term in order to have sufficient staff at the busier, end-of-the-term, supplemental workers can be hired later for very specific tasks and schedules. This can be done with students or nonstudents, depending on the institutional situation.

Training is the all-important function that integrates student workers into a department and informs them of expectations (Kathman and Kathman 1986;[25] Boone et al. 1991[26]). Checklists (with skills and procedures listed) can assist with training new workers, particularly when several people do the training and a record of what has been done must be passed on from person to person. If students are to work in more than one access services area, there must be cross-training. Clearly written procedure manuals, while no substitute for individual training, can serve as guides and resources to workers and be useful for further, self-paced learning.

Cubberley (1991)[27] provides instructions for writing a clear, succinct, direct procedure manual.

Library staff members who work with the public, especially at service counters, are often asked to be courteous and friendly when delivering services but are rarely given specific instructions as to how to do this. Hobson et al. (1987)[28] explicitly described six observable verbal and nonverbal characteristics of good service and demonstrated that patrons are acutely aware of the quality of the service they receive with regard to those specific behaviors. This opens the possibility of evaluating, by direct or indirect observations, the quality of service provided by access service workers through the measurement of these behaviors.

An example of triage management for this area might be: (1) urgent, critically wounded but treatable: timely, progressive training of all workers; (2) hopeless, mortally wounded: individual training of all workers by staff supervisors especially when large numbers of students must be trained at busy counter times; and (3) can wait, superficially wounded: activities designed to bolster student worker morale, which is often cyclical and might be expected to be worse at the busiest times.

MANSFIELD LIBRARY EXAMPLES

Access services at the University of Montana, Mansfield Library, consists of circulation/stack management, reserve, interlibrary loan, microforms, and copy service. Student workers are supervised by classified staff members, who in turn are supervised by the access services coordinator, which is a faculty position and reports to the dean of public services. The University of Montana is one of six institutions of higher learning in Montana, with a current enrollment of approximately 10,000 students. The materials collection consists of about 700,000 volumes (not counting government documents) and 5,000 active serial subscriptions. In addition to its undergraduate education obligations, the Mansfield Library provides support for 56 master degrees and 10 doctoral programs.

In 1990 a new manager of access services was installed as department head at the Mansfield Library. For this and other reasons, there was a need to gain a better understanding of the many and sometimes conflicting needs of the various areas within the department. Several years worth of annual reports were available for each area; however, no cumulative comparisons had ever been made, and no "ratio" comparisons of the work loads of each area existed. Faced with a stagnant or diminishing staff budget, there was a need to evaluate each area and prioritize access services budget requests, which became something of an exercise in triage management. The goal was to assign appropriate staff and resources to those areas most urgently in need while identifying services that were just "superficially wounded" in terms of their ability to be maintained in the restrictive budgetary situation.

Many of the requests for staff and resources made by the staff supervisors in each area appeared to be based on anecdotal evidence. The interlibrary loan supervisor asserted that ILL transactions were increasing astronomically and had far outpaced the staffing level. The circulation supervisor similarly stated that circulation business had increased and that more staff was required for the completion of the the many duties performed by that department. Additionally, the circulation supervisor claimed that circulation/stack maintenance staff were supervising far too many student workers. The reserve/ copy service supervisor also claimed to be supervising too many student workers.

In weighing the requests and comments from all the staff supervisors, the access services coordinator used the principles of triage. Various statistical categories were defined and each supervisor was asked to provide the last seven years worth of data in these categories for their areas. These data were compiled into tables of raw data (not shown) and simple descriptive analyses were then performed. The access services coordinator shared all of this information with the individuals involved before passing it on and incorporating it into the yearly budget request. The categories and the findings are presented in Table 1.

Predictably, the reaction to the analyses described in Table 1 correlated strongly with the positive or negative outcome of the results shown. That is, those staff members whose area appeared most in need approved of these analyses while those who appeared least in need were critical. Even so, no one disputed the methods used.

TABLE 1

A) InterLibrary Loan - Numerical Analysis

I) Total # of Transactions (borrowing/lending/canceled requests)
1984 - 85   7,624
1990 - 91   24,111   Percent change + 216%

II) Total # of Staff Hours
1984 - 85   2.0 FTE = 4160 Hours
1990 - 91   3.25 FTE = 6760 Hours   Percent change + 62%

III) Total # of Student Hours
1984 - 85   1,257 Hours
1990 - 91   2,394 Hours   Percent change + 90%

IV) Total # of Personnel Hours (Staff & Students)
1984 - 85   5,417 Hours
1990 - 91   9,154 Hours   Percent change + 69%

V) Ratio of Staff / Student Hours
1984 - 85   4,160/1,257 = 3.3   Decrease: about 3 staff
1990 - 91   6,760/2,394 = 2.8   hours to every one student
                                   hour

VI) Ratio of Transactions / Personnel
1984 - 85   7,624/5,417 = 1.4   Almost doubled: almost 3
1990 - 91   24,111/9,154 = 2.6   transactions per personnel
                                   hour

Comments:

* Over the last seven years, transactions increased 216% while the total number of personnel hours increased only 69%. This ever widening gap led to an almost doubling of transactions per personnel hour.

* Over the past year, personnel hours remained static while transactions increased 18%; this translates into the same amount of worker hours processing an additional 3,730 requests.

TABLE 1 (continued)

B) Reserve - Numerical Analysis

I) Total # of Check-outs (reserve items & theses/dissertations)
1985 - 86   39,193
1990 - 91   42,506   Percent change + 8%

II) Total # of Staff Hours
1984 - 85   1.0 FTE = 2080 Hours
1990 - 91   0.89 FTE = 1851 Hours   Percent change - 11%

III) Total # of Student Hours
1985 - 86   3,998 Hours
1990 - 91   3,709 Hours   Percent change - 7%

IV) Total # of Personnel Hours (Staff & Students)
1985 - 86   5,849 Hours
1990 - 91   5,560 Hours   Percent change - 5%

V) Ratio of Staff / Student Hours
1985 - 86   1,851/3,998 = .46   Static; about 1 staff hour
1990 - 91   1851/3709 = .49   to every two student hours

VI) Ratio of Transactions / Personnel
1985 - 86   39,193/5,849 = 6.7   Increased: about 7 trans-
1990 - 91   42,506/5,560 = 7.6   actions per personnel hour

Comments:

* Activity went up 8% while personnel hours decreased 5%.

* The ratio of staff to student hours remained relatively unchanged with student workers comprising 67% of total hours worked.

* The number of student hours in copy service is equal to or greater than the number in reserve. If those student hours are added to the staff/student ratio then the value is one staff hour for over four student hours. In other words the staff/student ratio was extremely high for the reserve/copy service supervisor.

C) Circulation - Numerical Analysis

I) Total # of Check-outs (monographs & serials)
1984 - 85   91,604
1990 - 91   86,248   Percent change - 6%

II) Total # of Staff Hours
1984 - 85   2.0 FTE = 4160 Hours
1990 - 91   2.75 FTE = 5720 Hours   Percent change + 38%

III) Total # of Student Hours (counter, shelving, special projects)
1984 - 85   11,719 Hours
1990 - 91   12,308 Hours   Percent change + 5%

TABLE 1 (continued)

IV) Total # of Personnel Hours (Staff & Students)
1984 - 85   15,879 Hours
1990 - 91   18,028 Hours   Percent change + 14%

V) Ratio of Staff / Student Hours
1984 - 85   4,160/11,719 = .35
1990 - 91   5720/12,308 = .46

decrease: Used to be almost 1 staff hour to 3 student hours; Currently about 1 staff hour to 2 student hours

VI) Ratio of Transactions / Personnel
1984 - 85   91,604/11,719 = 7.8
1990 - 91   86,248/12,308 = 7.0

decreased 7 transactions per personnel hour

Comments:

* Monograph and serial check-outs were measured rather than total transactions. Still, it was assumed that other material check-outs and related activities (reshelving, etc.) remained proportionally the same over the time period covered.

* Over the last seven years, check-outs decreased 6% while total personnel increased 14%.

* Furthermore, The staff-per-student ratio increased; 32% of all current personnel hours are staff, up from 26% seven years before.

It is true that not all factors can be captured by a quantitative snapshot such as these data provide. As part of the process, other qualitative factors that affect an operational area of access services should be identified and considered. For example, one obvious difference between areas is the reliance on student workers. Circulation areas rely very heavily on student workers while ILL areas rely mainly on staff members.

Although the analyses cited in this article are simple, descriptive comparisons, they were helpful in demonstrating comparative needs/staffing levels and identifying priorities. These trends had not been apparent in annual reports or elsewhere. Based upon the results found, the following immediate actions could be recommended: (1) an increase in staff hours for ILL, (2) a moratorium on requests for additional staff members in circulation, (3) the transfer of some student hours from circulation to other areas, and (4) relief for the reserve supervisor from supervision of copy service student workers.

Finally, comparisons with peer libraries can provide valuable baseline information and assist with further evaluations (Hartse and Lee 1992).[29] The access services coordinator provided a list of peer institutions and categories of data to collect, and asked all the access services staff supervisors to contact their colleagues for this information. This data allowed for additional comparisons and rankings, and should point out any historical imbalances or peculiarities that have occurred within certain areas at the Mansfield Library.

CONCLUSION

Data collection of carefully selected parameters with a subsequent quantitative evaluation and/or statistical breakdown into meaningful patterns is an important tool for the wise management of access services. The concept of triage which places the highest priority for attention on those cases that are in urgent need of critical treatment can be combined with useful evaluative measures for practical management decisions. Administrative and budgetary decisions, when based on quantitative evaluation, are easier to justify and more effective to use in explaining decisions to subordinates and in making requests to supervisors. In this time of budgetary stagnation in libraries, such data can also be used in assessing those services that are just superficially wounded and can wait, those that require urgent attention, and those that are hopeless in the existing budgetary situation. Although the principles of triage may seem harsh, so too is the economic reality of many library budgets today.

REFERENCE NOTES

1. Richard M. Dougherty, and Fred J. Heinritz, *Scientific Management of Library Operations,* Metuchen, NJ. (Scarecrow Press, 1982.)
2. Robert Swisher and Charles R. McClure, *Research for Decision Making: Methods for Librarians,* Chicago: (American Library Association, 1984).
3. F.W. Lancaster, *If You Want to Evaluate Your Library . . . ,* Champaign, IL: (University of Illinois, 1988).
4. John Vasi, *Use of Management Statistics,* SPEC KIT #153 (Association of Research Libraries, 1989).
5. F.W. Lancaster, *The Measurement and Evaluation of Library Services,* Information Resources Press, 1977.
6. Marcy Murphy, "Evaluating library public service," *Journal of Library Administration,* 12n1 (1990), 63-90.
7. Nancy A. Van House, Beth T. Weil, and Charles R. McClure, "Measuring Academic Library Performance: a Practical Approach," Chicago: American Library Association, 1990.
8. John Budd, "Libraries and Statistical Studies: an Equivocal Relationship," *The Journal of Academic Librarianship,* 8n5 (1982), 278-281.
9. John O. Christensen, "Use of Statistics by Librarians," *Journal of Library Administration,* 9n2 (1988), 85-90.
10. Sheila S. Intner, "Bibliographic Triage," *Technicalities* 7 (December, 1987): 10-12.
11. Marilyn Naito, "Management by the Mash Model," *Library Journal* (October 15, 1991): 45-47.
12. Dougherty and Heinritz, 1982.
13. William J. Hubbard, Stack Management, American Library Association, 1981.
14. David F. Kohl, "High Efficiency Inventorying through Predictive Data," *The Journal of Academic Librarianship* 8n2 (1982): 82-84.
15. Patricia M. Wallace, "Predicting future shelving needs," *Collection Management* 12n1/2 (1990): 95-107.
16. Pat Schabo and Diana Breuer, "Speed and Accuracy for Shelving," *Library Journal* (October 1, 1989): 67-68.

17. S. Celine Sharp, "A Library Shelver's Performance Evaluation as it Relates to Reshelving Accuracy." In Gregg Sapp, ed. "Access Services Management." (The Haworth Press, Inc. 1992).

18. John Costello and Charles Duffy, "Academic Interlibrary Loan in New York State: a Statistical Analysis," *Journal of Interlibrary Loan & Information Supply* 1n2 (1990): 41-43.

19. May M. Moore, "The Effects of Compact Disk Indexes on Interlibrary Loan Services at a University Library," *Journal of Interlibrary Loan & Information Supply*, 1n1 (1990): 25-42.

20. See D. Gyeszly and Gary Allen, "Effects of Online Periodical Indexes on Interlibrary Loan Services and Collection Development," *Journal of Interlibrary Loan & Information Supply*, 1n3 (1991): 39-48.

21. Thomas W. Shaughnessy, "From Ownership to Access: A Dilemma for Library Managers," *Journal of Library Administration* 14n1 (1991): 1-7.

22. Julie E. Wessling, "Benefits from Automated ILL Borrowing Records: Use of ILLRKS in an Academic Library," *RQ*, (Winter 1989): 209-218.

23. Jay G. Fuller, "Employing Library Student Assistants as Student Supervisors," *College & Research Libraries News* (October 1990): 855-857.

24. Mary Nagel and Jeanne Molloy, "In Praise of Students as Supervisors," *College & Research Libraries News* (October 1991): 577-578.

25. Michael D. Kathman and Jane M. Kathman, *Managing Student Workers in College Libraries* (Association of College and Research Libraries 1986): 182.

26. Morell D. Boone, Sandra G. Yee, and Rita Bullard, *Training Student Library Assistants* (American Library Association 1991): 110.

27. Carol W. Cubberley, "Write Procedure Manuals That Work," *Library Journal* (September 15, 1991): 42-45.

28. Charles J. Hobson, Robert F. Moran, Jr., and Arena L. Stevens, "Circulation/Reserve Desk Personnel Effectiveness," *The Journal of Academic Librarianship* 13n2 (1987): 93-98.

29. Merri A. Hartse and Daniel R. Lee (Changing Circulation Policies at an ARL Library: The Impact of Peer Institution Survey Data on the Process." In Gregg Sapp, ed. "Access Services Management" (The Haworth Press, Inc. 1992).

Access Services: The Development of a Holistic Approach to Convenience Information Services: An Editorial Essay on the Future of Access Services

Pat Weaver-Meyers
Virginia Steel

OVERVIEW OF THIS VOLUME

The collection of manuscripts in this volume represents a complex and continually evolving concept of access services. Rightly so. These works, in their diverse yet integrated viewpoint, paint a better picture of access services than any other collection or single article previously published. By approaching access services as a complete entity composed of related services, Gregg Sapp has brought together a group of articles that reflect the variety and vitality of access services departments of the nineties. This collection may open the gate for a flood of articles that describe how access services operations function and are managed. To date, however, the literature shows few articles or monographs that attempt to holistically describe access services departments.[1]

The articles in this volume reflect changes underway within libraries–academic, public, and special. The impact of electronic resources has been discussed for several years. As early as 1982,

---

Pat Weaver-Meyers, Head of Access Services at University of Oklahoma Libraries and Virginia Steel, Acting Head of Public Services at University of California, San Diego, were the consulting editors for this volume.

© 1992 by The Haworth Press, Inc. All rights reserved.

F.W. Lancaster predicted that technologies would foster major changes in libraries.[2] Others have even speculated that electronic information brokers will become the purloiners of the substance of librarianship. A recent feature on National Public Radio predicts just that, but we, as managers of access services operations, disagree. A more likely scenario, in our opinion, is that the reorganization of access services into an integrated department of diverse services may represent an organizational solution to such an unsettling specter for librarians as well as an opportunity for libraries to better meet the needs of their users.

While reading the articles in this collection, we took note of the increasing emphasis on providing efficient and timely services for library users, be they on-site or remote. Perhaps this is an outgrowth of the trend toward total quality management. Another explanation is that the access services model corresponds to convenience models introduced into the private sector.[3] "Convenience" is a word that often crops us in discussions about services, library or otherwise, these days. As Richard Dougherty stated, "The importance of convenience and timeliness can hardly be overstated in a society so accustomed to rapid communication and online systems. We demand quick, even instantaneous responses."[4]

CONVENIENCE MODELS

What is meant by the term "convenience models"? A brief review of marketing literature turns up a number of articles related to the concept of "convenience" but few thorough discussions of what "convenience" means. One of the most detailed discussions of the concept of "convenience" is in an article by L. G. Brown in which he describes five dimensions that are part of the concept of total convenience: (1) time dimension, (2) place dimension, (3) acquisition dimension, (4) use dimension, and (5) execution dimension. For each dimension there is a continuum ranging from "do-it-yourself" to "total convenience." Any given product or service may offer different levels of each dimension with the total product or service giving the desired degree of convenience. For example, Brown describes a pizza continuum which runs as follows:

DO IT YOURSELF

From scratch pizza
Boxed pizza mix
Frozen pizza
Pizza in restaurant
Pick up pizza
Home delivered pizza

TOTAL CONVENIENCE[5]

Based on this concept of convenience, several analogies for convenience services in libraries come to mind:

- Access services departments offer services similar to those offered by fast-food restaurants. If one views traditional reference services as the equivalent of reservations needed/ sit-down restaurants, access services can be considered the equivalent of McDonald's or Taco Bell, providers of information with easy pick-up or delivery. Fast-food restaurants continue to expand their menus while capturing an increasing share of the market for several reasons: their food is generally appetizing, ready within minutes, and inexpensive. McDonald's operating motto is "Q, S, C, and V–Quality, Service, Cleanliness, and Value."[6] Access services departments tend to have similar values, although frequently not articulated. The library units are expanding their offerings and modes of delivery for a broader information menu with products delivered quickly and at little or no cost.
- Another analogy that fits into the category of convenience models is the use of automated teller machines (ATMs) by the banking industry. F. W. Lancaster recognized the similarity between automated tellers and information services.[7] While not everyone uses a ATM, these have now become the accepted way to conduct much of one's banking activities. It is possible to deposit, withdraw, and transfer money between accounts without needing to interact with a human teller. In

libraries, the growing use of electronic tools that provide access to information corresponds to the rise in the use of ATMs. The need for interaction with a human being for reference assistance in the case of a library or for assistance with an account in the case of a bank will continue for the foreseeable future. However, for routine transactions, electronic access will substitute for in-person transactions. The library access services operations will be one of the departments most heavily involved in providing the support to deliver services and information remotely.

Convenience models have gained popularity for several reasons. They are usually inexpensive to use–fast food costs less than sit-down restaurants since the labor costs of hiring host- and waitpersons are eliminated; the menu is limited; and they respond to the needs of customers or clients quickly and at all hours of the day and night. They provide a uniform food product that can be consistently relied upon to be the same whether one is eating at McDonald's in Rhode Island or in southern California.

Another dimension of convenience that is important is the time dimension. Recent discussions about "lazy Americans" have revealed, surprisingly, that Americans work more hours now than they did in the 1950s, and there is a preponderance of dual-career couples. Leisure time is increasingly scarce, and often patrons of fast-food restaurants or ATMs use these because they save time that can be spent on other recreational activities. The same is true of access services. Fee-based services, interlibrary loan, document delivery, and more flexible loan periods are all ways in which library users can get the materials they need where and when they need them. Management emphasis is on *quality* service, and for access services quality translates into timely, efficient, inexpensive service. The popularity of telefacsimile and the enthusiasm for the newly introduced ARIEL software which transmits documents with high-quality resolution over the currently free Internet are two examples of ways in which access services is buying into the values of saving time and providing speedier service.

As convenience services become the bedrock of American business, from automated tellers to fast-food franchises, the modern information-seeker will continue to raise his or her expectations for convenient access. To meet these expectations, libraries must re-examine their policies and adopt more flexible service guidelines. Traditional library services are still in demand, but the user population demanding those services is shrinking. On college and university campuses, for example, faculty do not visit the library as often as they did just a few decades ago; instead they dial into the library's online catalog and submit electronic requests for document delivery and interlibrary loan. These services may fall into the execution dimension referred to earlier; it is no longer necessary for library users to come to the library. With the "library without walls" concept, information is delivered to a more convenient location such as an office or dorm.

In an overview of access services in academic libraries, Jo Bell Whitlatch identifies an unfulfilled desire on the part of information-seekers by reviewing several works on the importance of convenience. Convenience is a characteristic concern of the personal collecting of scholars as well as their use of branch libraries.[8] Some would say that convenience has become more important to restaurant patrons than the taste or nutritional value of the food. In a library setting, most reference librarians would admit that a sophomore researching an assignment due the following morning cares little for the quality of the information and is only interested in finding articles that are easily identified and retrieved–in other words, those that are convenient.

If these convenience models prove to be accurate analogies, then access services may well take on an even more clearly defined organizational structure. Historically, take-out from the traditional restaurant was insufficient to satisfy the convenience needs of the public. In response to the unmet demands, entire restaurants and restaurant chains which emphasized speedy delivery of food packaged and selected to be eaten on the go sprang up. Each meal may not be an eating adventure, but there are quality standards to which the restaurants adhere strictly. If access services follow the same model and developmental process, then it will become a more autonomous unit of the library comprised of services which deliver information quickly and on demand. Access services add value by adding convenience for the library customer. Organizationally, access services may very likely become a conglomeration of services based on adding convenience to standard information seeking and delivery.

THE FUTURE

Even as the articles in this volume have been written, more and more libraries are adopting an integrated access services model and are offering the types of services we have described. As user demands and expectations of library services increase, all libraries that wish to remain vital within their communities will be forced to join in. When they do, the organization that groups similar functions within one unit, access services, will avoid costly duplication and create a core group of experts on ready and rapid information delivery.

In keeping with this organizational change, individual expertise must be nurtured and attended so that libraries will have a cadre of specialists with expertise in networked and other electronic resources. Just as the development of online databases resulted in the creation of online searchers, so will the rise of network-accessed resources necessitate specialists devoted to reaching remote databases or instructing remote users on the resources available to them worldwide. Skeptics might bear in mind that traditionally it was the interlibrary loan librarian who knew more about the bibliography room than anyone else in the library.

As document delivery becomes a more commonly offered service, additional developments in value-added information will materialize. Quality management program will enable librarians to identify the components of excellent service. Service speed, information packaging, and delivery in whatever format is preferred by the user will add value by adding convenience. Overall, the outcome will be an increase in the availability of information.

Increasing the level of convenience will continue to be a major factor in maintaining the viability of library services. If patrons are less frustrated and find library services and collections to be more accessible than in the past, they will be more likely to become regular library users, if not supporters. The ease of obtaining materials will lead to increasing demands for remote reference assistance. When this happens, a close association between reference and access services will be critical as the menu and tutorial services may become more important and more frequent than face-to-face transactions in the library.

As workloads continue to increase, access services will adopt productivity standards and may in some cases take on an assembly-line persona. This will prove challenging for access services managers who will need to take care that staff are not dehumanized in the interests of providing services to a remote clientele. In addition to motivating the staff, access services managers will need to carefully analyze the changing information needs of information seekers using techniques perfected in the business world so that changes in the demand for information can be successfully handled by the library.

As these forces exert themselves, library administrators will find themselves straddling the funding fence. In this decade of decreasing funding and skyrocketing costs, hard decisions will be made about library services and collecting policies. The concept of access instead of ownership may force some institutions to reduce staffing in some areas such as acquisitions in favor of increasing staffing in other areas such as access services.

To avoid the possibility of creating information haves and have-nots, library administrators must find creative solutions to funding problems. These may include development of a cafeteria approach to services in which services are offered at differing costs depending on their value. To go back to the pizza continuum, pizza made from scratch is probably the least expensive in terms of ingredients, but it has a definite cost in terms of the value of the pizza-maker's time. The more expensive service of home-delivered pizza reduces the cost of the consumer's time but often slightly increases the cost of the pizza itself. Like pizza purveyors, libraries will not be able to continue to provide all services gratis, but they may retain the ideal of access to all by keeping charges so low that they are readily affordable to all but the most economically disadvantaged. Access services' contribution to this effort will be in maintaining efficient and effective production-line services that will keep costs down.

CONCLUSION

In some ways, the vision we have described of access services retains many of the qualities that have long existed in circulation operations. The most important of these may be that access services, like circulation services, is the only contact many library users will ever have with library personnel.[9] Therefore, measuring the quality of convenience services may be the only evaluation most library users will ever make about libraries, their services, and collections, in the information-rich years to come.

Emphasis on an integrated organizational structure for these convenience services should provide an effective and efficient provision of what will likely be a high demand service. The natural evolution of access services to a department which focuses on convenience services is an appropriate trend that parallels the development of convenience service providers in other industries. This volume's holistic focus on the organizational change taking place now will help managers create a service unit with the ability to satisfy the most time-conscious library user–if not the most discriminating information "palate."

REFERENCE NOTES

1. A recent search of the online database Library Literature with the free-text term "access(adj)services" produced only three citations. In fact, this index of journals in the discipline of librarianship has not yet created a subject heading for access services. However, research using a variety of more specific headings shows a wealth of literature on functions often incorporated into access services departments such as interlibrary loan, circulation, stack maintenance, serials, security, document delivery, fee-based services, among others, tend to come under this organizational umbrella. Clearly, as Deborah Carver suggests, the reorganization of these various areas under the broader rubric is still not yet institutionalized.

2. Lancaster, F. W. *Libraries and Librarians in an Age of Electronics* (Arlington, Va.: Information Resources Press, 1982).

3. Ibid, p. 155.

4. Dougherty, Richard M. "Needed: User-Responsive Research Libraries," *Library Journal* v116n1 (1991): 59-62.

5. Brown, L. G. "The Strategic and Tactical Implications of Convenience in Consumer Product Marketing," *Journal of Consumer Marketing* 6 (1989): 13-19.

6. Orr, D. G. (1983). "The Ethnography of Big Mac. In *Ronald Revisited: The World of Ronald McDonald* (Bowling Green: Bowling Green University Popular Press, 1983): 59-68.

7. Op. cit., p. 128.

8. Whitlatch, J. B. Access Services. In M. J. Lynch and A. Young (Eds.), *Academic Libraries Research Perspectives*. (Chicago: American Library Association, 1990): 67-105.

9. Hobson, C. J., Moran, R. F., & Stevens, A. L. Circulation/reserve desk personnel effectiveness. *Journal of Academic Librarianship* v13 n2 (1987): 93-98.

For Product Safety Concerns and Information please contact our EU
representative GPSR@taylorandfrancis.com
Taylor & Francis Verlag GmbH, Kaufingerstraße 24, 80331 München, Germany

www.ingramcontent.com/pod-product-compliance
Lightning Source LLC
Chambersburg PA
CBHW071821300426
44116CB00009B/1389